THE REVELS PLAYS

Former general editors
David Bevington
F. David Hoeniger
E. A. J. Honigmann
Clifford Leech
J. R. Mulryne
Eugene M. Waith
Martin White

General editors
Karen Britland, Richard Dutton, Alison Findlay,
Rory Loughnane, Helen Ostovich and Barbara Ravelhofer

THIERRY AND THEODORET

Manchester University Press

THE REVELS PLAYS

ANON *Thomas of Woodstock*
or King Richard the Second, Part One

BARRY *The Family of Love*

BEAUMONT *The Knight of the Burning Pestle*

BEAUMONT AND FLETCHER *A King and No King*
The Maid's Tragedy *Philaster, or Love Lies a-Bleeding*

CHAPMAN *All Fools*
Bussy d'Ambois *An Humorous Day's Mirth*

CHAPMAN, JONSON, MARSTON *Eastward Ho*

DEKKER *The Shoemaker's Holiday* *Old Fortunatus*

FLETCHER AND MASSINGER *The False One*
Love's Cure, or The Martial Maid

FORD *Love's Sacrifice* *The Lady's Trial*

HEYWOOD *The First and Second Parts of King Edward IV*

JONSON *The Alchemist* *The Devil Is an Ass*
Epicene, or The Silent Woman *Every Man In His Humour*
Every Man Out of His Humour *The Magnetic Lady*
The New Inn *Poetaster* *Sejanus: His Fall*
The Staple of News *Volpone*

LYLY *Campaspe* and *Sappho and Phao* *Endymion*
Galatea and *Midas* *Love's Metamorphosis*
Mother Bombie *The Woman in the Moon*

MARLOWE *Dido, Queen of Carthage* *Doctor Faustus*
Edward the Second
The Jew of Malta *The Massacre at Paris* *Tamburlaine the Great*

MARSTON *Antonio and Mellida*
Antonio's Revenge *The Malcontent*

MASSINGER *The Roman Actor*

MIDDLETON *A Game at Chess* *Michaelmas Term*
A Trick to Catch the Old One

MIDDLETON AND DEKKER *The Roaring Girl*

MUNDAY AND OTHERS *Sir Thomas More*

PEELE *The Troublesome Reign of John, King of England*
David and Bathsheba

SHIRLEY *Hyde Park*

WEBSTER *The Duchess of Malfi*

THE REVELS PLAYS

THIERRY AND THEODORET

JOHN FLETCHER,
PHILIP MASSINGER AND
NATHAN FIELD

edited by Domenico Lovascio

MANCHESTER
UNIVERSITY PRESS

Introduction, critical apparatus, etc.
© Domenico Lovascio 2024

The right of Domenico Lovascio to be identified as the author of this work has been asserted in accordance with the Copyright, Designs and Patents Act 1988.

Published by Manchester University Press
Oxford Road, Manchester, M13 9PL

www.manchesteruniversitypress.co.uk

British Library Cataloguing-in-Publication Data
A catalogue record for this book is available from the British Library

ISBN 978 1 5261 6420 9 hardback
ISBN 978 1 5261 9544 9 paperback

First published 2024
Paperback published 2026

The publisher has no responsibility for the persistence or accuracy of URLs for any external or third-party internet websites referred to in this book, and does not guarantee that any content on such websites is, or will remain, accurate or appropriate.

EU authorised representative for GPSR:
Easy Access System Europe – Mustamäe tee 50, 10621 Tallinn, Estonia
gpsr.requests@easproject.com

Typeset
by New Best-set Typesetters Ltd

*This book is dedicated to Luisa Villa and Lisa Hopkins.
I would have never become the scholar I am today without their
teaching, support, and encouragement.*

Contents

ILLUSTRATIONS	viii
GENERAL EDITORS' PREFACE	ix
ACKNOWLEDGEMENTS	xii
ABBREVIATIONS AND REFERENCES	xv
INTRODUCTION	1
Authorship	1
Dating and stage history	5
Sources	10
Defying genre expectations	22
Criticism	28
The text	40
This edition	45
THIERRY AND THEODORET	53
APPENDICES	195
1. Press variants in Q1	195
2. Overview of the historical events dramatized in the play, based on the *Chronique de Frédégaire* (seventh century)	200
3. 'The eldest son chargeth his mother with incestuous life': The Tale of the Lady of Cabrio in Fenton's *Tragical Discourses*	202
INDEX	207

Illustrations

1. Title page of Q1, courtesy of the Harry Ransom Center, University of Texas (Pforz 373) 2

2. Ordella, kneeling, implores Thierry to sacrifice her for the sake of France, while Thierry, horrified at the idea, lets fall his sword, in *The Dramatic Works of Beaumont and Fletcher*, edited by George Colman the elder, 10 vols (London: Evans and Elmsley, 1778), 10:124, courtesy of Württembergische Landesbibliothek Stuttgart (Fr.D.oct.61-10) 23

3. Thierry and Ordella sit together on their thrones under the eyes of Brunehaut, in *The Works of Mr Francis Beaumont and Mr John Fletcher*, 7 vols (London: Tonson, 1711), 7:3697, courtesy of Universitäts und Landesbibliothek Bonn (Fb 407) 35

4. Marked proof-sheet of sig. C1^v in Q1, courtesy of the Boston Public Library (G.3966.2) 42

General editors' preface

Clifford Leech conceived of the Revels Plays as a series in the mid-1950s, modelling the project on the New Arden Shakespeare. The aim, as he wrote in 1958, was 'to apply to Shakespeare's predecessors, contemporaries, and successors the methods that are now used in Shakespeare's editing'. The plays chosen were to include well-known works from the early Tudor period to about 1700, as well as others less familiar but of literary and theatrical merit. 'The plays included', Leech wrote, 'should be such as to deserve and indeed demand performance'. We owe it to Clifford Leech that the idea became reality. He set the high standards of the series, ensuring that editors of individual volumes produced work of lasting merit, equally useful for teachers and students, theatre directors and actors. Clifford Leech remained General Editor until 1971, and was succeeded by F. David Hoeniger, who retired in 1985.

Ever since then, the Revels Plays have been under the direction of four or five general editors: initially David Bevington, E. A. J. Honigmann, J. R. Mulryne, and E. M. Waith. E. A. J. Honigmann retired in 2000 and was succeeded by Richard Dutton. E. M. Waith retired in 2003 and was succeeded by Alison Findlay and Helen Ostovich. J. R. Mulryne retired in 2010, David Bevington passed away in 2019, and Martin White retired in the same year. They were succeeded by Karen Britland, Rory Loughnane, and Barbara Ravelhofer. Published originally by Methuen, the series is now published by the Manchester University Press, embodying essentially the same format, scholarly character, and high editorial standards of the series as first conceived. The series now concentrates on plays from the period 1558–1642. Some slight changes have been made: for example, starting in 1996 each index lists proper names and topics in the introduction and commentary, whereas earlier indexes focused only on words and phrases for which the commentary provided a gloss. Notes to the introduction are now placed together at the end, not at the foot of, the page. Collation and commentary notes continue, however, to appear on the relevant pages.

The introduction to each Revels play undertakes to offer, among other matters, a critical appraisal of the play's significant themes and images, its poetic and verbal fascinations, its historical context, its characteristics as a piece for the theatre, and its uses of the stage for which it was designed. Stage history is an important part of the story. In addition, the introduction presents as lucidly as possible the criteria for choice of copy-text and the editorial methods employed in presenting the play to a modern reader. The introduction also considers the play's date and, where relevant, its sources, together with its place in the work of the author and in the theatre of its time. If the play is by an author not previously represented in the series, a brief biography is provided.

The text of each Revels play, in accordance with established practice in the series, is edited afresh from the original text of best authority (in a few instances, texts), in modern spelling and punctuation and with speech headings that are consistent throughout. Elisions in the original are also silently regularised, except where metre would be affected by the change. Emendations, as distinguished from modernized spellings and punctuation, are introduced only in instances where error is patent or at least very probable, and where the corrected reading is persuasive. Act divisions are given only if they appear in the original, or if the structure of the play clearly points to them. Those act and scene divisions not in the original are provided in small type. Square brackets are also used for any other additions to, or changes in, the stage directions of the original.

Rather than provide a comprehensive and historical variorum collation, Revels Plays editions focus on those variants which require the critical attention of serious textual students. All departures of substance from the copy-text are listed, including any significant relineation and those changes in punctuation which involve to any degree a decision between alternative interpretations. The collation notes do not include such accidentals as turned letters or changes in the font. Additions to stage directions are not noted in the collations, since those additions are already made clear by the use of brackets. On the other hand, press corrections in the copy-text are duly collated, as based on a careful consultation of as many copies of the original edition or editions as are needed to ensure that the printing history of those originals is accurately reported. Of later emendations of the text by subsequent editors, only those are reported which still deserve attention as alternative readings.

One of the hallmarks of the Revels Plays is the thoroughness of their annotations. Besides explaining the meanings of difficult words and passages, the annotations provide commentary on customs or usage, on the text, on stage business – indeed, on anything that can be pertinent and helpful. On occasion, when long notes are required and are too lengthy to fit comfortably at the foot of the page below the text, they are printed at the end of the complete text.

Appendices are used to present any commendatory poems on the dramatist and play in question, documents about the play's reception and contemporary history, classical sources, casting analyses, music, and any other relevant material.

Each volume contains an index to the commentary, in which particular attention is drawn to meanings for words not listed in the OED, and (starting in 1996, as indicated above) an indexing of proper names and topics in the introduction and commentary.

Our hope is that plays edited in this fashion will promote further scholarly and theatrical investigation of one of the richest periods in theatrical history.

KAREN BRITLAND
RICHARD DUTTON
ALISON FINDLAY
RORY LOUGHNANE
HELEN OSTOVICH
BARBARA RAVELHOFER

Acknowledgements

The first acknowledgement must go out to Commissioning Editor Matthew Frost and to General Editors Karen Britland, Richard Dutton, Alison Findlay, Rory Loughnane, Helen Ostovich, and Barbara Ravelhofer, who gave me the opportunity to edit this bizarrely captivating, though unfortunately neglected, early modern play for the Revels Plays series.

I am grateful to several friends and colleagues who have commented on parts of the edition or have provided useful information, namely Marisa Cull, Lisa Hopkins, E. Wyn James, Peter Kirwan, Megan Lloyd, Eoin Price, Pervez Rizvi, Paul Russell, Emanuel Stelzer, and David Willis. Special thanks go to José A. Pérez Díez, who shared with me images of the copy of Q1 held in the Brotherton Library at Leeds University; to Darren Freebury-Jones, who kindly shared with me his unpublished research on authorship in the Fletcher canon; to Martin Wiggins, who made it possible for me to listen to the Zoom recording of the Reading Early Plays (REP) reading of *Thierry and Theodoret* by kindly having that play selected as one of the first five to be uploaded to the Replays section of the project website; and to Michela Compagnoni and Maddalena Repetto, who both checked my text against Q1 before submission and providentially spotted a few typos that I would not have identified without their help. Special thanks go to Andrew Kirk for his meticulous copy-editing and to Lianne Slavin for steering the publication process so competently and efficiently. All these people have made this a much better critical edition than it would have been otherwise, and if any errors remain, they are entirely my responsibility.

Colleagues teaching English at the Department of Modern Languages and Cultures at Genoa have been a delight to work with, and I owe deep gratitude to the staff of the Library at my Department, especially Franco Reuspi, Simona Basso, and Simone Tallone, who always respond promptly to my book orders and my requests for interlibrary loan materials. They have made my work so much easier.

My collation of the extant copies of Q1 has been made possible largely thanks to funding made available through the Malone

Society, to which I am grateful for generously supporting my work (again).

The Beinecke Library at Yale University, the Bodleian Library at the University of Oxford, the Chapin Library at Williams College, the Charles Patterson van Pelt Library at the University of Pennsylvania, and the Houghton Library at Harvard University all provided me with scans of their copies of Q1 free of charge. The British Library, the Harry Ransom Center at the University of Texas at Austin, the Huntington Library, Innerpefray Library, the Library at the University of Illinois Urbana-Champaign, the National Library of Scotland, the Trinity College Library at the University of Cambridge, and the Victoria and Albert Museum all fulfilled my order for scans of their copies of Q1 very promptly and efficiently. I extend my gratitude to all these institutions.

Thanks also go to the Universitäts- und Landesbibliothek Bonn and the Wuerttembergische Landesbibliothek Stuttgart for making images to reproduce in this volume available very rapidly. I am especially indebted to the Boston Public Library and the Harry Ransom Center at the University of Texas at Austin for kindly granting me permission to reuse their images in this book free of charge.

The Introduction incorporates (and elaborates upon) material from my open-access publication 'Unveiling Wives: Euripides' *Alcestis* and Two Plays in the Fletcher Canon', in *Classical Receptions in Early Modern English Drama*, edited by Silvia Bigliazzi and Tania Demetriou (University of Verona, 2024), https://doi.org/10.13136/TS.85, forthcoming in the series Skenè. Texts and Studies (Texts. DA), https://textsandstudies.skeneproject.it/index.php/TS/index. This is a CC-BY 4.0 publication (https://creativecommons.org/licenses/by/4.0/). The research presented in that essay was made possible thanks to funding made available by the Italian Ministry of Education, University, and Research (MIUR), which supported the project 'Classical Receptions in Early Modern English Drama' as a Research Project of National Interest (PRIN2017XAA3ZF).

I have had the rare privilege to have Richard Dutton as my General Editor for a second time after working with him on *The False One*. Having such a generous and formidable scholar guide me again with his patience, competence, and enthusiasm has made my work on this edition a truly exciting and unforgettable experience. If my skills as an editor have improved in any way since I started editing early modern English texts a few years ago, it is almost exclusively thanks to him. He has my enduring gratitude.

As always, my most heartfelt thanks go to my wonderful family: Giulia, our son Cesare, and our dog Juno.

DOMENICO LOVASCIO
GENOA, 21 JUNE 2023

Abbreviations and references

EDITIONS AND TEXTUAL REFERENCES

1711   *Thierry and Theodoret*, in vol. 7 of *The Works of Mr Francis Beaumont and Mr John Fletcher*, 7 vols (London: Tonson, 1711)

Bodleian   MS. Eng. misc. d.28, Bodleian Library, Oxford University, UK (c. 1622–25)

Coleridge   Samuel Taylor Coleridge, *Seven Lectures on Shakespeare and Milton* (London: Chapman and Hall, 1856)

Colman   *Thierry and Theodoret*, in vol. 10 of *The Dramatic Works of Beaumont and Fletcher, Collated with All the Former Editions and Corrected, with Notes, Critical and Explanatory, by Various Commentators; and Adorned with Fifty-four Original Engravings in Ten Volumes*, ed. George Colman the elder, 10 vols (London: Evans and Elmsley, 1778)

Cotgrave   John Cotgrave, *The English Treasury of Wit and Language* (London, 1655)

Deighton   K. Deighton, *Conjectural Readings on the Texts of Marston, Beaumont and Fletcher, Peele, Marlowe, Chapman, Heywood, Greene, Middleton, Dekker, Webster* (Westminster: Archibald Constable & Co., 1896)

Dyce   *Thierry and Theodoret*, in vol. 1 of *The Works of Beaumont and Fletcher: The Text Formed from a New Collation of the Early Editions, with Notes and a Biographical Memoir*, ed. Alexander Dyce, 11 vols (London: Moxon, 1844)

F2   *Thierry and Theodoret*, in *Fifty Comedies and Tragedies, Written by Francis Beaumont and John Fletcher, Gentlemen, All in One Volume, Published by the Authors' Original Copies, the*

	Songs to Each Play Being Added (London: J. Macock for John Martyn, Henry Herringman, and Richard Marriot, 1679)
Heath	Manuscript commentary by Benjamin Heath on the plays in the Beaumont and Fletcher Folios, mentioned in Dyce
Mason	John Monck Mason, *Comments on the Plays of Beaumont and Fletcher, with an Appendix Containing Some Further Observations on Shakespeare* (London: Harding, 1798)
Q1	*The Tragedy of Thierry, King of France, and His Brother Theodoret* (London: Nicholas Okes for Thomas Walkley, 1621)
Q2	*The Tragedy of Thierry, King of France, and His Brother Theodoret* (London: for Humphrey Moseley, 1648)
Seward	*Thierry and Theodoret*, in vol. 10 of *The Works of Mr Francis Beaumont and Mr John Fletcher*, ed. by Messrs Theobald, Seward and Sympson, 10 vols (London: Tonson and Draper, 1750)
Strachey	*Thierry and Theodoret*, in vol. 1 of *The Best Plays of the Old Dramatists: Beaumont and Fletcher*, ed. J. St. Loe Strachey, 2 vols (London: Vizetelly & Co., 1887)
Theobald	Lewis Theobald's conjectures, mentioned in Seward
Turner	*Thierry and Theodoret*, ed. Robert Kean Turner, in vol. 3 of *The Dramatic Works in the Beaumont and Fletcher Canon*, ed. Fredson Bowers, 10 vols (Cambridge University Press, 1976)
Weber	*Thierry and Theodoret*, in vol. 12 of *The Works of Beaumont and Fletcher, in Fourteen Volumes, with an Introduction and Explanatory Notes*, ed. Henry Weber, 14 vols (Edinburgh: Ballantyne, 1812)

FLETCHER'S WORKS

Quotations from other works in the canon of Fletcher and his collaborators are taken from *The Dramatic Works in the Beaumont and Fletcher Canon*, gen. ed. Fredson Bowers, 10 vols (Cambridge University Press, 1966–96), with the exception of Martin Wiggins's edition of *Valentinian*, in *Four Jacobean Sex Tragedies* (Oxford University Press, 1998) and the Revels Plays editions of *A King and No King* by Lee Bliss (Manchester University Press, 2004), *Love's Cure, or The Martial Maid* by José A. Pérez Díez (Manchester University Press, 2022), and *The False One* by Domenico Lovascio (Manchester University Press, 2022). Titles of Fletcher's works are abbreviated as follows:

Brother	The Elder Brother
Capt	The Captain
Corinth	The Queen of Corinth
CustCount	The Custom of the Country
FalseO	The False One
HMF	The Honest Man's Fortune
KNoK	A King and No King
LC	Love's Cure, or The Martial Maid
Lieut	Demetrius and Enanthe, or The Humorous Lieutenant
Loyal	The Loyal Subject
MadL	The Mad Lover
Malta	The Knight of Malta
Monsieur	Monsieur Thomas, or Father's Own Son
MT	The Maid's Tragedy
Phil	Philaster
Pilgrim	The Pilgrim
Progress	The Lovers' Progress
Proph	The Prophetess
Rollo	Rollo, or The Bloody Brother
SeaV	The Sea Voyage
SJVOB	Sir John van Olden Barnavelt
SpCur	The Spanish Curate
Val	Valentinian

MASSINGER'S WORKS

Quotations from Massinger's other works are taken from *The Plays and Poems of Philip Massinger*, ed. Philip Edwards and Colin Gibson, 5 vols (Oxford: Clarendon Press, 1976). Titles of Massinger's works are abbreviated as follows:

Bondman	The Bondman
Guardian	The Guardian
Renegado	The Renegado

xviii ABBREVIATIONS AND REFERENCES

SHAKESPEARE'S WORKS

Titles of Shakespeare's works are abbreviated as follows:

1H4	*King Henry IV Part 1*, ed. David Scott Kastan (London: Methuen for Arden Shakespeare, 2002)
A&C	*Antony and Cleopatra*, ed. David Bevington (Cambridge University Press, 2005, upd. edn)
Ham	*Hamlet*, ed. Ann Thompson and Neil Taylor (London: Bloomsbury Arden Shakespeare, 2016, rev. edn)
H8	*Henry VIII (All Is True)*, ed. Gordon McMullan (London: Methuen for Arden Shakespeare, 2000)
KL	*King Lear*, ed. R. A. Foakes (Walton-on-Thames: Nelson for Arden Shakespeare, 1997)
MWW	*The Merry Wives of Windsor*, ed. Giorgio Melchiori (Thomson for Arden Shakespeare, 2000)
Oth	*Othello, the Moor of Venice*, ed. Michael Neill (Oxford University Press, 2006)
Shrew	*The Taming of the Shrew*, ed. Barbara Hodgdon (London: Methuen for Arden Shakespeare, 2010)
WT	*The Winter's Tale*, ed. John Pitcher (London: A&C Black for Arden Shakespeare, 2010)

OTHER PRIMARY TEXTS

Aimoin	Aimoin of Fleury, *Libri quinque de gestis Francorum* (Paris, 1514)
Barnes, *Charter*	Barnabe Barnes, *The Devil's Charter* (London, 1607)
Beaumont, *Pestle*	Francis Beaumont, *The Knight of the Burning Pestle*, ed. Sheldon P. Zitner (Manchester University Press, 1984)
Belloy	Pierre de Belloy, *Examen du discours publié contre la maison royale de France* (Paris, 1587)

Bolton	Robert Bolton, *Some General Directions for a Comfortable Walking with God* (London, 1626)
Browne	Thomas Browne, *Pseudodoxia Epidemica, or Enquiries into Very Many Received Tenets and Commonly Presumed Truths* (London, 1646)
Caius	John Caius, *Of English Dogs: The Diversities, the Names, the Natures, and the Properties*, trans. Abraham Fleming (London, 1576)
Cotgrave, *Dictionary*	Randle Cotgrave, *A Dictionary of the French and English Tongues* (London, 1611)
Dodoens	Rembert Dodoens, *A New Herbal, or History of Plants* (London, 1578)
Fauchet	Claude Fauchet, *Recueil des antiquités gauloises et françaises* (Paris, 1579)
Fenton	Geoffrey Fenton, *Certain Tragical Discourses Written out of French and Latin* (London, 1567)
Flavigny	Charles de Flavigny, *Le Rois de France* (Geneva, 1593)
Frédégaire	*Chronicarum quae dicuntur Fredegarii Scholastici libri IV cum continuationibus*, ed. Bruno Krusch, in *Monumenta Germaniae historica. Scriptores rerum Merovingicarum*, vol. 11, *Fredegarii et aliorum chronica. Vitae sanctorum* (Hannover: Hahn, 1888), 1–193
Gentillet	Innocent Gentillet, *A Discourse upon the Means of Well Governing and Maintaining in Good Peace a Kingdom or Other Principality*, trans. Simon Patrick (London, 1602)
Goulart	Simon Goulart, *Mémoires de l'état de France sous Charles IX* (Meidelbourg, 1578)
Grimeston	Edward Grimeston, *A General Inventory of the History of France from the Beginning of That Monarchy unto the Treaty of Vervins in the Year 1598* (London, 1611, 2nd edn)
Jonson, *EMO*	*Every Man out of His Humour*, in *The Cambridge Edition of the Works of Ben Jonson*, gen. ed. David Bevington, Martin Butler, and Ian Donaldson, 7 vols (Cambridge University Press, 2012)
Leighton	Alexander Leighton, *An Appeal to the Parliament* (London, 1629)

Lucan, *Pharsalia*	Lucan, *The Civil War: Books I–X (Pharsalia)*, trans. J. D. Duff (London: Heinemann, 1962)
Machiavelli	Niccolò Machiavelli, *The Prince*, ed. Peter Bondanella (Oxford University Press, 2005)
Matthieu	Pierre Matthieu, *La conjuration de Conchine* (Paris, 1618)
O. B	O. B., *Questions of Profitable and Pleasant Concernings* (London, 1594)
Parkinson	John Parkinson, *Theatrum Botanicum* (London, 1640)
Pliny the Elder	Pliny the Elder, *The History of the World*, trans. Philemon Holland (London, 1601)
Prynne	William Prynne, *Histriomastix: The Player's Scourge, or Actor's Tragedy* (London, 1633)
Sala	Angelo Sala, *Opiologia, or A Treatise Concerning the Nature, Properties, True Preparation and Safe Use and Administration of Opium for the Comfort and Ease of All Such Persons as Are Inwardly Afflicted with Any Extreme Grief or Languishing Pain, Especially Such As Deprive the Body of All Natural Rest and Can Be Cured by No Other Means or Medicine Whatsoever* (London, 1618)
Schröder	Johann Schröder, *Zoologia, or The History of Animals* (London, 1659)
Sidney, *Arcadia*	Philip Sidney, *The Countess of Pembroke's Arcadia (The Old Arcadia)*, ed. Katherine Duncan-Jones (Oxford University Press, 1999)
Stafford	Anthony Stafford, *Meditations and Resolutions, Moral, Divine, Political* (London, 1612)
Statius, *Thebaid*	Statius, *Thebaid*, ed. and trans. D. R. Shackleton Bailey, 2 vols (Cambridge, MA: Harvard University Press, 2004)
Terence, *Andria*	Terence, *Andria*, ed. Sander M. Goldberg (Cambridge University Press, 2022)
Thomson, Ὀρθομεθοδος	George Thomson, Ὀρθομεθοδος Ἰατροχυμικη, *or The Direct Method of Curing Chemically* (London, 1675)
Tillet	Jean du Tillet, *Recueil des rois de France* (Paris, 1580)

Vicary	Thomas Vicary, *The English Man's Treasure with the True Anatomy of Man's Body* (London, 1596)
Vignier	Nicolas Vignier, *La Bibliotheque historiale* (Paris, 1587)
Walton	Izaak Walton, *The Complete Angler, or The Contemplative Man's Recreation* (London, 1653)
Williams, *Physical Rarities*	Ralph Williams, *Physical Rarities, Containing the Most Choice Receipts of Physick and Chirurgery for the Cure of All Diseases Incident to Man's Body* (London, 1651)
Woolley	Hannah Woolley, *A Supplement to The Queenlike Closet* (London, 1674)

OTHER REFERENCES

Adelman	Janet Adelman, *Suffocating Mothers: Fantasies of Maternal Origin in Shakespeare's Plays, Hamlet to The Tempest* (New York: Routledge, 1992)
Adler	Doris Adler, *Philip Massinger* (Boston, MA: Twayne, 1987)
Appleton	William W. Appleton, *Beaumont and Fletcher: A Critical Study* (London: Allen and Unwin, 1956)
Baldwin	Thomas Whitfield Baldwin, *The Organization and Personnel of the Shakespearean Company* (Princeton University Press, 1927)
Bevington	David Bevington, 'Textual Analysis', in *Antony and Cleopatra* by William Shakespeare (Cambridge University Press, 1990; updated edn 2005), 271–80
Blake	Norman Francis Blake, *A Grammar of Shakespeare's Language* (Basingstoke: Palgrave, 2002)
Blamires	Adrian Blamires, '"*Shrill cryings*" and "*often dyings*": Wedding Night Tragedy on the Renaissance Stage' (unpublished PhD thesis, University of Reading, UK, 2016)
Bliss, 'Introduction'	Lee Bliss, 'Introduction', in *A King and No King* by Francis Beaumont and John Fletcher (Manchester University Press, 2004), 1–55

Bliss, 'Romance'	Lee Bliss, 'Tragicomic Romance for the King's Men, 1609–1611: Shakespeare, Beaumont, and Fletcher', in *Comedy from Shakespeare to Sheridan: Change and Continuity in the English and European Dramatic Tradition*, ed. Albert R. Braunmuller and James C. Bulman (Newark, DE: University of Delaware Press, 1986), 148–64
Bowers, *Revenge*	Fredson Bowers, *Elizabethan Revenge Tragedy 1587–1642* (Princeton University Press, 1940)
Bowers, 'Short Lines'	Fredson Bowers, 'Establishing Shakespeare's Text: Notes on Short Lines and the Problem of Verse Division', *Studies in Bibliography*, 33 (1980), 74–130
Brown	Sarah Ann Brown, 'Welsh Characters in Renaissance Drama' (unpublished PhD thesis, Texas Tech University, USA, 2000)
Cameron	Kenneth Walter Cameron, '*Othello*, Quarto 1, Reconsidered', *PMLA*, 47 (1932), 671–83
Carlson	Marvin Carlson, *The Haunted Stage: The Theatre as Memory Machine* (Ann Arbor, MI: University of Michigan Press, 2002)
Cartwright	Robert Cartwright, *Shakespeare and Jonson: Dramatic, versus Wit-Combats. Auxiliary Forces: Beaumont and Fletcher, Marston, Dekker, Chapman, and Webster* (London: John Russell Smith, 1864)
Chelli	Maurice Chelli, *Étude sur la Collaboration de Massinger avec Fletcher et son groupe* (Paris: Presses Universitaires de France, 1926)
Clark	Sandra Clark, *The Plays of Beaumont and Fletcher: Sexual Themes and Dramatic Representation* (Hemel Hempstead: Harvester Wheatsheaf, 1994)
Coatalen	Guillaume Coatalen, 'Shakespeare and Other "Tragicall Discourses" in an Early-Seventeenth-Century Commonplace Book from Oriel College, Oxford', *English Manuscript Studies 1100–1700*, 13 (2007), 120–64
Clubb	Louise George Clubb, *Italian Drama in Shakespeare's Time* (New Haven, CT: Yale University Press, 1989)

Compagnoni	Michela Compagnoni, 'Blending Motherhoods: Volumnia and the Representation of Maternity in William Shakespeare's *Coriolanus*', in *Roman Women in Shakespeare and His Contemporaries*, ed. Domenico Lovascio (Kalamazoo, MI: Medieval Institute Publications, 2020), 39–58
'Conjuration'	'*Conjuration de Conchine* ou l'Histoire du mouvement dernier', *Le moniteur de la libraire*, 15 June 1842 (11), 12
Crystal and Crystal	Ben Crystal and David Crystal, *Shakespeare's Words: A Glossary and Language Companion* (Cambridge University Press, 2008)
Dessen and Thomson	Alan C. Dessen and Leslie Thomson, *A Dictionary of Stage Directions in English Drama, 1580–1642* (Cambridge University Press, 1999)
Dessen, *Elizabethan*	Alan C. Dessen, *Elizabethan Stage Conventions and Modern Interpreters* (Cambridge University Press, 1984)
Dessen, *Recovering*	Alan C. Dessen, *Recovering Shakespeare's Theatrical Vocabulary* (Cambridge University Press, 1995)
'Dramatic Records'	'Dramatic Records from the Privy Council Register, 1603–1642', *Malone Society Collections*, 1.4–5 (1911)
Dutton, 'Historical Allegory'	Richard Dutton, '*Thierry and Theodoret*: Historical Allegory and the Circumvention of Censorship', *Medieval and Renaissance Drama in England*, 37 (2024), forthcoming
Edwards	Robert R. Edwards, '"Lessons meete to be followed": The European Reception of Boccaccio's *Questioni d'amore*', *Textual Cultures*, 10 (2016), 146–63
ER	'Review of Dyce's *Beaumont and Fletcher*', *The Edinburgh Review*, 86 (1847), 42–67
Farmer and Henley	J. S. Farmer and W. E. Henley, *Slang and Its Analogues*, 7 vols (London: Routledge and Kegan Paul, 1890–1904)
Fleay	F. G. Fleay, *A Biographical Chronicle of the English Drama, 1559–1642*, 2 vols (London: Reeves and Turner, 1891)

Freebury-Jones, 'Attributions'	Darren Freebury-Jones, 'Authorship Attributions in the Fletcher Canon', *Medieval and Renaissance Drama in England*, 38 (2025), forthcoming
Freebury-Jones, 'Collaborator'	Darren Freebury-Jones, 'John Fletcher's Collaborator on *The Noble Gentleman*', *Studia Metrica et Poetica*, 7 (2020), 43–60
Galant	Justyna Galant, '*Thierry and Theodoret* by John Fletcher and Francis Beaumont: Reanimating Femininity', in *The Lives of Texts: Exploring the Metaphor*, ed. Katarzyna Pisarska and Andrzej Sławomir Kowalczyk (Newcastle upon Tyne: Cambridge Scholars Publishing, 2014), 207–26
Genest	John Genest, *Some Account of the English Stage, from the Restoration in 1660 to 1830, in Ten Volumes*, vol. 6 (Bath: Carrington, 1832)
Gill	Roma Gill, '"Necessitie of State": Massinger's *Believe As You List*', *English Studies*, 46 (1965), 407–17
Gossett	Suzanne Gossett, 'Introduction', in *Philaster*, by Francis Beaumont and John Fletcher (London: Methuen for Arden Shakespeare, 2009), 1–102
Gowing	Laura Gowing, *Common Bodies: Women, Touch and Power in Seventeenth-Century England* (New Haven, CT: Yale University Press, 2003)
Hall	Kim F. Hall, *Things of Darkness: Economies of Race and Gender in Early Modern England* (Ithaca, NY: Cornell University Press, 1995)
Hallissy	Margaret Hallissy, *Venomous Woman: Fear of the Female in Literature* (Westport, CT: Greenwood Press, 1987)
Hazlitt	William Hazlitt, *Lectures on the Dramatic Literature of the Age of Elizabeth* (New York: Wiley, 1849)
Hensman	Bertha Hensman, *The Shares of Fletcher, Field and Massinger in Twelve Plays of the Beaumont and Fletcher Canon*, 2 vols (Salzburg: Institut für Englische Sprache und Literatur, 1974)

Hirsh	James E. Hirsh, *The Structure of Shakespearean Scenes* (New Haven, CT: Yale University Press, 1981)
Honigmann	E. A. J. Honigmann, 'Re-Enter the Stage Direction: Shakespeare and Some Contemporaries', *Shakespeare Survey*, 29 (1976), 117–25
Hoy, 'Shares (III)'	Cyrus Hoy, 'The Shares of Fletcher and His Collaborators in the Beaumont and Fletcher Canon (III)', *Studies in Bibliography*, 11 (1958), 85–106
Hoy, 'Shares (IV)'	Cyrus Hoy, 'The Shares of Fletcher and His Collaborators in the Beaumont and Fletcher Canon (IV)', *Studies in Bibliography*, 12 (1959), 91–116
Ichikawa	Mariko Ichikawa, *Shakespearean Entrances* (Basingstoke: Palgrave Macmillan, 2002)
Jackson, *Records*	William A. Jackson, *Records of the Court of the Stationers' Company* (London: The Bibliographical Society, 1957)
Jackson, 'Tourneur'	MacDonald P. Jackson, 'Cyril Tourneur and *The Honest Man's Fortune*', *Medieval and Renaissance Drama in England*, 32 (2019), 203–18
Karim-Cooper	Farah Karim-Cooper, *Cosmetics in Shakespearean and Renaissance Drama* (Edinburgh University Press, 2006)
Kenny	Amy Kenny, *Humoral Wombs on the Shakespearean Stage* (Cham: Palgrave Macmillan, 2019)
Koeppel	Emil Koeppel, *Quellen-Studien zu den Dramen Ben Jonsons, John Marstons, und Beaumonts und Fletchers* (Erlangen: A. Deichert, 1895)
Lamb	Charles Lamb, *Specimens of English Dramatic Poets Who Lived about the Time of Shakespeare* (London: Longman, Hurst, Rees, and Orme, 1808)
Lang	Andrew Lang, *History of English Literature from Beowulf to Swinburne* (New York: Longmans, Green & Co., 1912)
Leech	Clifford Leech, *The John Fletcher Plays* (Cambridge, MA: Harvard University Press, 1962)

Le Long	Jacques Le Long, *Bibliothèque historique de la France* (Paris: Herissant, 1769)
Lewis	Edward Danby Lewis, 'John Fletcher: His Distinctive Structural and Stylistic Contribution to English Drama' (unpublished PhD thesis, Yale University, USA, 1941)
Lovascio, *Fletcher's Rome*	Domenico Lovascio, *John Fletcher's Rome: Questioning the Classics* (Manchester University Press, 2022)
Lovascio, 'Unveiling Wives'	Domenico Lovascio, 'Unveiling Wives: Euripides' *Alcestis* and Two Plays in the Fletcher Canon', in *Classical Receptions in Early Modern English Drama*, ed. Silvia Bigliazzi and Tania Demetriou (University of Verona, 2024), forthcoming
LPD	*Lost Plays Database*, ed. Roslyn L. Knutson, David McInnis, Matthew Steggle, and Misha Teramura (Washington, DC: Folger Shakespeare Library, 2009–)
Luis-Martinez	Zenón Luis-Martínez, *In Words and Deeds: The Spectacle of Incest in English Renaissance Tragedy* (Amsterdam: Rodopi, 2002)
Lupić and Greatley-Hirsch	Ivan Lupić and Brett Greatley-Hirsch, '"What stuff is here?": Edmond Malone and the 1778 Edition of Beaumont and Fletcher', *Papers of the Bibliographical Society of America*, 111 (2017), 287–315
Massai	Sonia Massai, *Shakespeare and the Rise of the Editor* (Cambridge University Press, 2007)
Maxwell	Baldwin Maxwell, *Studies in Beaumont, Fletcher, and Massinger* (Chapel Hill, NC: University of North Carolina Press, 1939)
McDonald	Russ McDonald, 'Fashion: Shakespeare and Beaumont and Fletcher', in *A Companion to Shakespeare's Works, Volume IV: The Poems, Problem Comedies, Late Plays*, ed. Richard Dutton and Jean E. Howard (Malden, MA: Blackwell, 2003), 150–74
McKeithan	Daniel Morley McKeithan, *The Debt to Shakespeare in the Beaumont-and-Fletcher Plays* (Austin: privately printed, 1938)

McInnis	David McInnis, *Shakespeare and Lost Plays: Reimagining Drama in Early Modern England* (Cambridge University Press, 2021)
McManus	Clare McManus, 'Introduction', in *The Island Princess*, by John Fletcher (London: Methuen for Arden Shakespeare, 2012), 1–95
McMillin	Scott McMillin, 'Introduction', in *The First Quarto of* Othello (Cambridge University Press, 2001), 1–47
Meads	Chris Meads, *Banquets Set Forth: Banqueting in English Renaissance Drama* (Manchester University Press, 2001)
Morley	Carol A. Morley, *The Plays and Poems of William Heminge* (Madison, NJ: Fairleigh Dickinson University Press, 2006)
Mousnier	Roland Mousnier, 'Le Roi-Soleil', *La France au temps de Louis XIV*, ed. Jacques Goimard (Paris: Hachette, 1965)
Munro, 'Plotting'	Lucy Munro, 'Plotting, Ambiguity and Community in the Plays of Beaumont and Fletcher', in *Community-Making in Early Stuart Theatres: Stage and Audience*, ed. Anthony W. Johnson, Roger D. Sell, and Helen Wilcox (Abingdon: Routledge, 2017), 255–74
Munro, '"Sblood!"'	Lucy Munro, '"Sblood!": Hamlet's Oaths and the Editing of Shakespeare's Plays', *Shakespeare Survey*, 70 (2017), 123–34
Nares	Robert Nares, *A Glossary, or Collection of Words, Phrases, Names, and Allusions to Customs, Proverbs, &c., which Have Been Thought to Require Illustration in the Works of English Authors, Particularly Shakespeare and His Contemporaries* (London: Robert Triphook, 1822)
O'Connell	James J. Mainard O'Connell, 'Hell Is Discovered', in *Renaissance Papers 2008*, ed. Christopher Cobb (Woodbridge: Boydell and Brewer, 2009), 65–88
Oliphant, 'Notes'	E. H. C. Oliphant, 'The Plays of Beaumont and Fletcher: Some Additional Notes', *Philological Quarterly*, 9 (1930), 7–22

Oliphant, *Plays*	E. H. C. Oliphant, *The Plays of Beaumont and Fletcher: An Attempt to Determine Their Respective Shares and the Shares of Others* (New Haven, CT: Yale University Press, 1927)
Panek	Jennifer Panek, *Widows and Suitors in Early Modern English Comedy* (Cambridge University Press, 2004)
Paster	Gail Kern Paster, *The Body Embarrassed: Drama and the Disciplines of Shame in Early Modern England* (Ithaca, NY: Cornell University Press, 1993)
Pearse	Nancy Cotton Pearse, *John Fletcher's Chastity Plays: Mirrors of Modesty* (Lewisburg, PA: Bucknell University Press, 1973)
Pérez Díez	José A. Pérez Díez, 'Introduction', in *Love's Cure, or The Martial Maid*, by John Fletcher and Philip Massinger (Manchester University Press, 2022), 1–61
Pitcher	John Pitcher, 'Introduction', in *The Winter's Tale*, by William Shakespeare (London: A&C Black for Arden Shakespeare, 2010), 1–135
PLRE	*Private Libraries in Renaissance England* (Washington, DC: Folger Shakespeare Library, 1992–), https://plre.folger.edu/
Pollard	Tanya Pollard, *Greek Tragic Women on Shakespearean Stages* (Oxford University Press, 2017)
Rochester	Joanne Rochester, *Staging Spectatorship in the Plays of Philip Massinger* (Farnham: Ashgate, 2010)
Schelling	Felix E. Schelling, *Elizabethan Drama, 1558–1642*, 2 vols (Boston, MA: Houghton, 1908)
Seward, 'Preface'	Thomas Seward, 'Preface' to *The Works of Mr Francis Beaumont and Mr John Fletcher*, 10 vols (London: Tonson and Draper, 1750), 1:v–lxxvi
Sherbo	Arthur Sherbo, '*The Knight of Malta* and Boccaccio's *Filocolo*', *English Studies*, 33 (1952), 254–7
Shrank and Werstine	Cathy L. Shrank and Paul Werstine, 'The Shakespeare Manuscripts', in *The Arden*

	Research Handbook of Shakespeare and Textual Studies, ed. Lukas Erne (London: Bloomsbury Arden Shakespeare, 2021), 53–70
Shuger	Deborah K. Shuger, *The Renaissance Bible: Scholarship, Sacrifice, and Subjectivity* (Berkeley, CA: University of California Press, 1994)
Squier	Charles L. Squier, *John Fletcher* (Boston, MA: Twayne, 1986)
Steggle	Matthew Steggle, *Laughing and Weeping in Early Modern Theatres* (Aldershot: Ashgate, 2007)
Swinburne	A. C. Swinburne, 'The Earlier Plays of Beaumont and Fletcher', *North American Review*, 191 (1910), 612–25
Thomson, 'Beds'	Leslie Thomson, 'Beds on the Early Modern Stage', *Early Theatre*, 19 (2016), 31–58
Thomson, '"Pass over the stage"'	Leslie Thomson, '"Pass over the stage"—Again', in *Staging Shakespeare: Essays in Honor of Alan C. Dessen*, ed. Lena Cowen Orlin and Miranda Johnson-Haddad (Newark, DE: University of Delaware Press, 2007), 23–44
Thorndike	Ashley H. Thorndike, *The Influence of Beaumont and Fletcher on Shakespeare* (Worcester, MA: Wood, 1901)
Turner, 'Introduction'	Robert Kean Turner, '*The Tragedy of Thierry and Theodoret*: Textual Introduction', in *The Dramatic Works in the Beaumont and Fletcher Canon*, gen. ed. Fredson Bowers, 10 vols (Cambridge University Press, 1966–96), 3:365–74
Turner, 'Notes'	Robert Kean Turner, 'Notes on the Text of *Thierry and Theodoret* Q1', *Studies in Bibliography*, 14 (1961), 218–31
Turner, 'Press-variants'	Robert Kean Turner, 'Press-variants in Q1', in *The Dramatic Works in the Beaumont and Fletcher Canon*, gen. ed. Fredson Bowers, 10 vols (Cambridge University Press, 1966–96), 3:460–3
Ulrich	Otto Ulrich, *Die pseudohistorischen Dramen Beaumonts und Fletchers:* Thierry and Theodoret, Valentinian, The Prophetess *und* The

	False One *und ihre Quellen* (Straßburg: Neuesten Nachrichten, 1913)
Waith	Eugene M. Waith, *The Pattern of Tragicomedy in Beaumont and Fletcher* (New Haven, CT: Yale University Press, 1952)
Ward	A. W. Ward, *A History of English Dramatic Literature to the Death of Queen Anne: Volume II* (London: Macmillan & Co., 1875)
Weber, 'Introduction'	Henry Weber, 'Introduction' to *The False One*, in *The Works of Beaumont and Fletcher*, 14 vols (Edinburgh: Ballantyne, 1812), 5.3–5
Wells	Stanley Wells, *Re-Editing Shakespeare for the Modern Reader* (Oxford: Clarendon Press, 1984)
Werstine	Paul Werstine, 'Line Division in Shakespeare's Dramatic Verse: An Editorial Problem', *Analytical and Enumerative Bibliography*, 8 (1984), 73–125
White	Martin White, 'Introduction', in *The Roman Actor*, by Philip Massinger (Manchester University Press, 2007), 1–67
Wiggins, *Catalogue*	Martin Wiggins, in association with Catherine Richardson, *British Drama, 1533–1642: A Catalogue*, 9 vols (Oxford University Press, 2012–18)
Wiggins, 'Four'	Martin Wiggins, 'Signs of the Four', *Around the Globe*, 57 (2014), 48–9
Williams, *Dictionary*	Gordon Williams, *A Dictionary of Sexual Language and Imagery in Shakespearean and Stuart Literature*, 3 vols (London: Athlone Press, 1994)
Williams, 'Field'	M. E. Williams, 'Field, Nathan (bap. 1587, d. 1619/20)', in *Oxford Dictionary of National Biography* (Oxford University Press, 2004), https://doi.org/10.1093/ref:odnb/9391 (accessed 14 July 2022)
Williams, 'Year's Contribution'	George Walton Williams, 'The Year's Contribution to Shakespearean Studies', *Shakespeare Survey*, 34 (1981), 191–3
Wright	George T. Wright, *Shakespeare's Metrical Art* (Berkeley, CA: University of California Press, 1988)

Wymer   Rowland Wymer, *Suicide and Despair in the Jacobean Drama* (Brighton: Harvester, 1986)

Quotations from all early modern English texts are modernized in spelling and punctuation or are taken from modernized editions.

The date limits and 'best guesses' for all the plays mentioned in the book are those provided by Wiggins, *Catalogue*, unless otherwise noted.

Introduction

AUTHORSHIP

The external evidence concerning the authorship of the play is rather weak. No authorial attribution is given on Q1's title page (see Figure 1). Q2 (1648) attributes the play to Fletcher, whereas its 1649 reissue assigns *Thierry and Theodoret* to Beaumont and Fletcher. It is therefore necessary to rely on internal evidence to try to establish the identities of the co-authors of the play. In his influential study of authorship in the Beaumont and Fletcher canon, Cyrus Hoy assigned 1.1, 2.2, 4.1, and 5.2 of *Thierry and Theodoret* to Fletcher; 1.2, 2.1, 2.3, and 4.2 to Massinger; 3.1–3 and 5.1 to Beaumont.[1] Hoy based his attributions on the examination of the appearance of typical stylistic traits of each playwright in the respective shares of the various plays. These traits range from linguistic preferences to patterns of versification, such as the presence/absence of Fletcher's typical pronominal 'ye', the use of 'hath' (Massinger) vs 'has' (Fletcher), the preference for either 'them' (Massinger) or '"em' (Fletcher), as well as Fletcher's characteristic recourse to such contractions as 'i'th", 'o'th", 'h'as', '"s' (for his), and 'let's', together with his tendency to use lines of iambic pentameter with a double ending (i.e., with an extra unstressed syllable at the end of the line). Distinguishing Fletcher from Massinger was relatively straightforward for Hoy, but things were more complicated in the case of Beaumont, whose hand was harder to identify because very few of his solo works are extant and because his writing style is not as recognizable as either Fletcher's or Massinger's. In the works of Beaumont, Hoy observed 'a tendency to employ together such distinctive linguistic forms as *ye*, *hath*, *doth*, and *'em*, without using any of these to any very marked degree'; in the share he assigns to him in *Thierry and Theodoret* he identifies 'single instances of *ye*, *hath*, and *doth*, while *'em* and *them* are used 6 times each'.[2]

Hoy's attribution of Fletcher's and Massinger's shares of *Thierry and Theodoret* has gone unchallenged, but the attribution to Beaumont has been disputed, chiefly because of the unquestionable presence of Massinger, which – as we now know – must exclude Beaumont on chronological grounds.[3] Massinger's earliest documented

THE
TRAGEDY
OF THIERRY KING OF
France, *and his Brother*
Theodoret.

As it was diuerſe times acted at the Blacke-
Friers by the Kings Maieſties
Seruants.

LONDON,
Printed for *Thomas Walkley*, and are to bee ſold at
his ſhop in *Britaines Burſe*, at the ſigne of
the Eagle and Child.
1621.

Figure 1 Title page of Q1

collaboration with Fletcher dates from 1613 in *The Honest Man's Fortune* (with Nathan Field and possibly Cyril Tourneur), but there is no known Beaumont-and-Fletcher play later than *The Captain* (1612); moreover, Beaumont suffered a debilitating stroke in 1613 and stopped writing altogether – he then died in 1616.[4]

The only possibility for having both Beaumont and Massinger as Fletcher's co-authors would be to posit a Massingerian revision of a play originally penned by Beaumont and Fletcher. Yet all known Massinger revisions of Fletcher's plays can be dated to the 1630s, and it would be difficult to explain why Massinger, a relatively inexperienced playwright in the 1610s, would have been entrusted with a revision of a Fletcherian play while Fletcher was still alive.[5]

If the third collaborator was *not* Beaumont, as seems overwhelmingly more likely, the question remains as to who partnered with Fletcher and Massinger to write *Thierry and Theodoret*. Even before Hoy's study, various candidates other than Beaumont had been proposed, ranging from George Chapman to John Webster to Nathan Field. Martin Wiggins labels this unidentified collaborator, who shares the 'negligible' stylistic traits of Beaumont, as the 'shadow Beaumont', and argues that differentiating him 'from the real one would be a useful task for future authorship research'.[6]

Darren Freebury-Jones has taken up the challenge. By using stylometric analysis on the basis of the results for automated searches of phrasal matches between plays in the publicly accessible electronic corpus of 527 plays dated between 1552 and 1657 developed by Pervez Rizvi (*Collocations and N-grams*), Freebury-Jones has managed to assign to Field sections of *Love's Pilgrimage* (1616, with Fletcher), *Beggars' Bush* (1616, with Fletcher and Massinger), *Rollo, Duke of Normandy, or The Bloody Brother* (1617, with Fletcher and Massinger), and *Thierry and Theodoret*. Thus, he has significantly augmented Field's canon beyond his two solo plays *A Woman is a Weathercock* (1609) and *Amends for Ladies* (1610), his collaboration with Massinger *The Fatal Dowry* (1619), and parts of *Four Plays, or Moral Representations, in One* (1613, with Fletcher), *The Honest Man's Fortune*, the lost 'The Jeweller of Amsterdam' (1616, with Fletcher and Massinger), *The Queen of Corinth* (1617, with Fletcher and Massinger), and *The Knight of Malta* (1618, with Fletcher and Massinger).[7] Sections of *Thierry and Theodoret* had already been attributed to Field by such scholars as F. G. Fleay, Maurice Chelli, William Wells, and Bertha Hensman, though with little or no accompanying discussion.[8]

The results of Freebury-Jones's investigation of matching verbal formulae are persuasive, even though it must be pointed out that some of the typical stylistic traits that are usually associated with Field are not as strongly visible in *Thierry and Theodoret* as in other plays in which he had a hand. Hoy argues that Field's linguistic pattern – though not as recognizable as either Fletcher's or Massinger's – is, in general terms, 'marked by the occasional use of *ye* and *y*', a fairly regular use of *hath* and *doth*, and a tendency to employ such contractions as *ha'* and combinations with *'ee* which, although present in certain of the Fletcher-Massinger collaborations, are not found in their unaided work'.[9] These characteristics are not particularly evident in Act 3 and Act 5, scene 1, of *Thierry and Theodoret*, but two further 'stylistic mannerisms' that Hoy identifies as typical of Field (and that Freebury-Jones does not discuss in any detail) are. One is Field's tendency to use 'grammatical inversions that generally accomplish the purpose of relegating some form of the verb to the end of the sentence or clause'; the other is 'Field's fondness for having characters speak in unison'.[10] As it happens, the third collaborator's share of *Thierry and Theodoret* features at least two instances of grammatical inversions of the kind described by Hoy: 'Which seeing alone may in your look be read' (3.1.32), and 'Who must alone her sex's want supply' (3.1.128). Moreover, six of the seven unison speeches that appear in the play (all headed '*Omnes.*' in Q1) are to be found in scenes penned by the third playwright (3.2 and 5.1).

The lives and careers of Fletcher (1579–1625) and Massinger (1583–1640) need not be covered here, as they have been illustrated in previous volumes of the Revels Plays series, but some basic information needs to be provided concerning Field.[11] Baptized on 17 October 1587 in the parish of St Giles Cripplegate in London, Nathan Field was the seventh of the seven children of the puritan Revd John Field. His acting career started in 1600. As a pupil at St Paul's School, he was recruited to the company of the Children of the Chapel Royal, with which he performed several roles over the years in such plays as Beaumont's *The Knight of the Burning Pestle* and Ben Jonson's *Poetaster* and *Epicene*, as well as in a number of city and court entertainments. A good friend of Jonson and of Fletcher, Field also wrote commendatory verses for *Volpone*, *The Faithful Shepherdess*, and *Catiline His Conspiracy*.

Field's playwriting career started with the comedy *A Woman is a Weathercock*, which was soon followed by another, *Amends for Ladies*.

In 1613 the Children of the Queen's Revels merged with Philip Henslowe's Lady Elizabeth's Men. Field became the leading figure of the new company. He appeared in Jonson's *Bartholomew Fair*, and he took part in the writing of (and performed in) *The Honest Man's Fortune* and *Four Plays, or Moral Representations, in One*. In 1616 Field defected to the King's Men, and by 28 April 1619 he had become a sharer of the company. From 1616 to 1619 he wrote several plays with Fletcher and Massinger, and he continued to act in the new and revived plays that the company staged – he is listed as one of the principal actors in Shakespeare's First Folio of 1623. His acting skills gained him a reputation as one of greatest players of the age, which endured until after the Restoration.

The date of Field's death is uncertain. He must have been dead by 2 August 1620, when his sister Dorcas was awarded administration of his estate, but he must have been alive as late as 19 May 1619, when he was fourth in a livery allowance list. The fact that Field is not mentioned in the manuscript of *Sir John van Olden Barnavelt* might indicate that he was dead by August 1619, but only a handful of actors are named in the manuscript, so that the absence of his name cannot be taken as incontrovertible evidence to narrow down the time frame during which he died.

Considerations of style and of chronology make Field the most likely fit for the profile of the third collaborator in *Thierry and Theodoret*, and this edition accordingly attributes the play to him alongside Fletcher and Massinger.

DATING AND STAGE HISTORY

Thierry and Theodoret is notably difficult to date. The publication of Q1 sets the upper limit for the composition of the play to 1621, while the presence of Massinger and the absence of Beaumont among the playwrights who collaborated in the writing sets the lower limit to 1613 (see AUTHORSHIP, above). The stage history offers no help towards dating the play more precisely. *Thierry and Theodoret* is advertised on Q1's title page as having been 'divers times acted at the Blackfriars by the King's Majesty's Servants', and that it was indeed primarily intended for the Blackfriars may be borne out by the type of stage trapdoor needed for Theodoret's assassination at the hands of Protaldi in Act 3, scene 2 (see Commentary at 3.2.119.1. SD); besides, by the second half of the 1610s the Blackfriars was clearly the more lucrative venue for the King's Men, so that it would have been more likely for new plays to be aimed at that playhouse rather than the Globe. Yet no performance is recorded either in the seventeenth or the following centuries, and Henry Weber provides neither evidence nor clarifications for his assertion that '[t]he tragedy used to be represented frequently in former times'.[12] Besides, the play has not been hitherto the subject of a staged reading as part of the Shakespeare's Globe 'Read Not Dead' programme.[13]

Within the 1613–21 time span, Martin Wiggins indicates 1617 as the 'best guess' for the play's composition on the grounds that such a date 'has the advantage of evening out Fletcher's workload during the third quarter of the decade', and because he identifies affinities between *Thierry and Theodoret* and other plays in the canon of Fletcher and his collaborators written around 1617, namely

> his other work with the unidentified third collaborator, *Love's Pilgrimage* and *Beggars' Bush*, the latter of which shares some of its thematic concerns and tonal qualities; *The Loyal Subject*, another thematic and tonal associate; *Rollo*, with which it shares aspects of its narrative and period setting; and *The Knight of Malta*, which features a semi-comical soldier role (Norandine) similar to that of de Vitry.[14]

Similarities with other dramatic specimens in the canon of Fletcher and his collaborators are not necessarily dependable when it comes to dating the play, as the fact that some common traits between *Thierry and Theodoret* and such plays as *A King and No King* (1611, with Beaumont), *Cupid's Revenge* (1607, with Beaumont), and *The Maid's Tragedy* (1611, with Beaumont) persuaded Ashley Thorndike that *Thierry and Theodoret* was an early Beaumont-and-Fletcher play. Thorndike points out that the sequence in which Martel kicks and deprives Protaldi of his sword replicates that between Bacurius and Bessus in *A King and No King*, just as de Vitry's beating of Protaldi recalls that of Bessus by Ligones.[15] As for *Cupid's Revenge*, the affinity stands in the denouement, as 'The hero [i.e., Leucippus] dies by the hand of the wicked queen-mother; the heroine [i.e., Urania] dies ... with her beloved; the wicked queen-mother [i.e., Bacha] commits suicide [though she does so on stage unlike Brunehaut]; and the faithful friend [i.e., Ismenus] is left to curse her and to lament his friend.'[16] Finally, Thorndike identifies in *Thierry and Theodoret* five character types that he thinks are to be found in *Philaster* (1609, with Beaumont), *The Maid's Tragedy*, *A King and No King*, and *Cupid's Revenge* too, namely the 'devoted, sacrificing, idyllic' maid (Ordella), the blunt and faithful friend (Martel), the 'poltroon' (Protaldi), the evil Queen mother (Brunehaut), and her royal, flawed son (Thierry).[17]

Clifford Leech adds that the failure to consummate a marriage on the wedding night makes *Thierry and Theodoret* akin to both *The Maid's Tragedy* and *A Wife for a Month* (1624). The situations and the scenes themselves are different – in *The Maid's Tragedy* the marriage cannot be consummated because Evadne is the King's mistress, her marriage with Amintor being just a set-up, and the audience is caught by surprise when they discover the affair; in *A Wife for a Month* (1624), Valerio and Evanthe cannot have sex because otherwise King Frederick, who wants her for himself, will have her beheaded – yet all three plays are also 'alike both in being rooted in the idea of a wedding-night disaster and in their power to embarrass and disturb'.[18]

The analogues listed by Thorndike and Leech, while helpful in placing *Thierry and Theodoret* in the larger context of Fletcher's dramatic art and craft, are of no use towards dating the play; they rather stand as testament to the indelible mark that the playwriting years with Beaumont (1606–12) had on the remainder of Fletcher's career, during which the latter kept redeploying motifs, tropes, and situations typical of the plays they had penned together. By contrast, the multiple connections that *Thierry and Theodoret* has with *Rollo* seem stronger and possibly more decisive in chronologically situating the play within Fletcher's oeuvre: first, both plays are set in medieval France; second, the widow Queen dowager Sophia emerges as the exact antithesis of Brunehaut in her attempt to reconcile her sons Rollo and Otto rather than divide them; third, Rollo's order to the kitchen staff to poison Otto's food in his failed attempt to murder him is similar to Brunehaut's use of an anaphrodisiac potion in a cup of wine to make Thierry impotent with the help of Lacure; fourth, the first half of the action concludes with the murder of one of the brothers in both plays; fifth, both tragedies criticize the practice of astrology and the belief in horoscopes; sixth, both plays end with the succession falling to the dead brothers' loyal and morally upright friend/kinsman (Martel/Aubrey); finally, *Thierry and Theodoret* displays several close verbal echoes from *Rollo*, which are detailed in the Commentary.

Wiggins, however, does not limit himself to discussing resemblances and affinities between plays in the Fletcher canon. He also interestingly adds that the character of de Vitry 'could be named after the assassin of Marshal d'Ancre, which would confirm a date later than April 1617'.[19] Wiggins is here referring to the arrest and murder of Concino Concini, the favourite of Maria de' Medici, Queen of France. Born in Florence, Concini moved to France in 1600 with his wife, Leonora Dori, the Queen's lady-in-waiting. In 1610 he purchased the marquisate of Ancre, and he became Maréchal (or Marshal) of France in 1613, even though he had never actually fought on the battlefield. From that moment on, his political decisions and his behaviour attracted the hostility of all social classes, especially the nobility. In 1617 King Louis XIII, who had formally ascended the throne in 1610 (with his mother acting as regent for several years while he was still a minor), gave the command to imprison him. Concini, however, was too powerful to be arrested (he had an army of 7,000 soldiers), and the King had to devise a plot with the assistance of the Duc de Luynes to have him killed. Concini was captured on the bridge of the Louvre castle on 24 April 1617, apparently resisted arrest, and was accordingly shot by Nicolas de L'Hôpital, Marquis and later Duc de Vitry, often referred to as Maréchal de Vitry. Concini's wife was also apprehended, charged with treason and sorcery – activities in which she had been apparently employed by the Queen – and finally beheaded on 8 July of the same year.

Fleay was the first to suggest that *Thierry and Theodoret* might have obliquely glanced at the murder of Concini: 'The astrology of Lacure and the name de Vitry distinctly point to the condemnation of Concini in 1617 for treason and sorcery. The whole play is a satire on the French Court under Marie de Medici. Vitri arrested the Maréchal d'Ancre and on his resistance killed him.'[20] Fleay's claim has been disputed repeatedly on the grounds that the name Vitry 'is too common to point very closely at the Vitri who arrested Maréchal d'Ancre', and that the way the play makes use of astrology does not seem to hint forcefully enough at the events in France, because, argues Thorndike, '[f]or a contemporary prototype of L[a]cure there is no need of going to France ... a much better example is to be found in the notorious Dr Simon Forman, of London'.[21]

However, no one has ever pointed out that an octavo French pamphlet probably written by Pierre Matthieu and published in Paris by Pierre Rocolet in late 1617, *La conjuration de Concino Concini* (reprinted in early 1618 as *La conjuration de Conchine*), draws an unexpected parallel between the historical Protade and Concini, the only known instance of an explicit comparison between the two personalities, which may have decisively inspired Fletcher and his collaborators (see SOURCES, below).[22]

The time frame for Fletcher to have had the possibility to read *La conjuration de Concino Concini* before writing the play is admittedly narrow, but Fletcher does seem to have had a propensity for drawing upon recently published books from the continent, especially from France and Spain.[23] It is impossible to demonstrate that he did read *La conjuration de Concino Concini*, but, if this is the case, then the date for the play's composition needs to be pushed forward to 1618 rather than 1617, though earlier than November 1618 if the four soldiers appearing in Act 5, scene 1, were to be played by what Wiggins has labelled the 'Gang of Four', namely 'a small ensemble of actors within the King's Men' who appeared in scenes together from 1613 to 1618 portraying 'distinct groups of four characters who interact primarily with one another and whose contribution to the play as a whole might not be felt to justify the deployment of quite so many actors'.[24] From 1614, these four actors are accompanied by a fifth in a configuration of 'Four Plus One', with 'the new recruit regularly [taking] the role of their leader, a semi-detached character who connects them to the wider world of the play at large', who in this case would be the actor playing de Vitry.[25]

A 1618 dating results in shifting Fletcher's workload to three plays in 1617 and four in 1618 rather than the other way around (and the proximity with *Rollo* and the other plays that Wiggins singles out as displaying affinities with it still holds), but it interestingly brings *Thierry and Theodoret* closer to *The Knight of Malta*, with which it curiously shares (apart from the partly comical soldier role mentioned above) the Euripidean theatregram of the presumably deceased veiled wife restored to her grieving husband from Euripides' *Alcestis* (see SOURCES, below), which Fletcher only uses in these two plays – the use of it in *The Knight of Malta* probably also functioning as a sort of comment upon the use he had made of it in the earlier play.[26]

I believe that the decisive element in the dating, however, must be the pamphlet. If we accept – as I incline to do – that Fletcher and his collaborators knew it, then the play cannot have been crafted before 1618. If we do not, then Wiggins's suggestion of 1617 seems likelier.

SOURCES

French accounts
The main plot of the play is based on medieval French history.[27] It deals with the events of the life of Brunhilda of Austrasia and her two grandsons, Theuderic II, King of Burgundy, and Theudebert II, King of Austrasia, between 599 and 613. The incidents dramatized in the play are reported in a wide array of historical accounts, the best-known ones being the *Chronique de Frédégaire* (seventh century), Aimoin of Fleury's *Historia Francorum* or *Libri quinque de gestis Francorum* (tenth century), Claude Fauchet's *Recueil des Antiquités gauloises et françaises* (1579), and Jean de Serres's *Inventaire général de l'histoire de France* (1597). Among these, as Felix E. Schelling first argued and Otto Ulrich later demonstrated, Fletcher and his collaborators almost certainly consulted Edward Grimeston's translation of de Serres's *Inventaire général*, published in 1607 with the title *A General Inventory of the History of France from the Beginning of That Monarchy unto the Treaty of Vervins in the Year 1598*.[28] A second edition appeared in 1611.

While all the older chroniclers relate the essential facts of the narrative that were employed by the playwrights, Ulrich points out that they do so in different places, some of which are far apart in the respective volumes, whereas de Serres (and, hence, Grimeston) offers in few pages an almost novel-like presentation of the same material.[29] Moreover, as Table 1 shows, comparing the names of the main characters in the play with those that appear in the several historical accounts decisively settles the matter. There are at least three crucial resemblances as far as names are concerned that point to Grimeston's translation as the main source of the play:

1. 'Thierri' and 'Theodebert' are the closest forms to those used in the play, namely, 'Thierry' and 'Theodoret'. The 1611 edition of Grimeston even spells the first name with a final '-y', which seems to weigh in favour of Fletcher and his collaborators' having consulted that edition;
2. 'Membergue' is much more similar to 'Memberge' than all other forms;
3. 'Dataric' is almost the same as 'Datarick'.

In addition, Theodoret's order that his mother go to a monastery to atone for her lasciviousness is only to be found in de Serres's account (and, hence, in Grimeston); finally, there are several other

Table 1

Frédégaire	Aimoin	Fauchet	De Serres	Grimeston	T&T
Teudericus	Theodericus	Thierry	Thierri	Thierri/Thierry (2nd edn)	Thierry
Teudebertus	Theodebertus	Thiebert	Theodebert	Theodebert	Theodoret
Brunechildis	Brunechildis	Brunehaut	Brunehault	Brunehault	Brunhalt
Ermenberga	Hermenberga	Hermanberge	Membergue	Membergue	Ordella
Betteric	Bertric	Bertrefred/Bertric	Dateric	Dataric	Datarick
—	—	—	—	—	Memberge

verbal affinities and resemblances in points of detail – duly noted in the Commentary – that clearly suggest that Grimeston's translation is the main narrative source of *Thierry and Theodoret*.

Fletcher and his collaborators compress, simplify, and alter de Serres/Grimeston's account in many ways. As Thorndike usefully sums up, in the play 'all the battles and their accessories, with which the historical narrative is filled, are omitted, and the scenes are pretty closely confined to the palaces of the two kings'.[30] The most evident variation is the playwrights' making Brunehaut Thierry and Theodoret's mother rather than their grandmother. Ulrich argues that the variation was necessary because the acts of Brunehaut can seem possible and understandable during the old age of a mother but scarcely during that of a grandmother.[31] Leech claims that the change was made not only 'in the interest of verisimilitude', but also to make 'the relation with *King Lear* more evident' (see below).[32] Carol A. Morley points out that, by changing their degree of kinship, 'Fletcher neatly elides a generation and disentangles the network of vendettas to follow a clear narrative line through the source material'.[33]

These explanations are all (more or less) plausible – and I would add that, thematically, having a mother rather than a grandmother opens up the potential for a wider array of allusions and implications, given the early modern obsession with monstrous motherhood (see CRITICISM, below) – but it has never been noted before that Grimeston himself (following de Serres) mistakenly refers to Brunehault as Theodebert's mother at least once, namely when relating how, in light of her relationship with Protade, Theodebert felt compelled 'to find a means to withdraw *his mother* from the view of the multitude, who were eyewitnesses of the filthiness of this shameless old woman and of the ignominy of his house'.[34] Grimeston's slip may have either confused the playwrights or inspired their alteration of the historical facts. But the playwrights also had other precedents that they might have followed in making Brunehaut the mother of Thierry and Theodoret. For example, Simon Goulart, in *Mémoires de l'état de France sous Charles IX* (1577), relates that Brunechilde 'nourri si mal ses propres enfants Theodebert et Theodoric' (so poorly raised her own sons Theodebert and Theodoric); in *La bibliotheque historiale* (1587), Nicholas Vignier refers to 'Rois Theodoric et Theodebert, et à la reine Brunechilde leur mère' (Kings Theodoric and Theodobert, and the Queen Brunechilde their mother – though Vignier later correctly describes her as Theodoric and Theodebert's 'aïeule', i.e., grandmother); while Innocent Gentillet's *A Discourse upon the Means of Well Governing and Maintaining in Good Peace a Kingdom or Other Principality*, translated by Simon Patrick (1602), refers to Theodoric and Theodebert as 'the children of the Queen Brunehaut'.[35] Fletcher need not have read any of these texts, but we know that Gentillet's book was familiar to him, as there is evidence that he used it for *Rollo* and probably for *The False One* (1620, with Massinger).[36]

Thierry and Theodoret also deviates from Grimeston in other respects: Thierry is the King of France rather than Burgundy; the King of Spain becomes the King of Aragon; Membergue's name is changed to Ordella, and the name Memberge is given to Theodoret's daughter, who is unnamed in Grimeston; in Grimeston, Thierry murders Theodebert after learning from Brunehault that Theodebert is apparently a bastard, whereas in the play Brunehaut first has Protaldi murder Theodoret, then falsely reveals to Thierry that Theodoret is a bastard; in the play, Thierry's wife is not sent back to Spain after the missed consummation of the marriage (so that Brunehaut's plot backfires), and she finally dies by his side; the use of drugs and potions, for which Brunehault herself is responsible in Grimeston, is displaced in the play on to Lacure; Thierry dies of poison-induced sleep deprivation in the play, and not of poison-induced dysentery as in Grimeston; in the play, Brunehaut dies offstage by suicide roughly at the same time as Thierry, rather than surviving him and being sentenced to death much later by being tied to the tail of a wild mare – Fletcher's solution being much more dramatically and morally effective. Adrian Blamires also interestingly notes that whereas 'Thierry is a lustful king in the historical source', his 'erotic experience in the play is less certain', in that, 'when Thierry expresses pride over his Herculean potency, it is to boast more of continence, of how he restrains himself from tyrannical sexual abuses'; overall, Blamires concludes, 'the playwrights present Thierry as a more virtuous figure than in the source, though not one without significant moral ambiguity'.[37]

A further notable alteration to the historical record is to be found in the characterization of Protaldi, and it deserves more detailed discussion. Variously described in the chronicles as 'argutissimus et strenuus in cunctis' (very clever and vigorous in everything) in the *Chronique de Frédégaire*, 'sensu argutissimus, ac in consiliis haberetur cum primis strenuus' (very clever in thought and regarded as especially vigorous in decisions) by Aimoin, 'homme subtil et habile en toutes ses actions' (a subtle and clever man in all his actions) by Fauchet, Protaldi becomes in the play a cowardly braggart.[38] This might simply be the playwrights' taking advantage of the vagueness of Grimeston's description in order to insert a variation of the *miles gloriosus* in their play – Grimeston only reports that Protade was 'a young courtier' and that Brunehaut 'advanced him beyond duty or desert' – but it could more interestingly reflect what can be found in the 1617 French pamphlet mentioned above, *La conjuration de Concino Concini*.[39] Protade is here described as 'Italien ... homme de basse condition et de nulle valeur', just as in the play, and he is remarkably likened to Concini: 'En ce Protade nous voyons justement l'image de ce siècle, car Conchine, Italien comme lui et petit compagnon comme lui, s'était empare de tout le gouvernement des finances et de forces du royaume en telle sorte qu'il avois réduit en toutes extrémité les grands et la noblesse' (in this Protade we see precisely the image of this century, because Concini, Italian like him and a base fellow like him, had seized control of the finances and forces of the kingdom in such a way that he would have reduced to extremities the great and the nobility) if the grace of God had not intervened.[40]

Given that the story of Protaldi in the play and the historical events that led to Concini's death do not display decisive resemblances – apart from the fact that they were both favourites of a French queen, that they are entrusted with a high military role in spite of their lack of experience, and that they are both captured by a character called de Vitry (which entails a significant deviation from Grimeston's account, in which Protade is murdered in his tent by French noblemen after Thierry and Theodebert's reconciliation) – it is striking to find a French pamphlet that makes an explicit connection between two personalities so far apart in history, and it significantly corroborates Fleay's case for a connection between *Thierry and Theodoret* and the murder of Maréchal d'Ancre. Interestingly, the form of the name used by Fletcher and his collaborators, Protaldi, is nowhere to be found in the historical accounts (in which he is variously known as Protade, Protadius, Proclade, or Proclaide) and may be viewed as having been intended subtly to point to the Italian provenance of the character after such well-known Italian names as Grimaldi and Ubaldi – though it must be noted that other historical accounts also state that Protade was Italian, and not only the 1617 pamphlet.[41]

INTRODUCTION 15

Moreover, nobody has hitherto commented upon the name chosen for Thierry's bastard son in the play, that is, Leonor. The name is an invention of the playwrights; the sources upon which Fletcher and his collaborators drew do not mention the names of any of the bastard sons of either Thierry or Theodoret; in addition, Leonor was a female name, which may be an oblique reference to Concini's wife Leonora. In a forthcoming article, Richard Dutton interestingly focuses on the correspondences between Brunehaut and Maria de' Medici: both act as regents for their royal sons, both wield power not usually entrusted to women in the early modern period, and both have a very public relationship with a favourite (though not of a sexual nature in Marie's case).[42]

As noted earlier (see DATING AND STAGE HISTORY, above), it is impossible to ascertain whether Fletcher and his co-adjutors did consult *La conjuration de Concino Concini*, but it would be a striking coincidence for a play in which the Italian-like-named Protaldi, a hateful favourite of the Queen dowager of France, is captured by a soldier named de Vitry not to have any connection to a pamphlet that likens Protade to Concini, an Italian favourite of the Queen of France, who was arrested and murdered by Maréchal de Vitry. True, the action does not mimic that of the killing of Maréchal d'Ancre, but the elements are so artfully rearranged that the roles of the Italian Protaldi and of de Vitry, the characterization of Brunehaut as Queen mother, and even the name Leonor line up to speak to the case. My guess is that Fletcher came into possession of a copy of the pamphlet through the channels he regularly used to obtain books from the continent, got the idea of the association Protade–Concini from there, and then went on to find the historical information that he needed to create *Thierry and Theodoret*, so as to conceive a play based on the story of Brunehaut and Protaldi that would look at the recent events in France in a way sufficiently aslant not to raise the censor's eyebrows.[43] When early modern English playwrights could not write openly on a topic, they were remarkably inventive in finding something that was just close enough to duck under the censorship – especially when handling material that might offend a foreign ambassador – but that would nonetheless invite the audience to make the necessary connections themselves.

Be that as it may, Fletcher and his collaborators might have drawn small details of the play from other French historical accounts as well. Thorndike claims that the character of Lacure 'is obviously suggested by Protald[i]'s companion in the chronicles', whom Fauchet describes as the 'premier médecin du roi'.[44] Finally, the idea that Theodoret was taken as a changeling because the Queen had no hope of conceiving other children might have been suggested by a passage in Charles de Flavigny's *Le Rois de France* (1593).[45]

King Lear, Henry IV Part 1, *and* Macbeth

Although the main source for the events dramatized in *Thierry and Theodoret* is indisputably Grimeston, Daniel Morley McKeithan has convincingly argued in favour of some important structural similarities between the play and Shakespeare's *King Lear*: first, *Thierry and Theodoret* reverses the Shakespearean pattern by opening with an irredeemably evil mother and her two decent (if flawed) sons instead of a kind (if confused) king and his two wicked daughters; second, after being reproached by Theodoret, Brunehaut furiously decides to go to her other son to find sympathy for her complaints, similarly to Lear going to Regan after falling out with Goneril; third, Brunehaut, argues McKeithan, resembles Goneril in several respects. In particular, she feels

> for Protald[i] a base love like that which Goneril has for Edmund. Goneril poisons Regan, plots her own husband's death, and then stabs herself when she sees Edmund mortally wounded. Brun[e]ha[u]t has Theodoret slain, plots Ordella's death, poisons Thierry, and then chokes herself when she sees Protald[i] tortured. The crimes of Goneril and of Brun[e]ha[u]t are discovered in the same way: from a letter taken from Oswald in one play, and from a letter taken from Protald[i] in the other. When charged with her crimes, Brun[e]ha[u]t, like Goneril, confesses and becomes defiant.[46]

Finally, McKeithan also correctly regards the reconciliation of Thierry and Ordella as bearing resemblances to that of Lear and Cordelia (though, as I argue below, the mediation of *The Winter's Tale* cannot be overlooked in this case), and he rightly argues that 'the cowardice of Protaldi is displayed in much the same manner as is Oswald's' (the verbal echoes are detailed in the Commentary).[47]

At least two of the scenes featuring Protaldi display echoes of *Henry IV Part 1* too. First, as Wiggins points out, 'Martel's ruse to expose Protaldi's cowardice by confronting him with a progressively diminishing number of imaginary assailants' in Act 2, scene 2, 'is an inversion of Falstaff's escalating sequence of buckram men' in Act 2, scene 4; second, as first remarked by McKeithan, the robbery of

Protaldi by de Vitry and the four soldiers in Act 5, scene 1, appears partly modelled after 'the robbery of the king's men by Falstaff and his cronies' in Act 2, scene 2.[48]

It has never been mentioned before that *Thierry and Theodoret* displays a less evident but still remarkable affinity to another play by Shakespeare, namely *Macbeth*. True, Thierry is not involved in the death of Theodoret, but several other elements do show parallels: a royal kinsman is treacherously slain; the laws of hospitality are brutally transgressed; an 'unnatural' woman (and queen) is ultimately responsible for the crime – though the unnaturalness of Brunehaut (expressed through her unchecked sexual appetite; see CRITICISM below) is different from that of Macbeth's wife (manifested in her deep-rooted lust for power); both queens commit suicide offstage.

Hamlet *and Fenton's novella of 'The Lady of Cabrio'*
McKeithan also identified similarities between the first scene of *Thierry and Theodoret*, in which Theodoret chides Brunehaut for her dissolute lifestyle, and the fourth scene of *Hamlet*'s Act 3, in which the Danish Prince famously reproaches his mother Gertrude for her unchaste conduct.[49] The situation is indeed similar, but Nancy Cotton Pearse has suggested that the opening scene of *Thierry and Theodoret* is in fact closer to a sequence in Geoffrey Fenton's retelling of a *novella* by Matteo Bandello in which 'The eldest son chargeth his mother with incestuous life'.[50] The tale is 'The impudent love of The Lady of Cabrio with her procurer Tolonio, together with the detestable murders committed between them', contained in *Certain Tragical Discourses Written out of French and Latin* (1567). A modernized transcription of the relevant section of the *novella* is offered in Appendix 3.

The resemblances are many. First, this is a tale in which a sexually insatiable mother murders her two sons to protect her licentious way of life. Second, in the scene in question the Lady's eldest son, just like Theodoret, reminds his mother that an individual of rank is 'bound in double sort to a wonderful care of integrity in living in himself, so as his authority and effects of upright conversation may serve as a line to lead the meaner sort'.[51] Third, the son commands his mother to mend her ways unless she desires the world to make 'open exclamation against [her] lascivious order of life'.[52] Fourth, the son promises that he will kill his mother's lover with his own hands, similarly to Theodoret's swearing that he will personally punish Brunehaut's minions. Fifth, the Lady, like Brunehaut, accuses her son of being 'credulous in every report' against his mother.⁵³ Sixth, both women falsely weep during the conversation. Finally, and most importantly, while Gertrude is moved by her son's speech, both the Lady of Cabrio and Brunehaut 'are impervious to persuasions to repentance'.⁵⁴ On balance, then, Fenton's adaptation of Bandello's *novella* seems more similar to the opening scene of *Thierry and Theodoret* than *Hamlet*, Act 3, scene 4.

The Winter's Tale *and* King Lear *(again)*

As fleetingly mentioned above, the final scene of *Thierry and Theodoret*, in which Thierry and Ordella are finally reunited, exhibits evident correspondences with the reunion between Leontes and Hermione in *The Winter's Tale*. A supposedly dead wife is returned veiled by a third party to her husband, who is at first incredulous and then ecstatic on recognizing her. The closeness between the two scenes even includes a direct verbal borrowing – 'she is warm' (5.2.167; cf. *WT* 5.3.109) – but there are also a few differences, such as the fact that in *Thierry and Theodoret* the third party is a man, the couple is childless, a much longer time elapses in *The Winter's Tale*, Ordella is not presented as a statue, she does talk to her husband, and they both die.

However, as I have remarked earlier, the reconciliation scene between Thierry and Ordella also has affinities with that between Lear and Cordelia in *King Lear*, because that play had itself helped Shakespeare to shape the denouement of *The Winter's Tale*, most evidently in the reworking in *The Winter's Tale*, Act 5, scene 3, of Lear's believing that Cordelia's lips have life in them during his delirium in *King Lear*, Act 5, scene 3.⁵⁵ McKeithan has usefully recorded the similarities between the reunion of Thierry and Ordella and the reconciliation of Lear and Cordelia in *King Lear*, Act 4, scene 7:

1. Ordella, like Cordelia, is cautioned to be gentle with the sick man.
2. Thierry, like Lear, takes the lady to be a spirit in bliss.
3. Lear kneels to Cordelia, and Thierry, though possibly too ill to kneel, commands the other characters present to kneel before Ordella.
4. Both Lear and Thierry think at first that the spirit has come to inflict punishment.
5. Each is amazed to see the spirit shedding tears.

6. Each soon recognizes his loved one and is overjoyed at having her again.
7. The name Ordella may possibly have been derived from the name of Cordelia.[56]

I believe that the reconciliation scene in Fletcher's play fuses material from at least two Shakespearean plays, the latter of which (*The Winter's Tale*) had been in turn influenced by the former (*King Lear*). Fletcher appears to be looking at *The Winter's Tale*'s denouement and consciously tracing its literary and dramatic roots. In doing so, he also recognizes that *The Winter's Tale* is in active conversation with Euripides' *Alcestis*, and he crafts the last moments of his own play accordingly.

Alcestis, *the story of Jephthah, and* Iphigenia in Aulis
That the final scene of *Thierry and Theodoret* has affinities with the story of Alcestis has been casually remarked by Pearse, who argues that 'the plot of *Thierry and Theodoret* implies that Ordella is a modern Alcestis' and notes a few similarities between the stories of the two women, though she never mentions Euripides himself or his play and rather refers generically to 'the Alcestis myth'.[57] Ordella indeed shares some traits with Alcestis: she voluntarily accepts the prospect of death for her husband and expresses love for the same husband who has brought the sentence about.

Another important resemblance is the fact that in *Thierry and Theodoret*, just as in *Alcestis* (and *The Winter's Tale*), a third party, Martel, guides the husband through a recognition scene with his supposedly dead wife. In all cases, the third party deliberately withholds information from the husband – especially the knowledge that the wife is in fact still alive. Moreover, the third party, as in *Alcestis*, tries to convince the husband to remarry, and these manoeuvres function as a prelude to the recognition scene. Interestingly, in *Thierry and Theodoret* the agent of restoration is a man, Martel, as is Hercules in *Alcestis*, rather than a woman, as is Paulina in *The Winter's Tale*. There is never any ambiguity, though, for the audience, as to Ordella's being still alive, unlike *Alcestis* or *The Winter's Tale*, in which the audience is surprised to see the heroine come back from real or apparent death. In addition, Thierry is more favourably presented than Admetus because he cannot bring himself to sacrifice his wife.

The crucial element, however, is the Euripidean theatregram of the presumed deceased veiled wife restored to her grieving husband, which Fletcher reproduces much more closely than Shakespeare. It is impossible to ascertain exactly how Fletcher became acquainted with the Euripidean motif. To be sure, even if we assume that Fletcher had no sufficient knowledge of ancient Greek to read *Alcestis*, at least one Latin translation by George Buchanan (1556) would have been available to him.[58] Whatever the route through which *Alcestis* reached Fletcher, the fact that ancient Greece was much on the minds of Fletcher and his collaborators as they wrote *Thierry and Theodoret* is also forcefully suggested by other Hellenizing details that more or less stridently clash with the Merovingian setting of the play and depart from Fletcher and his collaborators' main narrative source.

First, the characters repeatedly invoke the gods in the Greek pantheon: there are at least sixteen mentions or invocations of the 'gods' throughout the play, and Theodoret specifically refers to 'the Thunderer' (i.e., Zeus/Jupiter) while talking to Martel (1.2.9). Second, one of the key locations is the Temple of Diana/Artemis, which is clearly out of place in medieval France and obliquely recalls Shakespeare's self-consciousness in having 'Greek female institutions such as the Delphic oracle and the temple of Diana at Ephesus' in *The Winter's Tale* and *Pericles* (1607) respectively.[59] Third, when Martel resoundingly extols the virtue of the allegedly dead Ordella, he claims that in her 'All was that Athens, Rome or warlike Sparta / Have registered for good in their best women, / But nothing of their ill' (4.2.111–13). Fourth, Brunehaut conceptualizes the clash she herself has set up between her sons Thierry and Theodoret in terms of the hatred between Eteocles and Polynices, the sons of Oedipus and Jocasta, who had been doomed by their father to kill each other (2.1.15–17; see Commentary for more details). Fifth, in the opening scene, Theodoret violently reproaches his mother for her lascivious ways and, just before leaving the stage, bids Brunehaut to 'live like Niobe' (1.1.125), thus evoking again a figure belonging to Greek mythology. Sixth, Ordella intervenes to defuse a rapidly escalating quarrel between Martel and Protaldi that threatens to end in a duel by asking Thierry not to 'suffer / Our bridal night to be the Centaurs' feast' (2.3.103–4), with yet another explicit (and ominous) allusion to Greek mythology (see Commentary for further discussion).

Moreover, Fletcher's characterization of Ordella seems to glance sideways at a further Greek female myth – though not necessarily to a specific Greek play in this case – by virtue of a connection between the myth of Iphigenia and a biblical story. As Emil Koeppel first noticed, the scene in which Thierry and Martel wait outside the temple for the first woman to come out is redolent of the tale of Jephthah's daughter – and is absent from Grimeston.[60] After defeating the Ammonites in battle, Jephthah vowed that he would burn the first thing that came out of his house and offer it to Yahweh. The first thing that came out, however, was his daughter, who then encouraged her father to fulfil his vow, which he eventually did. Fletcher had already modelled on this story a passage of one of his solo plays, *The Mad Lover* (1616), set in Paphos, a coastal city in south-west Cyprus. There Cleanthe, the waiting-woman of the Princess Calis, bribes the Priestess of Venus to tell Calis that she should marry the first man she meets on leaving the temple of the goddess, and tells her brother Syphax to wait outside, all ready to marry her.[61]

The story of Jephthah's daughter had been revived relatively recently by the Lord Admiral's Men, who had staged the lost 'Jephthah' (1602) by Anthony Munday and Thomas Dekker.[62] Besides, the tale may have reached Fletcher not only via the Bible but also via *The Famous and Memorable Works of Josephus*, translated by Thomas Lodge (1602), or George Buchanan's older Latin play *Jephthes, sive Votum* (1542). This work is particularly interesting in this context, insofar as it is largely based on Euripides' *Iphigenia in Aulis*, in which the title character agrees to be sacrificed for the sake of the Greek nation by her father, General Agamemnon, after learning that according to a prophecy the Greek fleet will not be allowed to sail for Troy unless Agamemnon's daughter is immolated. In a tragicomic twist, however, Iphigenia disappears at the moment of sacrifice. She has been saved by Artemis, who sends a hind to replace her. The wind begins to blow again, and the Greeks can finally depart for Troy.

Although Buchanan's *Jephthes* does not share the unexpectedly happy resolution of *Iphigenia in Aulis*, the link between the two plays is further underscored by the fact that the daughter, unnamed in the Scriptures, became Iphis in Buchanan's play.[63] Another play of the same period, *Iephthae* (1543–47, probably 1544), which John Christopherson first wrote in Greek and then translated into Latin, significantly draws upon *Iphigenia in Aulis*. While Fletcher and his collaborators' familiarity with Christopherson's play (only available in manuscript at the time) is unlikely, this suggests that the association between Jephthah's nameless daughter and Iphigenia was customary in the early modern period, which strengthens the likelihood that Fletcher and his collaborators might have had both women in mind when creating Ordella.[64]

In heroically and enthusiastically accepting the prospect of being sacrificed for the sake of her country in Act 4, scene 1, as depicted in Figure 2 (the frontispiece of the 1778 edition of the play), Ordella comes off as an Iphigenia-figure who elicits sympathy through her expression of powerful emotion. To be sure, Ordella's willingness to sacrifice herself by means of suicide is largely irrelevant to the plot, but it enables Fletcher to create a very intense sequence in which the virginal, Iphigenia-like Ordella manages to mobilize the playgoers' feelings. Yet the emotional impact of the temple scene proves to be secondary, as we now shall see, to two other interrelated effects on the audience that the play seems to pursue through the reuse of the Euripidean theatregram.

DEFYING GENRE EXPECTATIONS

Fletcher shapes the final scene of *Thierry and Theodoret* largely after the corresponding segment of *The Winter's Tale*; at the same time, he anatomizes Shakespeare's scene, goes back to two of the models that stand behind it, namely Shakespeare's own *King Lear* and Euripides' *Alcestis*, and decides to set up a sequence to which all three texts become confluent contributors. In doing so, Fletcher creates an intricate architecture of allusions that self-consciously and triumphantly brings to the fore multiple layers of dramatic *contaminatio*, the practice of combining texts of different provenance to create something new. The self-aware dimension of this artistic stunt is probably to be viewed as a nod to the sophisticated palates of those playgoers who were *au fait* with ancient Greek drama and probably relished feeling so. It is as though Fletcher were metaphorically nudging their elbows, complacently asking: 'Do ye see what I did there?' Here, as elsewhere in his canon, the impression is that Fletcher wants the play's mechanics and building blocks to be conspicuously on view: he wants his artfulness to be exhibited, not concealed.

The effect could have been further enhanced if Thierry was played by Richard Burbage, the man who had brought Lear and Leontes to life on stage. We cannot be certain regarding who played Thierry in the play's first performance, but Act 4, scene 2, might provide a helpful hint.[65] When Thierry tears his hair and throws

Figure 2 Ordella, kneeling, implores Thierry to sacrifice her for the sake of France, while Thierry, horrified at the idea, lets fall his sword

himself on the ground as a reaction to his perceived misfortune, he cries out:

> Oh, such a scene of grief,
> And so set down – the world the stage to act on –
> May challenge a tragedian better practised
> Than I am to express it, for my cause
> Of passion is so strong and my performance
> So weak that, though the part be good, I fear
> Th'ill acting of it will defraud it of
> The poor reward it may deserve, men's pity. (4.2.58–65)

In this typically Massingerian metatheatrical sequence, Thierry modestly doubts his own abilities only to allow Burbage once more to demonstrate his skills.[66] What tragedian was 'better practised' than him? Thomas Whitfield Baldwin assigns Thierry's part to Field and Theodoret's to Burbage – perhaps on the grounds of age, given that it would be logical to have the older actor playing the elder brother – but Field did not always play young heroes, and his reputation is primarily associated with smart-talking, devious types such as Voltore in *Volpone* and Face in *The Alchemist* (both of whom he played post-1616) rather than with tragic characters.[67] If Burbage did play Thierry, his presence would have automatically evoked his old triumphs, most particularly in the channelling of Lear's heart-rending awakening to Cordelia in the final sequence. Burbage's presence would have awakened a complex interplay between character and audience memories, in that the play might have taken advantage of the ghostly echoes of prior and current performances carried by the actor who performed the individual roles. As Marvin Carlson argues, the 'recycled body of an actor' in a performance 'will almost inevitably in a new role evoke the ghost or ghosts of previous roles', and Fletcher and his collaborators may have consciously exploited this mechanism in their theatrical practice.[68] All this would have been further exacerbated if these plays were performed alongside each other in the King's Men's repertory, especially at the moment of the first performance of *Thierry and Theodoret*. The impact on audiences would have been exceptionally powerful and extraordinarily effective. Unfortunately, there is no evidence that this was the case – though we do know that *The Winter's Tale* was revived for a court performance on 7 April 1618 – but in a period of scanty records there are likely to have been many performances for which no documentation survives.

INTRODUCTION   25

To return to the appropriation of the Euripidean motif in *Thierry and Theodoret*, I believe it also serves another function in terms of the playwright's intended effect of the stage action on his audience. Fletcher had established himself as a successful playwright on the London scene by virtue of such influential tragicomedies as *Philaster* and *A King and No King*, both written with Beaumont – and a tragic outcome averted thanks to a sudden reversal of fortune in the nick of time had become one of his dramatic hallmarks. As José A. Pérez Díez points out, Fletcher customarily 'experiments with generic uncertainty', thereby exposing 'the frail boundaries between genres', not only 'nod[ding] to traditional generic constraints', but also bringing forward a 'playful questioning of [generic] definitions'.[69]

As it happens, Euripides is sometimes identified as the initiator of tragicomedy, and *Alcestis* itself has been frequently described as a tragicomedy rather than a tragedy because of the final reconciliation between Admetus and Alcestis (and the same applies to the above-mentioned *Iphigenia in Aulis* because of the final divine rescue of the title character). Fletcher appears to have been aware of this and to have teased the audience throughout the play with the prospect that tragedy might turn at some point into tragicomedy. As Charles Squier observes,

> [i]f Theodoret were to survive being stabbed, Brun[e]ha[u]t repent at the sight of Thierry's sleepless agony and produce an antidote, no harm would be done, least of all to the fabric of the play. Tragedy would become tragicomedy, but the essentials, the mood, the tone, and the dramatic feel of the play would not have been changed.[70]

The negative judgement that Squier passes on the play altogether (see CRITICISM, below) is, in my view, largely unjustified, but he has a point in this case. Fletcher plays with the audience's expectations that things might somehow turn out miraculously for the better, as his previous dramatic offerings had made them accustomed to with their sudden revelations and surprising twists of events; but tragicomedy never occurs in *Thierry and Theodoret*.

Hence, the powerful *coup de théâtre* that should have been achieved by the unveiling of the supposedly deceased wife turns out to be generically ineffective in *Thierry and Theodoret* because it fails to convert tragedy into tragicomedy as one might have expected: while 'the specter of Alcestis ... loom[s] so large in [Shakespeare's] tragicomic imagination', when Fletcher goes back to Euripides in this play, he cannot ward off tragedy.[71] No happy ending is in store for Thierry and Ordella. In this sense, their fate is closer to Lear and Cordelia's tragic one than Leontes and Hermione's or Admetus and Alcestis' unexpectedly happy one. Besides, the audience *know* all along that Ordella is alive, which inevitably lowers that potential for surprise of which Shakespeare's romance and Euripides' tragicomedy both take advantage.

It is a typical trait of Fletcher's dramaturgy 'to look at everything that has to do with classical antiquity with a measure of detachment, suspicion, and scepticism, as though the classical past was no longer able to provide viable models and examples'.[72] Here, I believe that Fletcher treats a very influential classical theatregram with characteristic distrust and irreverence by emptying it of its genre-changing power. The prospect of tragicomedy is suggested but averted; Fletcher teases the Greek precedent and deflates it; romance tries to intrude into tragedy but is effaced, blocked out by the death of the newlyweds. In a different context, Lucy Munro has called attention to how *Thierry and Theodoret* presents 'an offhand, even satiric treatment of generic convention, in which an expected response is shut off through disjunctions of narrative and tone', thus 'steering their spectators in alternative directions', especially as regards its 'odd, unclimactic fashion' of dramatizing death, in particular that of Theodoret – who is even 'denied the dignity of a final speech', which apparently 'mock[s] the tendency outlined by Michael Neill, in which death in early modern tragedy becomes a form of self-fashioning', as speech is in fact foreclosed by death.[73] Fredson Bowers reaches similar conclusions as concerns the play's misleading deployment of elements typical of the sub-genre of revenge tragedy. Bowers observes that *Thierry and Theodoret* features '[t]raditional characters of revenge tragedy', and that 'situations are begun which would normally lead to revenge as the motivation for the future course of the action, and then nothing happens'.[74] Bowers helpfully singles out a telling example:

> considerable pains have been taken to prepare the audience for Memberge in the role of the revenger for her own slain father [i.e., Theodoret]. But after her first furious demand to Thierry for vengeance, a scene in which she seems willing to contemplate incest with him if it will procure revenge, she does not appear again until it is time to stand mute beside the bed of the dying Thierry and receive Martel as a husband.[75]

Fletcher's treatment of the Euripidean model in the final scene of the play then appears to be the culmination of this strategy, a conscious effort systematically to defy the expectations of the audience in terms of genre and theatrical conventions.

That this is a deliberate move on Fletcher and his collaborators' part is more fully borne out by the fact that they used the same trope of the veiled woman apparently returning from death once more in *The Knight of Malta* – this time to fully tragicomic extent. Here, the reunion scene between the old Spaniard Gomera and his lost wife Oriana (*Malta* 5.2.88–147) recalls that between Admetus and Alcestis, as already remarked in passing by John Genest, as well as that between Leontes and Hermione.[76] This sequence rewrites the corresponding segment in the play's narrative source, namely the thirteenth 'Questione d'amore' from Book 4 of Giovanni Boccaccio's *Filocolo*, which Fletcher might have read in the 1567 English translation by H. G. (probably Henry Grantham) as *A Pleasant Disport of Divers Noble Personages*, reprinted as *Thirteen Most Pleasant and Delectable Questions* in 1571 and 1587.[77] In Boccaccio's *questione*, a woman comes back from apparent death with a new-born child, to the surprise of her husband, but she is not veiled. Apart from the veil, however, the passage from *The Knight of Malta* features other resemblances and points of contact with *Alcestis*.

Gomera, like Admetus, does not want to welcome the veiled woman brought into his house by another man, the virtuous knight Miranda, because he is still reeling under the loss of his wife; Oriana is described as an exceptionally virtuous woman and, as she is still veiled, Miranda informs Gomera that she was 'Born a Greek' (*Malta* 5.2.101), which appears to be a pointed reference to the Greek provenance of the motif of the veiled woman, another of those self-conscious allusions that Fletcher and his collaborators may have inserted for the benefit of the most learned section of the audience. As Pearse remarks, Miranda's 'act of restoration' of Oriana to her husband Gomera 'completes Miranda's purification. In the spectacular grand finale, the wicked Mountferrat is ceremonially degraded from the Order while the angelic Miranda is formally initiated as a Knight of Malta. The play concludes with a double ceremony of expulsion and apotheosis; lust is expelled and chastity triumphs.'[78] In *The Knight of Malta*, then, Fletcher and his collaborators – Act 5 is generally attributed to Field – reuse the structural trope of a grieving husband's acceptance of a veiled woman who turns out to be his allegedly dead wife to transform potential tragedy into tragicomedy, thus abiding by the original generic direction of the theatregram. The comparison between its two uses therefore brings into even starker relief the self-consciousness and dexterity of Fletcher's dramatic writing in the concluding segment of *Thierry and Theodoret*.

While discussing Fletcher's tragicomedies, Russ McDonald argues that a vital element of his dramaturgy was that he and his collaborators 'set out to make their audience aware of their awareness of conventions ... by identifying and exaggerating some of the topics and strategies of their contemporaries', while Lee Bliss observes that Fletcher's tragicomedy often 'draws attention to its artifice and to the playwrights' amused elaboration of a generic topos'.[79] *Thierry and Theodoret* provides a spectacular instantiation of Fletcher's penchant for setting up a hugely eclectic dramaturgy oozing with virtuoso artfulness and a heightened sense of theatricality in its deliberate exposure of the layers of literary mediation and adaptation that contributed to Shakespeare's creation of the final segment of *The Winter's Tale*. In so doing, the play gratifies the playgoers' desire to be in the know, while simultaneously teasing and defying their generic expectations by inhibiting the transition of tragedy into tragicomedy. True, in relying perhaps excessively on the arch self-consciousness and ironic strategies typical of Fletcherian drama, *Thierry and Theodoret* might not be among the most successful specimens of Fletcher's playwriting – and an excessive reliance 'on a shared knowledge of ... dramatic conventions' might have resulted in making a proportion of playgoers feel 'disconcerted or left behind' during the performance.[80] Whether one likes the play or not, though, matters less than its elaborate theatrical adroitness, which is both its cipher and its mainstay. *Thierry and Theodoret* might be many things, but it is definitely not theatre for the uninitiated.

CRITICISM

Early reception and aesthetic judgements
The extent of the play's success (if any) in the seventeenth century is impossible to gauge with any certainty – all the more so given the lack of information regarding its stage history (see DATING AND STAGE HISTORY, above) – and the publication of *Thierry and Theodoret* by Thomas Walkley 'after the "big three" Beaumont and Fletcher plays, *Philaster*, *The Maid's Tragedy*, and *A King and No King*' does not necessarily depend on the fact that 'it was initially held just below them in terms of interest or esteem', as Blamires

hypothesizes.[81] Early modern plays reached the printing press (or did not) for a wide variety of reasons, and it is misconceived to suggest that publication of early dramatic texts be taken at face value as an indication of their quality or early recognition.[82]

It is indisputable, however, that *Thierry and Theodoret* significantly influenced at least one other commercial play, namely William Heminges's tragedy *The Fatal Contract* (1638–39).[83] Moreover, four extracts from *Thierry and Theodoret* are to be found in an Oxford manuscript commonplace book (*c.* 1622–25) held in the Bodleian Library, and eight more are included in John Cotgrave's *The English Treasury of Wit and Language* (1655): this would appear to indicate at least a moderate popularity of the play as reading material, the passages in both anthologies being quoted from Q1.[84] Recorded owners of the play (either Q1 or Q2) in the seventeenth century are William Drummond of Hawthornden, Robert Burton, John Horne (Vicar of Headington), John Houghton (Brasenose College, Oxford), James Herne, Ralph Sheldon (an antiquary), and Richard Wingfield (an estate landowner).[85]

The first critical evaluations and discussions of the play date back to the nineteenth century, when *Thierry and Theodoret* generally enjoyed a favourable reception. Charles Lamb famously extolled Act 4, scene 1, as 'the finest scene in Fletcher, and Ordella [as] the most perfect idea of the female heroic character ... that has been embodied in fiction', though he also found 'the manner of it', as compared with Shakespeare, 'slow and languid' in being based on a 'circular, not progressive' motion.[86]

Lamb's praise of that scene was echoed by Weber, who argued that it was only inferior to Shakespeare's artistry. He too regarded Ordella as 'one of the most perfect female characters ever delineated' and identified the only reason why a character such as Brunehaut (whom he found 'atrocious and disgusting in too great a degree for the stage') could be tolerated as her function as a foil 'to set off the saint-like beauty of Ordella'; all in all, Weber concluded, with regard to 'the beauty of the diction, and the propriety of the sentiments, Fletcher has seldom surpassed this ... production of his genius'.[87]

An anonymous reviewer of Alexander Dyce's edition of Beaumont and Fletcher voiced a dissenting opinion in *The Edinburgh Review* in 1847 by highlighting that the play was 'a piece stuffed full of horrors, and abounding in strained situations'.[88] Later in the century, however, E. H. C. Oliphant considered *Thierry and Theodoret* a 'very fine tragedy', and A. W. Ward celebrated the concluding scene, 'in which the sleepless misery of the poisoned Thierry is pictured with marvellous dramatic truth, unpolluted by realistic grossness'.[89]

The early twentieth century first saw Schelling describe the play as 'powerful if disagreeable', but it soon after witnessed A. C. Swinburne sing what are probably the play's highest praises ever.[90] He commended *Thierry and Theodoret* as 'about the finest and the fullest evidence left us of Fletcher's magnificent but far from supreme power as a tragic poet', and he identified the main strength of the play in the contrast between the 'abnormal wickedness' of Brunehaut and 'the abnormal goodness' of Ordella, which makes the audience's engagement with the play 'unflaggingly sustained'; moreover, he regarded 'the style ... as admirable in its impulsive fashion as is the style of Marlowe and Shakespeare and Webster in the nobler and more serious manner appropriate to higher and sincerer inspiration'.[91]

Following Swinburne, value judgements on the play became less and less positive. Andrew Lang deemed it 'rancid with the humours of the lowest London haunts, marked by wild anachronisms ... and crammed with impossible crimes'; Eugene M. Waith found it 'intense and gripping', but 'pervaded by factitious sensationalism'; William W. Appleton was even more critical, regarding *Thierry and Theodoret* as 'little more than a pastiche of elements from tragi-comedies' that lacks 'a well-conceived tragic figure [or] a consistently developed tragic situation'; yet he too had to acknowledge the power of Act 4, scene 1, which he considered 'notable ... in its mood of Roman pathos and resignation', if too readily detachable from the rest of the play.[92]

The ambivalence that informed Waith's comments was shared by Leech in the 1960s. He placed *Thierry and Theodoret* among Fletcher's 'best plays' but pronounced himself sceptical of its 'stage-worthiness' in modern times. In addition, he remarked that, although the plot has the potential to 'dull the sensibilities' with 'its sequence of villainous contrivances', yet the play somehow 'does not ... have this effect' and should 'command respect' even though it is 'less skilled ... than *The Maid's Tragedy* [and] a less dispassionate study of the mind than *Valentinian*'.[93]

Scholars writing about the play from the 1980s onwards have aired even more negative views. Squier sees the play as 'wild and woolly', 'packed with sensational materials', and set in a world that is 'violent, lurid, and unnatural, but ... not tragic in the larger sense of the word', unable as it is to offer any 'larger vision of life'; along similar lines, Doris Adler regards *Thierry and Theodoret* as 'extremely sensational and highly artificial'; while Blamires, writing in the twenty-first century, believes that '[w]ith its submissive heroine, obtuse hero and thinly-motivated villain it is hard to see *Thierry and Theodoret* finding much favour again'.[94]

As it happens, *Thierry and Theodoret* has probably never been as obscure and unpopular as it is today, but the emergence of a few critical takes that manage to push beyond mere value judgements raises hopes as to the possibility of a comprehensive critical reappraisal of the play.

Suicide, incest, and the carnivalesque
Sustained scholarly interpretations of the play are not many, but I believe it is important to offer a brief account of what scholars have argued about how the play is informed by such major critical issues as suicide, incest, and the carnivalesque. The play's representation of suicide is tackled by Roland Wymer, who identifies in Act 4, scene 1, an 'acute expression of the equivocal Christian attitude to voluntary death', in that the prospect of Ordella's sacrifice is praised as martyrdom, but that of her suicide is abhorred as self-slaughter.[95] The offstage suicide of Brunehaut is seen by Wymer partly as a conventional early modern dramatic device used in order that the deaths of evil characters not be preceded by any 'conscience-stricken speeches', so that they can be stripped 'of either redemptive or heroic connotations'.[96] This way, Fletcher leaves the audience 'with a general image of the self-destructiveness of evil', trenchantly conveying the idea that '[t]he retribution that evil brings on itself is the only lesson to be drawn from' Brunehaut's death, while at the same time 'solving the problem of how to punish her', since 'female criminals ... could not so readily be killed in battle or single combat in the manner of their male counterparts'.[97]

Looking at the play through a psychoanalytical lens, Zenón Luis-Martínez focuses on the issue of 'maternal jealousy' and Brunehaut's 'refusal to conform to the demands of the Oedipal mythos', by which she should renounce her sexuality.[98] Brunehaut's desire, he argues, 'is the fulcrum of tragic conflict', but the 'ultimate object' of her hindered desire actually becomes 'the possession of her son's desire, that is, the control of his sexuality', which she effects not only by impeding the consummation of his marriage with Ordella, but also through becoming herself 'the addressee of the confession' of

Thierry regarding his impotence, thereby subduing him 'as object of [her] incestuous knowledge'.[99]

From a different viewpoint, Justyna Galant examines the play within a Bakhtinian framework. She describes Brunehaut as 'a character multiplied, externalized and allegorized in the figures of her attendants', Bawdbert, Lacure, and Protaldi, 'who epitomize her chief vices' and are 'parasites materially reliant on' her, while she in turn 'recourses to them for the fulfilment of her needs'.[100] The three minions, Galant suggests, can be seen as partly 'allegorical characters – signs which refer to the features of Brun[e]ha[u]t': each of them 'refers back to the main sign in its entirety'; accordingly, Brunehaut 'is a synecdoche referring to the particular signs'.[101] In Galant's view, it is the connection between these 'carnivalized multiplied bodies' that 'draws attention to the very aberrant relationship between the heroine and her sons', inasmuch as, by 'subverting the usual order of things', Brunehaut 'replaces the maternal attitude to her children with the complex love–disdain tie she establishes with her cronies'.[102] Among them, Protaldi emerges as the one who is 'repeatedly subject to hierarchical elevation and carnivalesque "thrashing," turning from the allegedly bravest fighter in France to a clownish pathetic figure'.[103] Ultimately, Galant contends that the Bakhtinian 'logic of opposites' that is inherent in the carnivalesque tradition is embodied in *Thierry and Theodoret* by means of the polarization of the two main female characters and their 'mutual dependence ... in their struggle for the dominant semiotic order of reality', inasmuch as it appears that both of them 'advocate lifestyles and worldviews which are unacceptable to Thierry and Theodoret and which are both well out of the mainstream of common existence'.[104]

Misogyny and fragile masculinity
Sandra Clark has interestingly focused on the play's depiction of gender dynamics. She finds *Thierry and Theodoret* a 'distinctly misogynistic play' that 'revolves round the polarisation of woman as supremely virtuous or supremely vicious', as embodied in the contraposition of Ordella's 'deficient' and Brunehaut's 'excessive' sexual appetites.[105] The world of the play, Clark suggests, values women only insofar as they are 'submissive and chaste, like Memberge, ... who is preserved so as to marry Martel ... and continue the royal line', while 'the possibility of her ruling in her own right is never entertained, although she is the only direct descendant'.[106] Moreover, 'Theodoret is willing to offer up Memberge's life to prevent war,

and Thierry to kill an unknown woman in order to restore his sexual potency', which forcefully suggests that *Thierry and Theodoret* takes it for granted 'that women may be sacrificed to serve men's needs'.[107]

The play's misogynistic attitude, Clark adds, is also evident in the portrayal of Brunehaut as uncontrollably lustful, which 'raises the grim spectre of the monstrous woman who refuses to conform' to the norms of patriarchy (see below).[108] By contrast, the saint-like virtue of Ordella – who is even compared to the unfallen Eve for her contentment with continence – consists in her suppression of her sexual instincts, which brings her as far as first 'to accept that [Thierry] cannot make love to her', then to take 'upon herself responsibility for his impotence', and finally to express her willingness 'to die so that he can make love to someone else'.[109] Facing her husband's sexual incapacity on their wedding night is a supreme test of her chastity, the underlying assumption being that no woman would be able to repress her sexual urges at such a time. As Clark argues, the character of Ordella serves to exorcise 'the spectre of a man's inability to satisfy a woman's sexual appetite' through her reassuring 'combination of continence and selfless love'.[110] Masculinity consequently emerges as anxious and fragile in *Thierry and Theodoret*. 'The play has no example of manliness', contends Clark, as Brunehaut 'has Theodoret ... killed off, and renders Thierry impotent before torturing him to death'; and while Protaldi is described as a 'stallion', the only arena in which he proves his manhood is the bedroom: his cowardice is comically exposed by Martel.[111]

The fragility of Thierry's masculinity is evident from his reaction to what follows the unconsummated wedding night as explored by Blamires, who remarks that, even though on the surface 'Thierry embraces celibacy ... we sense how torn he is: however desirable a state of innocent fellowship might be, it leaves something to be desired'.[112] Thierry apparently renounces sex with elation because he 'finds a new faith in austere female purity' and in 'an ascetic or gnostic rejection of the body in favour of spiritual aspiration'.[113] The platonic rapture of the newlyweds is effectively portrayed in Figure 3 (the frontispiece of the 1711 edition of the play), which shows Thierry and Ordella blissfully sitting side by side under the livid, disappointed eyes of Brunehaut. Yet Thierry's excessively enthusiastic reaction before the court invites us 'to cast a sceptical eye over his idolatry', and this scepticism is confirmed by how easily he changes his mind when Brunehaut 'entices [him] with the prospect of fruitful sex with Ordella'.[114] Within a single scene, argues Blamires, Thierry 'both embraces and rejects a strict marital continence, swiftly traversing centuries of scholastic debate'.[115]

Thierry's desire for sexual satisfaction and procreation becomes even more obvious in his willingness to sacrifice a life to reacquire his potency in the bedroom. As Blamires remarks, 'Thierry has no apparent moral qualms over this', and his 'ready acceptance of this proposal ... smacks of the tyranny he earlier held in abeyance', though the fact that Martel – who is otherwise 'a moral touchstone' in the play – also takes part in this enterprise might suggest that this sacrifice is held acceptable because it is done for the benefit of France.[116] When Ordella appears to the two men, she is veiled, 'very much the bride (of death)', and she is more than willing to be sacrificed; in fact, Blamires observes, 'she never seems more alive than on the threshold of this marriage-to-death'.[117] When Thierry recognizes Ordella, however, he cannot bring himself to kill her, but she 'feels cheated, ... robbed of martyrological glory'.[118] Ordella, contends Blamires, is presented 'as a saint of matrimony', but her nuptial union with Thierry can only be 'achieved in death, the pair fainting together' in a very quiet consummation that sharply contrasts with the 'hellish offstage analogue' of Brunehaut's choking herself, unable to tolerate the sight of Protaldi being tortured to death amid 'cries and roars' (5.2.143).[119]

Brunehaut, or the scariest villainess in early modern English drama
As by far the most powerful character in the play, Brunehaut has attracted her fair share of critical commentary. Leech observes that through her depiction, 'Fletcher seems to have determined to consider the ultimate in evil, in monstrous egotism, and to trace its effects'; Pearse believes that her 'villainies are psychologically improbable in the extreme, but, as lust was considered the root of all evil, no wickedness done by an unchaste woman would surprise a Jacobean audience'; Squier argues that Brunehaut is both a 'sexy villainess' and 'a comic fishwife' from whose 'natural and unmotivated malignity' the action of the plays flows out and, though she moves 'in a twilight world of comedy and true evil', she definitely 'ranks high among Fletcher's depraved women'; for Clark, Brunehaut is portrayed as 'a witch, a sexual monstrosity, and a perversion of the sacred ideal of motherhood' for her over-indulgence 'in her inordinate sexual desires'.[120]

Figure 3 Thierry and Ordella sit together on their thrones under the eyes of Brunehaut

In Clark's opinion, Brunehaut's wicked actions are depicted with a view to giving 'vent to the misogynistic fear of woman whose appetites, if not regulated, recognise no limits of decency or morality, and affirms the need for male control and order'.[121] In addition, Clark remarks, Brunehaut appears to confuse the idea of 'power' with 'the free exercise of the will': in the concluding scene of the play, she describes herself as 'A woman in her liberal will defeated, / In all her greatness crossed, in pleasure blasted' (5.2.115–16). As a matter of fact, *Thierry and Theodoret* seems to define 'authority and social control ... only in terms of the expression and/or limitation of sexuality': never in the play does Brunehaut 'rebel against the patriarchal system that has conferred kingdoms on her two sons yet left her apparently a royal widow without other official status'.[122]

Clark rightly identifies some important aspects of how powerful a challenge Brunehaut poses to the Merovingian (and, by extension, the Jacobean) society's views concerning the representation of female sexuality, but I believe that so far the radical elements of Brunehaut's opposition to the norms of patriarchal society have not been fully appreciated by scholarship. Not only does Brunehaut lack the selfless and unconditional love of her children that is supposed to be inherent in every mother, perversely valuing her sexual urges well above the love of her two sons; more importantly, in relentlessly pursuing self-determination she opposes what Laura Gowing describes as the 'project of enclosing and controlling the female body' that 'was central to gender ideologies' in the early modern era.[123] Although medical literature valued female pleasure in sexual intercourse as necessary for conception, Gowing adds, this 'did not legitimate the idea of an active female sexual body: sexual initiative was socially men's prerogative, and female sexual assertion could always be associated with whorishness, witchcraft and sin'.[124] In forcefully advocating sexual initiative for herself in a context in which 'the female body was a public affair, the target of official regulation', Brunehaut accordingly embodies a very significant threat to patriarchal society.[125] She inappropriately places the private claims of her body natural above the public claims of her body politic as Queen dowager; in a reality in which the private dimension of the lives of people in power was so inextricably intertwined with their public image, Brunehaut's conduct becomes even more glaringly improper and threatening.

The subversiveness of Brunehaut's machinations, however, extends beyond her refusing to be controlled by men into her challenging the essence itself of gender relationships within the patriarchal order: her rage makes her pursue the control of the male body, as well as the destruction of legitimate (and potentially productive) sexuality. In the world of the play only Brunehaut is allowed to have sex: she commands men to satisfy her lust and enthusiastically revels in her own sexuality. She repeatedly threatens her minions with gelding, she tries to have her sons fight against each other, she has Protaldi stab Theodoret to death – the killing knife also traditionally signifying the penis, so that Brunehaut can be said to be vicariously and unnaturally penetrating her son, a man – and she tampers with Thierry's natural bodily functions with the help of Lacure: first, she resorts to a potion that she assumes will sink his marriage by hampering his erection, thus giving substance to what Michela Compagnoni describes as 'the nightmare of maternal malevolence as intrinsically attempting to contaminate (filial) masculinity' that 'is often detected and staged by early modern playwrights'; then, she uses poison to bring Thierry prematurely to his deathbed by depriving him of sleep.[126] 'Unnatural parricide, cruel, bloody woman!' (5.1.229–30), 'Wicked, wicked Brunehaut!' (5.1.235), de Vitry cries out after discovering Brunehaut's plot; 'Thou old impiety, / Made up by lust and mischief' (3.2.198–9), Martel comments after she persuades Thierry that Theodoret is a changeling. Brunehaut's viciousness as a mother is unparalleled in early modern drama: Shakespearean mothers such as Gertrude and Volumnia, for instance, disappoint or limit the freedom of their offspring; Brunehaut physically gets rid of her sons. Even worse, her successful attempt to control the male body and its natural functions in this case does not merely lead her to kill her own son: it is the King that she murders. Thierry's death is not as bloody and violent as Evadne's stabbing of the King while he is tied to the bed in *The Maid's Tragedy*, Act 5, scene 2, but it is equally momentous and potentially incendiary on a political level. Finally, Brunehaut reclaims the ultimate control of her own body by killing herself offstage: no one will be able to take pleasure from vindictively torturing her further than Martel's hitting her to keep her awake while Protaldi suffers on the wheel. That Martel himself is the only significant male figure to elude her control throughout the play repeatedly maddens her.

As for Brunehaut's hypersexuality, it may depend in part on her status as a widow. The lustful widow is a popular character in early modern drama, but she usually appears in comedies rather than tragedies.[127] Besides, Brunehaut is an atypical dramatic widow, in that her objective is not to remarry: she just wants to live her sexuality as freely as possible. She has had many lovers, and Protaldi is merely an object of pleasure, not a potential match or, in other words, someone who could, as it were, subdue her in marriage and win her wealth, as would normally occur in comedies, in which the widow frequently embodies 'the threat of a woman who [is] legally, economically, and sexually independent'.[128] In *Thierry and Theodoret* we are on the whole far from the world of comedy, and Protaldi's sexual prowess is unable to neutralize the threat Brunehaut poses to the male ego and to patriarchal society.

Finally, by trafficking with anaphrodisiac potions and poisoned objects, Brunehaut comes across as displaying features of what Margaret Hallissy describes as the archetype of the *venefica*, or potion-maker, that is, a female character 'who concocts a potion to be administered to a victim, usually male', just as Brunehaut does with Thierry (albeit with the support of Lacure).[129] The *venefica* embodies the 'fear of female power to deceive and destroy men' and 'represents the dark and devious underside of legitimate feminine roles: nurturer and healer', an aspect that is foregrounded in the case of Brunehaut's violence against her sons.[130] The use of poison makes woman particularly devious, Hallissy argues, because the 'poisoner uses superior secret knowledge to compensate for physical inferiority'.[131] Brunehaut certainly embodies at least some of these aspects. Besides, 'the *venefica* is [often] associated with witchcraft' in the early modern period, and Brunehaut's ability to cause Thierry's impotence does bring her close to the realm of magic.[132]

The nexus of poison, impotence, and (suspected) sorcery would have come across as eerily familiar to the audience through its resonance with a famous recent scandal surrounding Lady Frances Howard. Howard had been married to Robert Devereux, 3rd Earl of Essex, when they were 14 and 13 respectively, with a view to cementing a political union, but they were separated soon after the wedding. Essex went on a European tour. When he came back, Howard consistently avoided him, as she had fallen in love with Robert Carr, 1st Earl of Somerset. In 1613 Howard obtained a sensational annulment of her marriage to Essex. It was demonstrated by a committee of ten matrons and two midwives that she was still a virgin, and King James I granted the annulment on 25 September 1613 on the grounds of Essex's selective impotence towards his wife, which was seen as the result of his having been bewitched by what was termed *'maleficium versus hanc'*.[133] Howard then married Somerset on 26 December 1613. But more was to follow. In 1615 Howard was tried and convicted for the murder of Sir Thomas Overbury two years earlier. Overbury had opposed her marriage to Somerset. Poison and witchcraft were central to the case, and it emerged that she had managed to poison Overbury with an enema laced with mercury chloride through an intermediary. The Somersets were arrested for the murder in mid-October 1615. As a result of the investigation, the Somersets were tried along with four accomplices in late 1615 and early 1616. Howard was found guilty of murder and her husband of being an accessory for burning incriminating documents and bribing various people to cover everything up. The four accomplices were all hanged for conspiracy to commit murder. The Somersets were initially sentenced to death too, but they were then confined to the Tower, from where they were eventually released in early 1622 after being pardoned by the King. This second scandal was even more sensational than the first, since it caused the fall of Somerset, James's first major favourite, and precipitated the end of the Howards' influence in the Privy Council.

The affinities between these events and those dramatized in *Thierry and Theodoret* should not lead anyone to claim that the play was intended as a direct comment on the Howard scandals; yet it would have certainly been odd for playgoers in the second half of the 1610s not to make a connection. As Dutton suggests, in some sense the play overlays the allusions to the Maréchal d'Ancre with those to Frances Howard – sensation upon sensation – but always in a way that leaves ample room for plausible deniability with the then Master of the Revels, Sir George Buc.[134] All in all, though there are many tragedies from the second half of James's reign that can be said to allude at some level to the Howard scandals, *Thierry and Theodoret* seems to do so more comprehensively than most in capturing the themes of impotence, poison, and (suspected) sorcery in the actions of the unblinkingly evil Queen mother.

At any rate, for all Brunehaut's cruelty, her uncompromising attitude and her boldness in defying the norms of society seem to have elicited a hint of admiration from Fletcher. 'I live honest? / He may as well bid dead men walk' (1.1.165–6), she thunders after Theodoret has suggested that she should retire to a monastery for the rest of her life, her powerful, monosyllabic adynaton shaking the boards and making the audience shudder at the intensity of her lust and the magnitude of her urge to self-determination. Brunehaut is a formidable villain, an evil force to be reckoned with: she never repents in the play, never begs for mercy, never surrenders; defiant to the end in the face of a world that threatens severely to curtail her sexual freedom, she is defeated only because she mistakenly entrusts Protaldi with the delivery of the letters that would have finally brought her plot to successful completion, had not the cowardice and ineptitude of her lover thwarted her ultimate plan to seize power for herself after Thierry's death.

THE TEXT

No manuscript of *Thierry and Theodoret* survives. Thomas Walkley first published the play anonymously in quarto in 1621 (Q1) without having previously entered it in the Stationers' Register. The printer is unnamed, but the title page bears the type ornaments of Nicholas Okes. *Thierry and Theodoret*'s Q1 collates A^2 B–K^4 and was set by two compositors, as Robert Kean Turner has cogently demonstrated. His painstaking analysis provides illuminating insights into the production of Q1.[135]

Turner examined the running titles, spelling preferences, cases of type shortage (W), and broken and deformed types throughout Q1 to conclude that the compositors used two skeleton-formes: Skeleton I was employed to impose B (*inner*), C (*outer*), and D (*inner* and *outer*); Skeleton II was employed to impose B (*outer*), C (*inner*), E (*inner* and *outer*), and all ensuing formes, although '[f]rom Sheet E on the printing was carried out in only one skeleton-forme'.[136] Turner also argues that, 'since types from both formes of B reappear in both formes of C, printing was suspended for a time between the last forme of B to be machined and the first forme of C'; after that, Compositor B continued by himself, 'apparently setting by formes, outer first, through H (*inner*). In Sheet I, however, the inner forme seems to have been the first composed.'[137] Towards the end of the book, the compositor started 'to set short one-line speeches in the same line of type as the concluding line of preceding speeches' whenever he could and to squeeze in as many lines as possible per page, evidently because he did not want to use any additional sheets after imposing K4^v.[138] By comparing the spelling preferences of *Thierry and Theodoret*'s Q1 with those in the first quarto of *The Maid's Tragedy* (which Okes produced with another unidentified printer for Francis Constable and Richard Higginbotham), Turner was able to determine that one of the two compositors who set

Thierry and Theodoret was probably 'not a regular compositor but a person who had other duties in Okes's establishment' and who also 'set most of sheet G of *The Maid's Tragedy* Q1'.[139] In both cases, that individual appears to have stepped in to complete a task that one of the regular compositors was unable to finish.

While discussing *Philaster*, Suzanne Gossett points out that '[i]t has long been noticed that between 1619 and 1622 there was a flurry of publication of plays owned by the King's Men' aside from the Pavier Quartos, namely *The Maid's Tragedy*'s Q1 (1619), *A King and No King*'s Q1 (1619), and *Philaster*'s Q1 (1620), together with *Thierry and Theodoret*'s Q1 and Shakespeare's *Othello*'s Q1 (1622).[140] All of these were published by Walkley except for *The Maid's Tragedy*, which was issued by Constable and Higginbotham. Curiously, *Thierry and Theodoret* is the only one of these texts to have been published with no authorship attribution and not to have been reprinted shortly thereafter in enlarged and improved editions. As it happens, Constable issued *The Maid's Tragedy*'s Q2 in 1622; Walkley published *Philaster*'s Q2 in 1622 and *A King and No King*'s Q2 in 1625; *Othello* was included in the Folio of *Mr William Shakespeare's Comedies, Histories, & Tragedies* in 1623. Gossett also remarks that *Thierry and Theodoret* is unique among these plays in its not having 'been performed in the 1612–13 season of celebrations for the wedding of Princess Elizabeth and Frederick the Elector Palatine'.[141]

Thierry and Theodoret also stands out among the other plays published by Walkley around this time because it lacks a preface or an epistle to the reader – which are instead to be found in *A King and No King*'s Q1, *Philaster*'s Q2, and *Othello*'s Q1. This complicates any attempt to define the nature of the underlying manuscript of *Thierry and Theodoret*'s Q1, though it remains possible to make some informed conjectures based on the available evidence.

First, the press variants in the extant copies (a fuller account of which is given in Appendix 1) are 'quite routine', argues Turner, as also suggested by a marked proof-sheet of sig. C1^v that survives in the copy held at the Boston Public Library (Figure 4); in general, there is no 'indication in the text of Q1 that the copy from which it was set was illegible enough to cause more than occasional difficulties'.[142] The problems in lineation – with some verse mislined as prose, and passages of prose printed with capitals at the beginning of each line, as if verse – though hardly negligible, are not as pervasive as to argue in favour of a largely corrupt manuscript; in addition, mislineation is rather glaring only in the share of Field and therefore cannot be attributed entirely to the compositors, so that at least

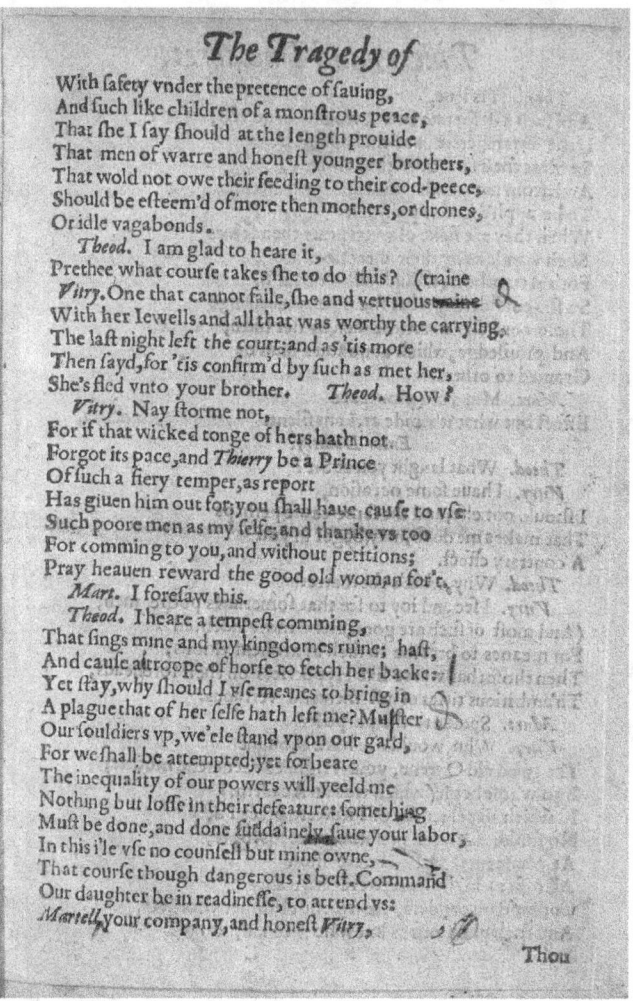

Figure 4 Marked proof-sheet of sig. C1ᵛ in Q1

some sheets of the manuscript copy must have been messy enough to mislead them.

Second, even though it is true, as Cathy L. Shrank and Paul Werstine remark, that 'some playhouse manuscripts contain so little mark-up that it is entirely possible that manuscripts with no mark-up whatsoever could have been used to guide production', the complete absence of professional stage directions (SDs) in Q1 seems to argue against a playhouse manuscript, as does the presence of several permissive SDs 'calling for an indefinite number of characters', as well as 'directions employing the formula &c.', which indicates that while the scene begins with the characters listed in the SD, other characters enter later.[143]

Third, the linguistic traits in the shares of the three authors are preserved with considerable accuracy, especially in the cases of Fletcher and Massinger; in this sense, the abundance of parentheses in Massinger's share is especially striking, as parentheses are a typical stylistic marker of his and are used only once in the other playwrights' shares of the play.[144]

This kind of evidence, alongside the dearth of evidence for theatrical annotation, would seem to lead towards the conclusion that the underlying manuscript was not significantly modified from the script as it had been completed by the playwrights. Yet the fact that the text also displays a certain uniformity across different authorial shares, together with its division into acts (and, though erratically so, into scenes), appears to indicate that Q1 was based on a transcript of an authorial draft (though not a particularly polished one). In particular, certain speech prefixes are consistent throughout (e.g., *Theod.*, *Brun.*, *Ordella*, *Lecure*), and, when Martel and Protaldi enter at 2.2.49.1 and 2.3.53 respectively, 'Q1 omits the prefix for their immediately following speeches (although elsewhere in the same situation prefixes are provided); the former scene is Fletcher's and the latter is Massinger's', as Turner observes.[145] In addition, the mysterious appearance of the speech prefix '*Deui.*' (instead of '*Mart.*') at 4.1.159 is probably to be attributed to a scribe, as it seems nearly impossible that the error was the compositor's (given that the most recent appearance of de Vitry was in Act 3, scene 2) or even Fletcher's (as de Vitry does not reappear in Fletcher's share until Act 5, scene 2). Finally, the SD at 3.2.45.1 reads '*Enter Protaldy, a Lady, and Reuellers.*' As Turner points out, '[i]t is difficult to see how the compositor could have been guilty of placing a direction forty lines early'; it seems more likely to posit either 'an authorial error during revision' or 'a scribal rationalization of a marginal direction whose exact location was unclear'.[146] Given that 'authorial characteristics do not overlap', adds Turner, 'it seems unlikely that one of the writers copied out the work of the other two', so that one is left to assume that Q1 was based on a scribal transcript of an authorial draft.[147]

Concurring support for this conclusion comes from the strong likelihood that Walkley had *A King and No King* printed from a transcript that may have been made for Sir Henry Neville (1588–1629) and that had been obtained from a private source, perhaps Neville himself.[148] There is no reason to assume, though, that Walkley obtained the transcript in any underhand way or without the initial knowledge of the King's Men: 'the absence of any clamor over' the publication by Walkley of the quarto texts listed above after the letter that the Lord Chamberlain sent to the Court of the Stationer's Company on 13 May 1619 – in response to which the Court declared that '[i]t is thought fit and so ordered that no plays that His Majesty's players do play shall be printed without consent of some of them' – appears to be, as Kenneth Walter Cameron argues, 'a clear indication that the quartos were published with the consent of the company'.[149] As Sonia Massai suggests, Walkley may have actually 'had a working relation with the company or with one of their patrons'.[150]

Subsequent editions of *Thierry and Theodoret* have no textual authority. Accordingly, the copy-text of this edition is Q1. In 1648 – a crucial time in the English Civil War, mere months before King Charles I's beheading – Moseley published a second edition in quarto (Q2) in a double-column layout. The title page assigns the play to Fletcher. While it does not represent an independent witness, Q2 at times offers several sensible emendations that clarify some details in the text of Q1. The nature and the scope of the changes do not seem to suggest that they are the result of authorial revision – and all three authors had long been dead by 1648 – but they constitute proximate efforts to interpret Q1 in some places where it needs interpretation. The reviser of the text of Q1 must have been an educated reader with a solid knowledge of early modern drama who was collaborating with the printing shop, but probably no more than that. The book was reissued a year later with a cancel bifolium replacing leaf A1, the text being identical to Q2 of 1648, with a new title page attributing the play to Beaumont and Fletcher, a list of *dramatis personae*, a Prologue, and an Epilogue. The latter two, however, refer in fact to Fletcher and John Ford's *The Noble Gentleman* (1626) and to James Shirley's *Changes* (1632) respectively.[151] *Thierry and Theodoret* was then included in the Folio of 1679 (F2) with the omission of the text from 'drench' (5.2.10) to '*Enter* Messenger' (5.2.126.1. SD), which was probably caused by 'a fault in the printing rather than a defect in the copy'.[152] *Thierry and Theodoret* later appeared in editions of the plays in the (Beaumont and) Fletcher canon in 1711 (with an introduction frequently and misleadingly attributed to Gerald Langbaine the younger), 1750 (edited by Thomas Seward), 1778 (edited by George Colman), 1812 (edited by Weber), 1844 (edited by Dyce), 1887 (edited by John St Loe Strachey), and 1976 (edited by Turner).[153] George Darley's 1839 edition reprinted the text established by Weber with very few variations and no annotation, while the text in the Cambridge edition by Arnold Glover and A. R. Waller (1905–12) simply transcribes F2 with minor typographical corrections. Accordingly, these two editions have been excluded from the historical collation.

THIS EDITION

This book presents readers with the first modern-spelling single-volume annotated edition of *Thierry and Theodoret*. The control-text for the present edition is one of the copies of Q1 held in the Harry Ransom Humanities Research Center at the University of Texas at Austin. I have silently modernized spelling and punctuation in line with series policy, recording in the collation all editorial departures from the copy-text as far as substantive readings are concerned, without providing the full textual history of a reading. Sometimes the lineation of the verse has also required editorial intervention.

Modernizing punctuation has been especially challenging. Fletcher often wrote long, loosely structured periods, with explanatory insertions, parenthetical clauses, and allusive sub-clauses that make it difficult to determine where ideas begin and end, or even to see the shape of the whole passage at a first glance.[154] Massinger arguably organizes ideas more lucidly and displays a stronger grip on the syntax of his writing, but he resorts to parenthetical clauses even more frequently than Fletcher. I have done my best to furnish the text with the pointing that I believe will best clarify its meaning for contemporary readers, encouraging them to pause and take stock, though I am aware that any intervention on punctuation is interpretative and that sometimes it is impossible to resolve ambiguities satisfactorily. Hence, despite the currently widespread notion that brackets should have no place in theatrical texts and editors of early modern drama ought to make do without them, I have employed brackets on several occasions, often in combination with dashes and semicolons, to help readers navigate the syntactical convolution of Fletcher and the parenthetical neurosis of Massinger.

My treatment of SDs also deserves some discussion. It is my firm conviction that a modernized edition of a sixteenth- or seventeenth-century play should aim at the largest possible readership and not be addressed only to a restricted number of privileged, initiated readers. I believe it is the job of the editor to make the onstage action as intelligible as possible to as many people as possible – including those not particularly familiar with the conventions of early modern drama: what is immediately and unambiguously evident to one reader may not be to another, and several actions that are implicit (and apparently obvious) in the text might be easily overlooked in reading without an editorial SD.

Accordingly, I have been generous in expanding original SDs and adding new ones to assist readers to envision the play's basic action as indicated in the dialogue – even if this might result occasionally in insulting the intelligence of fellow specialists, or in unaesthetically clogging the page with more SDs than one would like there to be. Editorial SDs (or amendments to the original ones) are indicated in the text by square brackets and should be viewed not as prescriptions, but as informed suggestions to readers.

I have made my best efforts, however, not to underestimate the text's openness to interpretation. Hence, I have refrained from adding bracketed SDs that would limit the options of plausible stage action. In general, I have tried to make readers aware of potential alternative actions in the Commentary and I have attempted not to abuse the 'asides', limiting their use to those situations in which it seemed to me uncontroversial that a line could be effective or logical only when delivered that way. I have also abundantly indicated to whom speeches are addressed whenever a speech is clearly not addressed to the preceding speaker. Again, sometimes this will look unnecessary to some, but it will be helpful for others. No edition can be final or definitive, and it is probably impossible for any single one to satisfy the needs of all potential users, but I hope the present volume will at least satisfy the needs of some.

NOTES

1 Hoy, 'Shares' (III), 97.
2 Hoy, 'Shares' (III), 97.
3 Wiggins, *Catalogue*, #1848, 59.
4 Jackson, 'Tourneur'.
5 Wiggins, *Catalogue*, #1848, 59.
6 Wiggins, *Catalogue*, #1799, 516.

INTRODUCTION   47

7 Freebury-Jones, 'Attributions', forthcoming.
8 Fleay, 205; Chelli, 128–9; Oliphant, 'Notes', 12; Hensman, 1.10.
9 Hoy, 'Shares' (IV), 95.
10 Hoy, 'Shares' (IV), 96.
11 Most of the following section draws upon Williams, 'Field'. For Fletcher, see Bliss, 'Introduction', 1–5; for Massinger, see White, 1–8.
12 Weber, 'Introduction', 270.
13 The play, however, has been read publicly three times: first, as part of the Beaumont and Fletcher Marathon on 19 June 2013; second, as part of the Massinger Marathon on 13 June 2018; and, third, as part of the Reading Early Plays project on 5 November 2020, all under the aegis of Martin Wiggins.
14 Wiggins, *Catalogue*, #1848, 59.
15 Thorndike, 80.
16 Thorndike, 80–1.
17 Thorndike, 81.
18 Leech, 122.
19 Wiggins, *Catalogue*, #1848, 59.
20 Fleay, 205. That English playwrights might want to stage, more or less explicitly, the events of contemporary French politics around 1617 is absolutely plausible, as suggested by the fact that the Privy Council did suppress such a play. A letter registered 22 June 1617 (that is, a mere eight days after D'Ancre's death) and addressed to the Master of the Revels, Sir George Buc, reads: 'We are informed that there are certain players or comedians – we know not of what company – that go about to play some interlude concerning the late Marquis d'Ancre, which for many respects we think not fit to be suffered. We do therefore require you upon your peril to take order that the same be not represented or played in any place about this city or elsewhere where you have authority. And hereof have you a special care' ('Dramatic Records', 376; see also *LPD*, https://lostplays.folger.edu/Marquis_d%E2%80%99Ancre, accessed 22 July 2022; Wiggins, *Catalogue*, #1834, 41). This play can hardly have been *Thierry and Theodoret*, though, as there is no evidence that the latter was ever suppressed.
21 Thorndike, 79.
22 No copy of the first edition is extant; hence all quotations come from the 1618 edition. The second edition contains the *privilège du Roi* dated 9 November 1617. For more information, see Le Long, 412–13; 'Conjuration'.
23 Lovascio, *Fletcher's Rome*, 50–1.
24 Wiggins, 'Four', 48.
25 Wiggins, 'Four', 48.
26 The term 'theatergram' was introduced in the late 1980s by Louise George Clubb to refer to well-established units of repertoire, prominent action and character clusters, or compelling bits of stage business that can migrate across plays (Clubb, 6).
27 Earlier scholars hypothesized that *Thierry and Theodoret* might have drawn upon the lost 'Branhowlte', staged in 1597 at the Rose by the Lord Admiral's Men, but this is pure speculation.
28 Schelling, 1.423–4; Ulrich, 10–19.

29 Ulrich, 10.
30 Thorndike, 112–13.
31 Ulrich, 19.
32 Leech, 132.
33 Morley, 279.
34 Grimeston, sig. D4^r (emphasis mine).
35 Goulart, 2.340^r; Vignier, 2.232; Gentillet, 72.
36 Lovascio, *Fletcher's Rome*, 33–4.
37 Blamires, 212.
38 Frédégaire, 4.27; Aimoin, 3.92; Fauchet, 5.3.153.
39 Grimeston, D4^r.
40 Matthieu, 67.
41 Tillet, sig. 2bvi^r; Goulart, 2.339^v; Belloy, sig. Rii^r.
42 Dutton, 'Historical Allegory', forthcoming.
43 For possible ways by which Fletcher might have acquired books printed on the continent, see Lovascio, *Fletcher's Rome*, 51.
44 Fauchet, 5.3.153.
45 Flavigny, sig. G3^r. See also Commentary, 3.2.158–76.
46 McKeithan, 144.
47 McKeithan, 142. See Commentary, 2.2.52–125, 2.3.92–101.
48 Wiggins, *Catalogue*, #1848; McKeithan, 148.
49 McKeithan, 147–8.
50 Pearse, 166–8.
51 Fenton, sig. 2Biii^r.
52 Fenton, sig. 2Biiii^r.
53 Fenton, sig. 2Biiii^v.
54 Pearse, 168.
55 Pitcher, 19–20; *WT* 5.3.76–7; *KL* 5.3.109–10.
56 McKeithan, 144–5.
57 Pearse, 228, 170–1, 171n20.
58 Pollard, 179–80.
59 Pollard, 14.
60 Koeppel, 36; Judges 11:30–39.
61 *MadL* 3.6.21–32, 4.3.25–6.
62 See *LPD*, https://lostplays.folger.edu/Jephthah, accessed 22 July 2022.
63 Pollard, 45.
64 See also Shuger, 134–66.
65 This section on Burbage develops an insightful suggestion by Richard Dutton.
66 On Massinger's use of metatheatrical elements, see, among others, White, 'Introduction', 29–46; Rochester, 15–51.
67 Baldwin, casting charts, 198–9.
68 Carlson, 8.
69 Pérez Díez, 5, 37.
70 Squier, 112.
71 Pollard, 178.
72 Lovascio, *Fletcher's Rome*, 9.
73 Munro, 'Plotting', 269.
74 Bowers, *Revenge*, 168.
75 Bowers, *Revenge*, 169.

INTRODUCTION 49

76 Genest, 273; see also Pearse, 171n20, 189; Cartwright, 89.
77 Sherbo; Edwards, 151.
78 Pearse, 189. A veiled wife returning from presumed death also appears in Field's 'The Triumph of Love' in *Four Plays in One*. The situation in this play, however, is different from what occurs in either *Alcestis* or *The Winter's Tale*. The wife, Cornelia, does not really return from another place: she has been hiding all along in Milan, where the story is set, after the Duke, her husband, has been exiled by a usurping tyrant, and she only unveils after the rightful Duke has been restored to his throne. Hence, it is technically the husband who comes back rather than the wife. Besides, there is no third party involved in facilitating the recognition of Cornelia by the Duke: she acts on her own initiative.
79 McDonald, 165; Bliss, 'Romance', 160.
80 Munro, 'Plotting', 271.
81 Blamires, 195.
82 McInnis, 2–11.
83 Bowers, *Revenge*, 239; Morley, 278–81.
84 The passages in Bodleian (cols. 704–5, in Coatalen) are 1.1.19–25, 2.1.38–46, 4.1.58–61, and 5.2.104–10. The excerpts in Cotgrave are 3.3.50–3 (sig. B8^v), 4.1.95–111 (sigs. F3^v–F4^r), 4.1.216–7 (sig. F7^v), 1.1.102–6 (sig. G2^r), 3.1.96–8 (sig. H8^v), 1.2.20–5 (sigs. L7^v–L8^r), 1.2.60–4 (sig. R8^r), 4.2.267–70 (sig. S7^r). Several of these extracts display small variations and additions to the text of Q1, mostly insignificant. The significant ones are recorded in the Collation or discussed in the Commentary.
85 Wiggins, *Catalogue*, #1848; *PLRE*, https://plre.folger.edu/booksDetail.php?id=13542, accessed 22 July 2022.
86 Lamb, 403n100.
87 Weber, 'Introduction', 270.
88 Oliphant, *Plays*, 274; *ER*, 382.
89 Ward, 174.
90 Schelling, 1.425.
91 Swinburne, 613–14.
92 Lang, 195; Waith, 129; Appleton, 86–7.
93 Leech, 5, 134, 136.
94 Squier, 90, 109; Adler, 19; Blamires, 221.
95 Wymer, 28.
96 Wymer, 47.
97 Wymer, 47–8.
98 Luis-Martinez, 267, 270.
99 Luis-Martinez, 266–8.
100 Galant, 209.
101 Galant, 210.
102 Galant, 211.
103 Galant, 210.
104 Galant, 226.
105 Clark, 90.
106 Clark, 90.
107 Clark, 91.
108 Clark, 91.

109 Clark, 94.
110 Clark, 38.
111 Clark, 92.
112 Blamires, 214.
113 Blamires, 215.
114 Blamires, 215–16.
115 Blamires, 216.
116 Blamires, 216–18.
117 Blamires, 218.
118 Blamires, 219.
119 Blamires, 221, 220.
120 Leech, 134; Pearse, 167; Squier, 109, 112; Clark, 91.
121 Clark, 91.
122 Clark, 91–2.
123 Gowing, 7.
124 Gowing, 85.
125 Gowing, 16.
126 Compagnoni, 40. See also Adelman, 130–64.
127 As Jennifer Panek, 5, points out, 'Nearly all the well-known theatrical names of the first quarter of the seventeenth century produced at least one comic remarrying widow plot: Chapman, Jonson, and Rowley wrote two apiece; Beaumont and Fletcher, two, and Fletcher, alone, one; Middleton turned out an astonishing seven; Dekker, Massinger, Brome, Field, Cooke, and Barry all tried their hands at one, and Haughton contributed a widow subplot to the collaborative *Patient Grissil* (1600).'
128 Panek, 7.
129 Hallissy, 60.
130 Hallissy, xi, 60.
131 Hallissy, 6.
132 Hallissy, 60.
133 Hallissy, 65.
134 Dutton, 'Historical Allegory', forthcoming.
135 Turner, 'Notes'; Turner, 'Introduction'.
136 Turner, 'Introduction', 366–7.
137 Turner, 'Introduction', 366–7.
138 Turner, 'Introduction', 367.
139 Turner, 'Notes', 223. Okes also produced *The Knight of the Burning Pestle* (1613) and *Philaster*'s Q1 (1620) and Q2 (1622).
140 Gossett, 83.
141 Gossett, 83.
142 Turner, 'Introduction', 368.
143 Shrank and Werstine, 59; Turner, 'Introduction', 368.
144 Turner, 'Introduction', 368–9.
145 It must be noted that '[t]here is also some small variation in the designation of the characters', e.g., de Vitry is both spelled 'Vitry' and 'Devitry', while Lefort is spelled both 'Forte' and 'Leforte' (Turner, 'Introduction', 368). For the characters entering at 2.2.39, who are referred to both as 'Huntsmen' and as 'Keepers', see the relevant Commentary note to 'Keepers' in the list of Characters in the Play.

146 Turner, 'Introduction', 369–70.
147 Turner, 'Introduction', 369.
148 Turner, 'Introduction', 370–1; McMillin, 16.
149 Jackson, *Records*, 110; Cameron, 673.
150 Massai, 120.
151 For the attribution to Ford, see Freebury-Jones, 'Collaborator'.
152 Turner, 'Introduction', 373.
153 On the mistaken association between Langbaine and the 1711 edition, see Lupić and Greatley-Hirsch, 293n18.
154 As Clare McManus, 89, explains, 'One significant challenge facing an editor of Fletcher is the punctuating of his idiomatic, parenthetical line. Fletcher's verse makes allusive, emotional sense but it often falls beyond immediate explanation, leading editors to suspect problems in the printing process. Sometimes … editors sense the presence of lost lines beneath the convoluted structure. At other times, they reorder to try to make clearer sense of the text and to smooth out its deviations. However … Leech identifies Fletcher's characteristic burying of his central point in the midst of a tangle of parentheses … this enacts an allusive, indirect approach to meaning, requiring a particular effort from the reader, if less so from the listener.'

THIERRY AND THEODORET

Characters in the Play

THIERRY, King of France, Theodoret's elder brother
THEODORET, King of Austrasia, Thierry's younger brother

Characters in the Play] Q1 does not provide a list of roles. The 1649 reissue of Q2 gives an incomplete list of '*Dramatis Personae*' (lightly emended by successive editors), which offers mostly unsatisfactory descriptions of the characters and abides by the seventeenth-century convention according to which characters were listed based on social rank rather than dramatic prominence. Female roles always came after male ones, often following a space signalling that they belonged to a discrete (and secondary) hierarchy. This conventional subordination was probably strengthened by the fact that female parts were played by young male players. At the end of the list, F2 adds the following information: 'The Scene France'. We cannot know for sure who played which roles. Baldwin (casting charts, 198–9) proposed Nathan Field as Thierry, Richard Burbage as Theodoret, Richard Sharpe as Ordella, G. Lowin (by which name Baldwin may perhaps have meant George Birch) as Memberge, John Lowin as Martel, Henry Condell as de Vitry, Richard Robinson as Brunehaut, William Ecclestone as Protaldi, John Underwood as Bawdbert, and Nicholas Tooley as Lacure. For the possibility that Thierry was played by Burbage, see Introduction, 22–4. Further insights on casting are expected to arise from the 'Reading Early Plays' project currently being led by Martin Wiggins.

1. THIERRY] Theuderic II (587–613), King of Burgundy (595–613), the second-born son of Childebert II, from whom he inherited the kingdom, with its capital at Orléans. He is also known in the historical sources as Teudericus or Thierri/y. See Appendix 2 for further historical details. This is the largest role in the play with 683 lines (Baldwin, casting charts, 198–9). The name is sometimes pronounced as two, sometimes as three syllables.

2. THEODORET] Theudebert II (586–612), King of Austrasia (595–612), the first-born son of Childebert II, from whom he inherited the kingdom, with its capital at Metz. The historical sources record his name also as Teudebertus, Theodebertus, or Thiebert. See Appendix 2 for further historical details. As he dies in Act 3, Theodoret only has the fourth largest role in the play with 240 lines (Baldwin, casting charts, 198–9). The name is sometimes pronounced as three, sometimes as four syllables. In this list of characters, the designation of 'King' has been chosen for Theodoret because he refers to himself as a 'king' or to his territories as a 'kingdom', as other characters do (see 1.2.7, 9, 20, 34, 39, 118; 2.3.91). Yet it must be pointed out that the play confusingly labels his dominions as a 'dukedom' twice (2.1.113, 3.3.31), perhaps to make it clear that Theodoret's kingdom is smaller than Thierry's.

ORDELLA, daughter to the King of Aragon, Thierry's wife
MEMBERGE, Theodoret's daughter
MARTEL, a soldier, follower and friend to Theodoret and
    Thierry   5
DE VITRY, a former soldier
Four SOLDIERS, following de Vitry

BRUNEHAUT, the old Queen of France, mother to Thierry
    and Theodoret

---

3. ORDELLA] The daughter of Dataric (also known as Betteric, Bertric, Dateric, or Bertefred in the historical accounts), King of Spain (Aragon in the play), recorded as Ermenberga, Hermenberga, Hermanberge, or Membergue in the sources, the name used in the play for Theodoret's daughter. See Appendix 2 for further historical details. The name Ordella is perhaps reminiscent of 'Cordella' in the anonymous *King Leir* (c. 1589) or perhaps intended to play on the noun 'ordeal' – a common early modern English spelling thereof being 'ordell' (cf. *OED* n.) – which would be particularly apt considering the extreme trials of chastity and wifely obedience to which she is submitted. Despite the centrality of her role, she only speaks 153 lines (Baldwin, casting charts, 198–9), fewer than Protaldi (229) and de Vitry (194), and only slightly more than Bawdbert (133).

4. MEMBERGE] Theodoret's daughter, unnamed in the historical sources.

5. MARTEL] An unhistorical character, with the third largest role in the play (397 lines, as per Baldwin, casting charts, 198–9). Dyce points out that Brunehaut speaks of Martel as 'base', but this does not seem to be an accurate description of his social rank. At the same time, there seems to be no evidence in the text for the notion that Martel is Thierry and Theodoret's 'kinsman' as suggested in the list of '*Dramatis Personae*' in the 1649 reissue of Q2. The playwrights could have found the name 'Martel' in Grimeston, though it is probably also intended to imply the adjective 'martial'.

6. DE VITRY] an unhistorical character whose name might allude to Nicolas de L'Hôpital, Marquis and later Duc de Vitry, usually known as Maréchal (or Marshal) de Vitry, the man who arrested and killed Concino Concini, 1st Marquis d'Ancre, on 24 April 1617. See Introduction, 7–9.

8. BRUNEHAUT] Brunhilda (c. 543–613), also known as Brunechildis or Brunehault in the sources. See Appendix 2 for further historical details. This is the second largest role in the play at 441 lines (Baldwin, casting charts, 198–9). Brunhilda's name has several different forms, too many to list here. The choice has fallen on 'Brunehaut' because it is the most widely used present-day French form of the name and is also very close to the spelling found in Q1 (i.e., Brunhalt) and in Grimeston (i.e., Brunehault). The form 'Brunhild' has been avoided because it may mislead readers into thinking that this is the character from Germanic heroic legend, widely known via Richard Wagner's *Der Ring des Nibelungen*. Some of the sources mistakenly describe Brunehaut as the mother of Theuderic and Theodebert rather than their grandmother, which may have inspired Fletcher and his collaborators to change their relationship. See Introduction, 12–13.

PROTALDI, Brunehaut's minion and paramour
BAWDBERT, Brunehaut's minion and pander   10
LACURE, Brunehaut's minion and physician
A SERVANT, attending Bawdbert

A POST
Two KEEPERS
A LADY   15
REVELLERS
Three COURTIERS
Two DOCTORS, attending Thierry
Two MESSENGERS
Attendants   20
Guards
Soldiers
Courtiers
Two Men
A Priest   25

---

9. PROTALDI] Protade (also known as 'Protadius' or 'Proclaide' in the historical accounts), the favourite and lover of Brunhilda. See Appendix 2 for further historical details. Some of the sources describe Protade as Italian (see Introduction, 13–14), which may explain why Fletcher and his collaborators changed the name of the character to 'Protaldye', a form resembling such Italian surnames as 'Grimaldi', 'Vivaldi', 'Ubaldi', 'Baraldi', 'Garibaldi', etc.; hence the modernized form 'Protaldi'.

10. BAWDBERT] An unhistorical character. I have modernized Q1's 'Bawdber' to 'Bawdbert' because the name, with its '-ber' suffix and its stress on the second syllable, seems intended to make the name sound French on the model of such names as 'Robert', 'Albert', 'Gilbert', etc.

11. LACURE] An unhistorical character. I have modernized Q1's 'Lecure' to 'Lacure' because 'cure' is a feminine noun in French and therefore grammatically requires the definite article 'la' rather than 'le'.

14. KEEPERS] Although 2.2.39. SD3 in Q1 refers to these two characters as '2 *Huntsmen*', 2.2.49.1. SD labels them as 'Keepers'. Moreover, they call themselves 'keepers' (2.2.41) in the dialogue, as does Protaldi: 'How now, keepers?' (2.2.47). The SPs at 2.2.39, 41, 43, 45, and 48 in Q1 are not helpful, as they only designate the characters by numbers ('1.' and '2.').

ACT I

SCENE I

Enter THEODORET, BRUNEHAUT [*and*] BAWDBERT.

SCENE 1] *Q1* (Act. 1. Scoe. 1). 0.1. SD] *Q1; Enter* Theodoret, Brunhalt, Bawdber [*with her*]. *Turner*.

1.1.0.] Generally held to be a Fletcher scene. Weber adds the setting: '*Austracia. An apartment in* Theodoret's *palace*'. This scene develops Grimeston, sigs D4ʳ: 'He [i.e., Childebert] left two sons, Theodebert and Thierry. The first had for his portion the realm of Austrasia, the second of Bourgogne. Brunehaut his mother survived him [i.e., Childebert] and kept at Metz with the eldest ... But the malice of Brunehaut ... must now divide the brethren ... This old bitch ... found still means to follow his beastly lust, and then had she got a young courtier called Protade for a stallion, whom she entertained in view and knowledge of the whole court, and advanced him beyond duty or desert. The dislike of this unchaste conversation, offensive to the whole world, doth in the end force Theodebert to find a means to withdraw his mother from the view of the multitude, who were eyewitnesses of the filthiness of this shameless old woman and of the ignomiry of his house. He supposed to send her away with policy, persuading her she should do best to retire herself into some goodly monastery, there to lead a godly life and to seek for rest befitting her age. This admonition caused her to leave the court and state of Theodebert, but not change her mind.' However, the opening scene may also recall *Hamlet*. Just as the Prince of Denmark reproaches his mother Gertrude for marrying Claudius too soon after the death of her former husband, Theodoret chides his mother Brunehaut for her unchaste behaviour. Yet Brunheaut does not respond like Gertrude. She is furious and vows revenge. The conversation between Theodoret and Brunehaut in fact seems closer to that between the Lady of Cabrio and her eldest son in Geoffrey Fenton's 'The Impudent Love of the Lady of Cabrio with Her Procurer Tolonio, together with the Detestable Murders Committed between Them' in *Certain Tragical Discourses Written out of French and Latin* (1567) – a retelling of Matteo Bandello's 1554 *novella* XXXIII 'Infortunato ed infausto amore di madama di Cabrio provenzale con un suo procuratore, e morte di molti' – in which a sexually insatiable mother murders her two sons in order to protect her licentious lifestyle. See Introduction, 17–18, and Appendix 3.

Brunehaut. Tax me with these hot taintures?
Theodoret.   You are too sudden.
    I do but gently tell you what becomes you
    And what may bend your honour, how these courses
    Of loose and lazy pleasures — not suspected,
    But done and known — your mind, that grants no limit,   5
    And all your actions follows, which loose people
    That see but through a mist of circumstance
    Dare term ambitious: all your ways hide sores
    Opening in the end to nothing but ulcers.
    Your instruments, like these, may call the world,   10
    And with a fearful clamour, to examine
    Why and to what we govern. From example,
    If not for virtue's sake, ye may be honest:

---

1. taintures] *Q1c, Colman, Weber, Dyce, Strachey*; tainters *Q1u, Q2, F2, 1711, Seward, Turner.*

---

1. *Tax ... taintures*] Brunehaut's furiously aggrieved question (with a strong accent on 'me') makes for a very effective opening of the play, having the merit both of captivating the audience's attention *in medias res* and of channeling the anger, bitterness, and resentment that will characterize Brunehaut and determine her actions for the entire play.

Tax ... with] charge me with, accuse me of.

hot] angry, full of hatred.

taintures] imputations of dishonour, foul allegations. In defence of 'tainters' (i.e., tenters), Turner argues that '[t]he proof-reader probably directed a change to the more conventional "taintures" and the compositor miscorrected to "tainturs".' Yet 'tainture' (with the same or a similar meaning to that in *T&T*) is to be found in three Fletcher solo plays, namely *Tamer* 2.5.113: 'To make the tainture most notorious'; *Val* 1.3.210: 'I hear these taintures'; and *Lieut* 3.7.39: 'Without the too much tainture of our honours'. By contrast, 'tainter' is to be found only in *Chase* 3.1.405: 'a tainter of your honour', with the meaning of 'one who taints'.

2. *becomes*] befits.

3. *bend*] pervert from the right purpose.

courses] 'ways of action, proceedings; personal conduct or behaviour, esp. of a reprehensible kind' (*OED* n. 22b).

4. *loose*] dissolute.

4–5. *not ... known*] referred to 'courses' in the previous line.

6. *follows*] As Blake points out, verbs in the 'plural could also end in <-(e)s> or <(e)th>, and examples are not infrequent' (90). The subjects of the verb are 'mind' and 'actions'; 'courses' is the direct object.

loose] 'lax in principle, conduct, or speech' (*OED* adj. 7).

10. *instruments*] minions (*OED* n. 3a). Cf. 2.1.68, 5.2.191.

> There have been great ones good ones, and 'tis
>   necessary —
> Because you are yourself and, by yourself,   15
> A self piece from the touch of power and justice —
> You should command yourself. You may imagine
> (Which cozens all the world, but chiefly women)
> The name of greatness glorifies your actions
> And strong power like a penthouse promises   20
> To shade you from opinion. Take heed, mother,
> And let us all take heed: these most abuse us.
> The sins we do people behold through optics,
> Which shows 'em ten times more than common vices
> And often multiplies 'em. Then what justice   25
> Dare we inflict upon the weak offenders
> When we are thieves ourselves?
> *Brunehaut.*   This is Martel,
> Studied and penned unto you, whose base person
> I charge you (by the love you owe a mother
> And as you hope for blessings from her prayers)   30
> Neither to give belief to nor allowance.
> Next, I tell you, sir — you, from whom obedience
> Is so far fled that you dare tax a mother,

---

14. ones good] *this edn;* ones, good *Q1*.   22. take] *Q1c;* rake *Q1u*.   26. inflict] *Q1c;* afflict *Q1u*.

---

14. *great ones good ones*] that is, great ones who are also good ones.
16. *self ... justice*] a piece taken from the touchstone of power and justice itself (which should accordingly be a hallmark of virtue).
18. *cozens*] deceives.
20. *penthouse*] awning, canopy.
21–2. *Take heed ... take heed*] Be careful. The repetition of the injunction 'take heed' is a very typical stylistic feature of Fletcher's writing. Cf., among others, *MadL* 4.4.19–20: 'Take heed, for honour's sake, take heed: the bramble / No wise man ever planted by the rose'; *FalseO* 4.3.34–5: 'You, that have Roman hearts, take heed of falsehood, / Take heed of blood, take heed of foul ingratitude'. See also *CustCount* 1.1.11–12; *Princess* 4.1.56; *Loyal* 4.3.147–9; *MT* 4.1.239–40; *Rollo* 2.1.15–20, 5.2.78–80; *SeaV* 4.2.190–1; *Val* 3.3.137.
22. *these*] i.e., greatness (l. 19) and power (l. 20).
abuse] deceive.
23. *optics*] magnifying glasses.
28. *Studied ... unto*] contrived and written upon.
31. *allowance*] approval, acceptance.
33. *tax*] censure.

Nay, further, brand her honour with your slanders
And break into the treasures of her credit — 35
Your easiness is abusèd, your faith freighted
With lies, malicious lies, your merchant mischief,
He that never knew more trade than tales and tumbling
Suspicions into honest hearts; what you, or he,
Or all the world dare lay upon my worth, 40
This for your poor opinions: I am she —
And so will bear myself — whose truth and whiteness
Shall ever stand as far from these detections
As you from duty. Get you better servants,
People of honest actions, without ends, 45
And whip these knaves away: they eat your favours
And turn 'em unto poisons. My known credit,
Whom all the courts a this side Nile have envied
(And happy she could cite me), brought in question
Now, in my hours of age and reverence, 50
When rather superstition should be rendered?

---

39. Suspicions] *1711;* Suspitious *Q1*.

35. *credit*] reputation.
36. *easiness*] kindness, but also the quality of being easily influenced. *freighted*] loaded.
37. *your ... mischief*] mischief is your merchant, i.e., the one who supplies you with lies, that is, Martel. The commercial metaphor is developed over three lines with 'freighted' (36), 'merchant' (37), and 'trade' (38).
38. *tumbling*] tossing.
41. *This*] The deictic might indicate that Brunehaut is supposed to deliver a derisory gesture here (the 'finger', possibly), or it may simply introduce her following sentence.
42. *whiteness*] moral purity.
43. *detections*] exposures, accusations (*OED* n. 1).
45. *ends*] aims, purposes (i.e., surreptitious ones).
47. *unto*] into.
credit] reputation.
48. *a*] on.
49. *she ... me*] that woman 'who could cite or quote me as a precedent to her behaviour' (Seward).
51. *superstition*] 'extravagant quasi-religious devotion to a non-religious object' (*OED* n. 6b). Cf. *Brother* 3.5.163-5: 'The old man shall not love his heaps of gold / With a more doting superstition / Than I'll love you'; *Progress* 3.3.59-61: 'May I not kiss ye now in superstition? / For you appear a thing that I would kneel to: / Let me err that way'.
rendered] offered up.

And by a rush that one day's warmth
Hath shot up to this swelling? Give me justice,
Which is his life.
Theodoret.   This is an impudence —
And he must tell you that till now, mother,   55
Brought ye a son's obedience and now breaks it —
Above the sufferance of a son.
Bawdbert.   [*Aside*] Bless us!
For I do now begin to feel myself
Turning into a halter, and the ladder
Turning from me, one pulling at my legs too.   60
Theodoret. These truths are no man's tales, but all men's
    troubles.
They are, though your strange greatness would outstare
    'em.
Witness the daily libels, almost ballads,
In every place, almost in every province,

---

52. warmth] *Q1;* sudden warmth *conj Deighton.*   57. SD] *Weber; not in Q1.*
59. Turning] *Q1;* Girning *conj Deighton;* Tucking *Seward.*

---

52. *a rush*] i.e., Martel. The line is two syllables short. Dyce notes that 'An epithet to "rush" or to "warmth" has dropped out'. This may well be the case, but it is impossible to reconstruct which adjective might have been intended, so that Deighton's conjecture 'sudden warmth', though attractive, cannot be accepted into the text. It might even be the case that the short line is somehow intended to mimic the sudden growth.

55. *he*] Theodoret means himself.
tell you] i.e., tell you so.
57. *sufferance*] endurance.
59. *Turning ... halter*] Seward regarded the expression as unnatural for the English language and the repetition of 'Turning' at the beginning of ll. 59 and 60 as the result of 'a false glance of the printer's eye'. He therefore emended to 'Tucking into a halter' as 'not only a more common and better expression, but more droll and in character'. Weber countered Seward's argument by pointing out that Seward had failed to 'recollect the common phrase of turning into bed, which is here ludicrously applied to the halter'. There is no necessity to emend the verb, and repetitions such as this one are not infrequent in the canon of Fletcher and his collaborators. Moreover, hanging was commonly effected up a ladder, attaching a halter (i.e., a rope with a noose), then pulling the ladder away, that is, with no drop. This left the convict strangling in mid-air rather than breaking his neck – pulling the legs was a kindness to effect death more quickly.
62. *strange*] 'difficult to take in or account for; ... surprising, unaccountable' (*OED* adj. 10a).
64. *every place*] i.e., 'every place in the metropolis' (Weber).

    Are made upon your lust, tavern discourses,   65
    Crowds crammed with whispers; nay, the holy temples
    Are not without your curses. Now you would blush,
    But your black-tainted blood dare not appear
    For fear I should fright that too.
Brunehaut.   O ye gods!
Theodoret. Do not abuse their names. They see your actions,   70
    And your concealed sins, though you work like moles,
    Lies level to their justice.
Brunehaut.   Art thou a son?
Theodoret. The more my shame is of so bad a mother,
    And more your wretchedness you let me be so.
    But, woman — for a mother's name hath left me   75
    Since you have left your honour — mend these ruins
    And build again that broken fame, and fairly.
    Your most intemperate fires have burnt, and quickly.
    Within these ten days take a monastery,
    A most strict house, a house where none may whisper,   80
    Where no more light is known but what may make ye
    Believe there is a day, where no hope dwells
    Nor comfort but in tears.
Brunehaut.   Oh, misery!
Theodoret. And there to cold repentance and starved penance
    Tie your succeeding days, or curse me heaven   85
    If all your gilded knaves, brokers and bedders —

---

   65. *Are made upon*] that are made about.
   66. *temples*] In spite of the Merovingian setting, the characters clearly move in a pre-Christian religious framework, and they repeatedly invoke the gods in the Greek pantheon. See Introduction, 20.
   67–9. *Now ... too*] Cf. *Ham* 3.4.73: 'O shame, where is thy blush?'
   72. *Lies*] See 1.1.6.
   level] plain, obvious, manifest.
   78.] According to humoral theory (see 2.1.256–7), ageing was associated with coolness and dryness; hence, Brunehaut's 'most intemperate fires' are especially inappropriate.
   80. *strict*] rigorous in discipline.
   86. *gilded*] adorned or embellished so as to seem attractive (*OED* adj. 3); perhaps wearing clothes covered with gold embroidery.
   brokers] bawds, pimps.
   bedders] the meaning appears to be 'fornicators', though *OED* defines 'bedder' as 'One who puts to bed; one who litters cattle' (n. 1), providing this passage as the only example.

        Even he you built from nothing, strong Protaldi —
        Be not made ambling geldings; all your maids,
        If that name do not shame 'em, fed with sponges
        To suck away their rankness; and yourself   90
        Only to empty pictures and dead arras
        Offer your old desires.
Brunehaut.   I will not curse you
        Nor lay a prophecy upon your pride,
        Though heaven might grant me both, unthankful, no.
        I nourished ye, 'twas I, poor I groaned for you;   95
        'Twas I felt what you suffered, I lamented
        When sickness or sad hours held back your sweetness;
        'Twas I paid for your sleeps, I watched your wakings,
        My daily cares and fears that rid, played, walked,
        Discoursed, discovered, fed and fashioned you   100
        To what you are, and am I thus rewarded?   [*Weeps.*]
Theodoret. But that I know these tears, I could dote on 'em
        And kneel to catch 'em as they fall, then knit 'em
        Into an armlet ever to be honoured;
        But, woman, they are dangerous drops, deceitful,   105

---

98. *paid*] *Q1*; pray'd *Seward.* *watched*] *F2*; watch *Q1.*   101. SD] *this edn; not in Q1.*

---

  88. *geldings*] castrated men, eunuchs (*OED* n.1 2).
  90. *rankness*] rottenness, lustfulness
  95–101.] Cf. *Rollo* 1.1.245–51: 'Dare you remember that you had a mother / Or look on these grey hairs, made so with tears / For both your goods, and not with age, and yet / Stand doubtful to obey her? From me you had / Life, nerves and faculties to use these weapons, / And dare you raise them against her to whom / You owe the means of being what you are?'
  95. *groaned*] that groaned (probably during labour).
  96. *felt*] that felt.
  lamented] that lamented.
  98. *paid ... sleeps*] Seward correctly interprets as 'I paid for your sleeps at the price of my own watchings' but unnecessarily emends the verb to 'prayed' because 'a metaphor of that nature would require a further explanation', which it does not.
  99. *rid*] rode.
  100. *discoursed*] brought by means of discourse or talk (*OED* v. 1g).
  discovered] brought to light, revealed.
  fashioned] shaped, moulded.

    Full of the weeper's anger and ill nature.
Brunehaut. In my last hours despised?
Theodoret.   That text should tell
    How ugly it becomes you to err thus.
    Your flames are spent; nothing but smoke maintains ye;
    And those your favour and your bounty suffers   110
    Lie not with you, they do but lay lust on you
    And then embrace you as they caught a palsy;
    Your power they may love, and like Spanish jennets
    Commit with such a gust.
Bawdbert.   *[Aside]* I would take whipping
    And pay a fine now.   *Exit.*
Theodoret.   But, were ye once disgraced   115
    Or fallen in wealth, like leaves they would fly from you
    And become browse for every beast. You willed me
    To stock myself with better friends and servants.
    With what face dare you see me or any mankind,
    That keep a race of such unheard-of relics,   120

---

106. weeper's anger] *Cotgrave;* weeper, anger *Q1.*   114. SD] *Weber; not in Q1.*   115. SD] *this edn; Exit Bawdber. Q1*

---

    106. *weeper's*] 'Compare the omission of terminal letters by Q1 at 1.2.54; 2.1.[241]; 2.2.5; 2.3.[75]; 3.1.32 (press corrected), 93; 4.1.16; 5.1.[112]. Because the present reading is in the work of Compositor *A* and the rest in that of Compositor *B*, it seems likely that occasional obscurity in the representation of terminals was a characteristic of the manuscript' (Turner).
    107. *That text*] the words you have just uttered.
    108. *ugly*] uglily.
    becomes] befits.
    110. *suffers*] tolerates. See 1.1.6.
    112. *as ... palsy*] as if they were catching some infirmity.
    113. *jennets*] studs. Jennets were small Spanish horses, and, as Williams (*Dictionary*, 2:733) points out, 'The sexual reputation of the jennet includes the stallion.'
    114. *gust*] enjoyment.
    114–15. *take ... now*] the most usual punishments for bawds.
    117. *browse*] 'vegetation suitable for browsing by animals' (*OED* n.1 1b).
    119. *see*] examine, scrutinize.
    mankind] men.
    120. *That*] The antecedent is 'you' in the preceding line.
    race] group of people.
    relics] remnants.

Bawds, lechers, leeches, female fornicators
And children in their rudiments to vices,
Old men to show examples and, lest art
Should lose herself in act, to call back custom?
Leave these, and live like Niobe. I told you how, 125
And, when your eyes have dropped away remembrance
Of what you were, I am your son. Perform it.   [*Exit.*]
Brunehaut. Am I a woman, and no more power in me
To tie this tiger up? A soul to no end?
Have I got shame and lost my will? Brunehaut, 130
From this accursèd hour forget thou bor'st him
Or any part of thy blood gave him living.
Let him be to thee an antipathy,
A thing thy nature sweats at and turns backward;
Throw all the mischiefs on him that thyself 135
Or women worse than thou art have invented,
And kill him drunk or doubtful.

   Enter BAWDBERT, [*again, with*] PROTALDI
   [*and*] LACURE.

---

121. lechers, leeches] *Colman;* Letchers, Leaches *Q1c;* Leachers, Letchecs *Q1u.* fornicators] *this edn;* fornications *Q1.* 127. SD] *1711; not in Q1.*
137. SD1] *Dyce (subst); Enter Bawdber, Protaldye, Lecure. Q1.*

---

 121. *lechers, leeches*] Williams (*Dictionary*, 2:794) argues that 'there seems to be an intended quibble on lecher and leech (presumably one who sticks to another, sexually, for the purpose of gain)'.
 122. *in ... vices*] beginning to learn about.
 125. *Niobe*] a Theban heroine who boasted that her sons and daughters were fairer than Leto's children Apollo and Artemis; as a result, the two gods slew all Niobe's children. Devastated by grief, she was finally turned into stone by Zeus but continued to weep unceasingly. She thus became a symbol of sorrow (cf. *Ham* 1.2.149: 'Like Niobe, all tears'). As Clark remarks, '[t]he reference to Niobe as the model for the chaste and grieving widows highlights Brun[e]ha[u]t's behaviour as doubly inappropriate, for a widow and for a queen' (92).
 129. *tiger*] cruel person.
 to no end] with no purpose.
 133. *antipathy*] an object of antipathy.
 137. *drunk or doubtful*] i.e., even if drunk or full of fear, that is, in a vulnerable state, possibly redolent of Hamlet's desire to murder Claudius 'When he is drunk asleep' (*Ham* 3.3.89).

Bawdbert. [*Aside to* PROTALDI *and* LACURE] Such a sweat
   I never was in yet: clipped of my minstrels,
   My toys to prick up wenches withal? Uphold me:
   It runs like snowballs through me.
Brunehaut.   Now, my varlets,   140
   My slaves, my running thoughts, my executions —
Bawdbert. [*Aside*] Lord, how she looks!
Brunehaut. Hell take ye all.
Bawdbert. [*Aside to* PROTALDI *and* LACURE] We shall be gelt.
Brunehaut.   Your mistress,
   Your old and honoured mistress, you tired curtals,
   Suffers for your base sins. I must be cloistered,   145
   Mewed up to make me virtuous. Who can help this?
   Now you stand still like statues. — Come, Protaldi,
   One kiss before I perish. Kiss me strongly. [*He kisses her.*]
   Another. [*He kisses her.*] And a third. [*He kisses her.*]
Lacure.   [*Aside to* BAWDBERT] I fear not gelding
   As long as she holds this way.
Brunehaut.   [*To* PROTALDI] The young courser,   150

SD2] *this edn; aside Turner; not in Q1.* 141. executions —] *Turner;* executions. *Q1.* 142. SD] *Turner; not in Q1.* 143. SD] *this edn; aside Turner; not in Q1.* 148. SD] *this edn; not in Q1.* 149. SD1] *this edn; not in Q1.* SD2] *Dyce (subst); not in Q1.* SD3] *this edn; aside Turner; not in Q1.* 150. SD] *this edn; not in Q1.*

---

138. *clipped ... minstrels*] deprived of my genital organs.
139. *prick up*] penetrate.
Uphold me] Keep me from falling. Probably accompanied by Bawdbert's simulated swoon in the arms of Protaldi and Lacure.
140. *varlets*] attendants, but also knaves, rogues.
143. *gelt*] castrated.
144. *curtals*] A curtal was 'a horse with its tail cut short or docked (and sometimes the ears cropped)' (*OED* n. 1). The word was also used as 'a term of derision or opprobrium' (*OED* n. 3c).
145. *cloistered*] enclosed in a cloister.
146. *Mewed up*] confined, shut away.
150–1. *The ... mistress*] 'The allusion is evidently to a horse-race, and the simple meaning seems to be that he will win her from Protald[i], or, as Mason ... explains it, "will make you lose her, will separate you from her"' (Weber).
150. *courser*] 'a large powerful horse, ridden in battle, in a tournament, etc.' (*OED* n.2 1a).

SC 1]   THIERRY AND THEODORET   67

            That unlicked lump of mine, will win thy mistress.
            Must I be chaste, Protaldi?
Protaldi.   Thus. [*Kisses her.*] And thus, lady. [*Kisses her.*]
Brunehaut. It shall be so. Let him seek fools for vestals.
            Here is my cloister.
Lacure.   But what safety, madam,
            Find you in staying here?
Brunehaut.   Thou hast hit my meaning.   155
            I will to Thierry, son of my blessings,
            And there complain me, tell my tale so subtly
            That the cold stones shall sweat and statues mourn. —
            And thou shalt weep, Protaldi, in my witness,
            And there forswear.
Protaldi.   Yes, anything but gelding.   160
            I am not yet in quiet, noble lady.
            Let it be done tonight, for without doubt
            Tomorrow we are capons.
Brunehaut.   Sleep shall not seize me,
            Nor any food befriend me but thy kisses
            Ere I forsake this desert. — I live honest?   165
            He may as well bid dead men walk. I humbled

152. SD1] *this edn; not in Q1.* SD2] *Weber; not in Q1.* 160. SP *Protaldi*] *Dyce; Bawd. Q1.*

---

151. *unlicked ... mine*] The familiar proverbial belief (originating from antiquity) that mother bears needed gradually to lick their cubs into their proper shape because they were thought to be born as formless lumps was also sometimes applied to other animals, including horses, as in this case. Brunehaut describes Theodoret as 'unlicked', thus suggesting that she feels she has failed to fashion him properly.

153-4. *Let ... cloister*] Cf. *A&C* 1.1.34-5: 'Let Rome in Tiber melt, and the wide arch / Of the ranged empire fall. Here is my space.'

153. *vestals*] i.e., vestal virgins, the priestesses (originally four, then six) who tended the sacred fire in the temple of the goddess Vesta in ancient Rome.

155. *my meaning*] 'the intended sense or underlying point of [my] words' (*OED* n.2 2c).

156. *will*] will go.

160. *forswear*] commit perjury.

163. *capons*] a capon is a gelded cock; hence, the figurative meaning of eunuch or unperforming husband (Williams, *Dictionary*, 1:202).

165. *honest*] respectably, virtuously.

166. *He ... walk*] The monosyllabic delivery makes Brunehaut's statement all the more chillingly effective.

68   THIERRY AND THEODORET   [ACT I

    Or bent below my power? Let night-dogs tear me
    And goblins ride me in my sleep to jelly
    Ere I forsake my sphere.
Lacure. This place you will.
Brunehaut.   What's that to you or any?   170
    Ye dose, you powdered pig's bones, rhubarb clyster,

---

171. dose] *Dyce;* Dross *Seward;* Dolt *conj Seward;* doss *F2;* dosse *Q1.*

    167. *night-dogs*] *OED* is unhelpful in this case, but night-dogs are likely what John Caius (C2ᵛ) describes as 'thievish dogs' or 'night-curs': 'the thievish dog ... at the mandate and bidding of his master fleereth and leereth abroad in the night, hunting conies ... During all which space of his hunting he will not bark, lest he should be prejudicial to his own advantage. And thus watcheth and snatcheth up in course as many conies as his master will suffer him, and beareth them to his master's standing. The farmers of the country and uplandish dwellers call this kind of dog a night-cur, because he hunteth in the dark.' Cf. also *MWW* 5.5.231: 'When night-dogs run, all sorts of deer are chased'.
    168. *goblins ... jelly*] Goblins were believed to be 'small, ugly, gnome-like creature[s] of folklore, fairy tales, and fantasy fiction; in early use considered as malevolent or demonic' (*OED* goblin n.1 1a). Brunehaut's words are based on the old belief that nightmares were provoked by spirits or monsters that 'settle[d] on and produce[d] a feeling of suffocation in a sleeping person' (*OED* nightmare n. 1a).
    169. *sphere*] both 'place, position, or station in society' (*OED* n. 5a) and 'province or domain in which one's activities or faculties find scope or exercise' (*OED* n. 6a).
    170. *This ... will*] This is a 'squinting' or 'amphibious' half-line, meaning it can form a full verse line either with the preceding or the following half-line. On balance, it seems to have a stronger link with Brunehaut's ensuing spiteful question, which needs to follow Lacure's remark right away. On amphibious lines, see Bevington, 276; Bowers, 'Short Lines'; Werstine; Williams, 'Year's Contribution'.
    171. *dose*] Q1 reads 'dosse', which has been interpreted by several editors as a corruption of another word. Seward, for instance, proposed either 'dross' or 'dolt'. In fact, there is no need to hypothesize corruption, 'dosse' being a seventeenth-century spelling variant of 'dose', which is here used with the meaning of 'a definite quantity of a medicine or drug given or prescribed to be given at one time' (*OED* n. 1a), as can be inferred by the fact that Brunehaut insults Lacure by applying opprobriously to him three types of early modern medical treatments ('dose', 'powdered pig's bones', and 'rhubarb clyster', see below.)
    powdered] pulverized.
    rhubarb] known for its laxative properties.
    clyster] *OED* (n. 3) gives this as the only example for 'a contemptuous name for a medical practitioner', but the presence of 'rhubarb' makes the usual sense of enema or suppository more applicable.

SC 2]   THIERRY AND THEODORET   69

  Must you know my designs? A college on you
  The proverb makes but fools.
Protaldi.   But, noble lady —
Brunehaut. You are a saucy ass too. — Off I will not,
  If you but anger me, till a sow-gelder   175
  Have cut you all like colts. [*To* PROTALDI] Hold me
   and kiss me,
  For I am too much troubled.   [*He does so.*]
  [*To* BAWDBERT *and* LACURE] Make up my treasure,
  And get me horses private. Come, about it! *Exeunt.*

SCENE 2

Enter THEODORET, MARTEL [*and* Attendants].

Theodoret. Though I assure myself, Martel, your counsel
  Had no end but allegiance and my honour,

---

173. lady—] *Colman;* Lady. *Q1.* 174. are] *Seward; not in Q1.* 175. till] *F2;*
tell *Q1.* 176. SD] *this edn; not in Q1.* 177. SD1] *this edn; not in Q1.*
SD2] *this edn; not in Q1.*

SCENE 2] *Q1* (Act. 1. Scoe. 2). 0.1. SD] *Weber; Enter Theodoret, Martell.
&c. Q1.* 1. Though] *Q2;* Thought *Q1.*

---

 172. *on*] of.
 173. *proverb*] The proverb referred here seems to be 'Every man is either
a fool or a physician' (Dent M125). Cf., among others, O. B., sig. G^r: 'this
old proverb: "Either a fool or a physician"'; Barnes, *Charter*, sig. L3^r: 'Either
mere fools or good physicians all'; Stafford, sig. E4^r: 'It is a common speech
that every man is either a fool or a physician'; Bolton, sig. O2^r: 'Hence that
proverb hath its probability: "Every man is either a fool or a physician."'
 174. *saucy*] insolent.
 175. *sow-gelder*] 'one whose business it is to geld or spay sows' (*OED* n.
a).
 176. *cut ... colts*] castrated you all like young horses.
 177. *Make up*] prepare.
 178. *private*] secretly.
 about it] Set about it.

 1.2.0.] Generally held to be a Massinger scene. Weber adds the setting:
'*Another in the same*', i.e., another apartment in Theodoret's palace. The first
half of the scene (1–78) develops Grimeston, sig. D4^r: 'She retires then from
Metz and comes into Bourgogne to her son, full of choler, and, finding
Thierry ill affected against his brother, she presently kindles the unfortunate
fire of dissention betwixt them.'

  Yet I am jealous I have passed the bounds
  Of a son's duty; for, suppose her worse
  Than your report (not by bare circumstance
  But evident proof confirmed) has given her out,
  Yet, since all weaknesses in a kingdom are
  No more to be severely punished than
  The faults of kings are by the Thunderer,
  As oft as they offend, to be revenged,
  If not for piety, yet for policy
  (Since some are of necessity to be spared)
  I might, and now I wish I had not looked
  With such strict eyes into her follies.
Martel.   Sir,
  A duty well discharged is never followed
  By sad repentance, nor did your highness ever
  Make payment of the debt you owed her better
  Than in your late reproofs not of her but
  Those crimes that made her worthy of reproof.
  The most remarkable point in which kings differ
  From private men is that they not alone
  Stand bound to be in themselves innocent,
  But that all such as are allied to them
  In nearness or dependence by their care
  Should be free from suspicion of all crime,
  And you have reaped a double benefit
  From this last great act: first, in the restraint
  Of her lost pleasures you remove th'example

---

5. your] *Seward;* you *Q1*. 14–15. With ... Sir, | A ... followed] *Seward; Q1 lines* With ... follies. | Sir, ... follow'd.

---

 3. *jealous*] fearful, doubtful.
 6. *given ... out*] proclaimed her.
 9. *the Thunderer*] i.e., Jupiter, the ruler of the Roman gods, who wielded thunderbolts to exert his authority.
 13. *I might*] i.e., I might spare her.
 15. *discharged*] performed.
 15–16. *is ... By*] never results in.
 18. *reproofs*] censures.
 28. *lost*] Seward glosses as 'abandoned, lost to all goodness'; Mason interprets as 'pleasures now lost to her, which she is compelled to relinquish'. I incline towards Seward's interpretation.

	From others of the like licentiousness;	
	Then, when 'tis known that your severity	30
	Extended to your mother, who dares hope for	
	The least indulgence or connivance in	
	The easiest slips that may prove dangerous	
	To you or to the kingdom?	
Theodoret.	I must grant	
	Your reasons good, Martel, if as she is	35
	My mother she had been my subject or	
	That only here she could make challenge to	
	A place of being, but I know her temper,	
	And fear (if such a word become a king)	
	That in discovering her I have let loose	40
	A tigress whose rage being shut up in darkness	
	Was grievous only to herself, which brought	
	Into the view of light — her cruelty	
	Provoked by her own shame — will turn on him	
	That foolishly presumed to let her see	45
	The loathed shape of her own deformity.	
Martel.	Beasts of that nature, when rebellious threats	
	Begin to appear only in their eyes	
	(Or any motion that may give suspicion	
	Of the least violence), should be chained up —	50
	Their fangs and teeth, and all their means of hurt,	
	Pared off and knocked out — and so made unable	
	To do ill: they would soon begin to loathe it.	

---

29. *like*] same.
33. *easiest slips*] smallest instances of moral fault.
37–8. *That ... being*] if my palace were the only place in which she could demand as her right to make her dwelling.
39. *become*] befits.
41. *A tigress*] Cf. Fenton, sig. 2Bvi^r: 'the tigress his mother'. In the sense of 'A fierce, cruel, or tiger-like woman' (*OED* n. 2a), both instances predate *OED*'s first recorded usage.
42. *grievous*] 'having injurious effects; causing hurt or pain' (*OED* adj. 2a).
48. *appear*] pronounced as three syllables.
52. *Pared off*] removed by cutting.
knocked out] dashed out by a blow.

  I'll apply nothing, but, had your grace done
  Or would do yet what your less forward zeal   55
  In words did only threaten, far less danger
  Would grow from acting it on her than may
  Perhaps have being from her apprehension
  Of what may once be practised, for — believe it —
  Who, confident of his own power, presumes   60
  To spend threats on an enemy that hath means
  To shun the worst they can effect gives armour
  To keep off his own strength, nay, more, disarms
  Himself and lies unguarded 'gainst all harms
  Or doubt or malice may produce.
Theodoret.   'Tis true,   65
  And such a desperate cure I would have used
  If the intemperate patient had not been
  So near me as a mother; but to her —
  And from me! — gentle unguents only were
  To be applied, and, as physicians,   70
  When they are sick of fevers, eat themselves
  Such viands as by their directions are
  Forbid to others, though alike diseased,
  So she, considering what she is, may challenge
  Those cordials to restore her by her birth   75
  And privilege which at no suit must be

---

54. your] *Q2;* you *Q1.*   61. an enemy] *Q1c;* an nimy *Q1u.*

 54. *apply*] make ready, prepare (*OED* v. 21).
 58. *apprehension*] anticipation.
 60–5. *Who ... produce*] All those who, being overconfident in their own might, attempt to threaten an enemy who is capable of averting even the most terrible of their attacks end up providing that enemy with means of defence against themselves, to the point of losing their own weapons and remaining unprotected from all the damage that can be done by either doubt or hatred.
 70. *physicians*] pronounced as four syllables.
 73. *Forbid*] forbidden.
 74. *challenge*] have a natural claim to (*OED* v. 6). Cf. *SpCur* 3.3.76–78: 'Whose honest cause, when 'tis related truly, / Will challenge justice'.
 75. *cordials*] a 'food or (esp. alcoholic) drink with medicinal or health-giving properties, esp. one that is thought to invigorate the heart, stimulate the circulation, or provide comfort' (*OED* n. 1a).
 76. *suit*] petition.

Granted to others.
Martel.   May your pious care
Effect but what it aimed at. I am silent.

   Enter DE VITRY [*laughing and then composing himself*].

Theodoret. What laughed you at, sir?
de Vitry.   I have some occasion —
I should not else — and the same cause perhaps   80
That makes me do so may beget in you
A contrary effect.
Theodoret.   Why, what's the matter?
de Vitry. I see — and joy to see — that sometimes poor men
(And most of such are good) stand more indebted
For means to breathe to such as are held vicious   85
Than those that wear like hypocrites on their foreheads
Th'ambitious titles of just men and virtuous.
Martel. Speak to the purpose.
de Vitry.   Who would e'er have thought
The good old Queen, your highness's reverend mother,
Into whose house (which was an Academe   90

78.1. SD] *this edn; Enter* DE VITRY, *laughing. Weber; Enter* Deuitry. *Q1.*
89. highness's] *Colman;* Highnesse *Q1.*

78.1. SD laughing ... himself] It is possible that de Vitry has started laughing offstage (loud enough to be heard by the audience) and that he has composed himself by the time he enters, but it would be more dramatically effective to have him still laugh and try to control himself as he walks forward. In any case, he must have stopped laughing by the time he enters conversation with Theodoret because of the past tense used ('laughed') at l. 79.
   81. *beget*] engender.
   88–103. *Who ... vagabonds*] Who could ever think that Brunehaut – whose house is a den of immorality and sin (and accordingly no fitting place for a soldier to be in) and who has managed to have important offices conferred on panders, people devoted to lust, physicians with a questionable set of morals, and other similar individuals bred in a depraved age of peace – would eventually take measures to ensure that soldiers and younger brothers unwilling to prostitute themselves would enjoy a higher reputation than moths, drones, or lazy vagabonds?
   90. *Academe*] brothel (*OED* academy n. 4c). 'The implication is of an establishment learned in vice' (Williams, *Dictionary*, 1:3). The spelling 'academe' has been retained for the sake of the metre.

In which all principles of lust were practised)
No soldier might presume to set his foot,
At whose most blessèd intercession
All offices in the state were charitably
Conferred on panders, o'erworn chamber-wrestlers   95
And such physicians as knew how to kill
With safety under the pretence of saving,
And suchlike children of a monstrous peace,
That she — I say — should at the length provide
That men of war and honest younger brothers   100
That would not owe their feeding to their codpiece
Should be esteemed of more than moths or drones,

---

102. moths] *Seward;* mothers *Q1.*

---

93. *intercession*] pronounced as five syllables.
95. *o'erworn*] exhausted.
chamber-wrestlers] people who practise the art of wrestling in the bedroom, i.e., spend much time in sexual activities. The noun 'chamber' is here used attributively, with the sense 'of or relating to the bedroom as a place of sexual activity; sexual, wanton', also perhaps 'with implications of effeminacy' (*OED* n. C2).
98. *suchlike*] of a similar kind.
monstrous] depraved and absurd.
99. *provide*] take measures to ensure.
100. *men of war*] warriors, soldiers.
101. *codpiece*] The codpiece was 'a (padded) pouch attached to the front of a man's close-fitting hose or breeches to cover the genitals, commonly worn in the 15th and 16th centuries' (*OED* n. 1a). By extension, it could be used as a euphemism for the penis (*OED* n. 2a).
102. *moths*] Q1's 'mothers' seems a misreading error. It is true that theoretically, as Richard Dutton (pers. comm.) points out, 'mothers' might actually work, given that 'de Vitry's speech is scornfully ironic about the status of true soldiers in Brunehaut's household', so that it would be 'a nice touch to describe them as "esteemed of more than *mothers*, or drones, / Or idle vagabonds" (especially with the sense of 'mothers' as *bawds*), a side-swipe at Brunehaut that resonates with the play's general preoccupation with vicious and virtuous motherhood'. Yet not only were moths typically associated with parasitic behaviour, 'moths' is in fact also metrically more correct, and its collocation with the word 'drones' is attested multiple times in early modern texts, whereas the combination 'mothers'–'drones' is not. Cf., for example, Johnson, *EMO* 1.3.95-6: 'Are bees / Bound to keep life in drones and idle moths?'; Leighton, 121: 'what a numberless number of moths, drones, and caterpillars they keep in their cathedral and collegiate church'; Prynne, 145: 'the very moths, the drones, and cankerworms of the commonwealth'.

Or idle vagabonds?
Theodoret. I am glad to hear it.
  Prithee, what course takes she to do this?
de Vitry. One
  That cannot fail: she and her virtuous train, 105
  With her jewels and all that was worthy the carrying,
  The last night left the court; and, as 'tis more
  Than said (for 'tis confirmed by such as met her),
  She's fled unto your brother.
Theodoret. How!
de Vitry. Nay, storm not,
  For, if that wicked tongue of hers hath not 110
  Forgot its pace and Thierry be a prince
  Of such a fiery temper as report
  Has given him out for, you shall have cause to use
  Such poor men as myself (and thank us too)
  For coming to you, and without petitions. 115
  Pray heaven reward the good old woman for't.
Martel. I foresaw this.
Theodoret. I hear a tempest coming
  That sings mine and my kingdom's ruin. Haste,
  And cause a troop of horse to fetch her back.
  Yet stay. Why should I use means to bring in 120
  A plague that of herself hath left me? Muster
  Our soldiers up: we'll stand upon our guard,
  For we shall be attempted. Yet forbear.
  The inequality of our powers will yield me
  Nothing but loss in their defeature. Something 125
  Must be done, and done suddenly. Save your labour:
  In this I'll use no counsel but mine own.

104–5. Prithee ... One | That ... train] *Colman; Q1 lines* Prethee ... this? | One ... traine. 105. her ... train] *F2;* vertuous traine *Q1c;* vertuoustraine traine *Q1u.* 106. worthy] *Q1;* worth *Seward.*

---

105. *her*] F2's emendation creates a perfectly decasyllabic line.
111. *Forgot*] forgotten.
113. *given ... out*] proclaimed him.
115. *without petitions*] without being requested to do so.
118. *sings*] resonantly proclaims.
124. *powers*] armies.
125. *defeature*] defeat, ruin.

That course, though dangerous, is best.
                            [*To* Attendants] Command
Our daughter be in readiness to attend us.
                                  [*Exeunt* Attendants.]
Martel, your company. — And, honest Vitry,   130
Thou wilt along with me?
de Vitry.   Yes, anywhere.
To be worse than I am here is past my fear.   *Exeunt.*

---

128. SD] *this edn; not in Q1.* 129.1. SD] *this edn; not in Q1.* 131. me?] *Colman;* me. *Q1.*

---

128. *That course*] i.e., going personally to Thierry's court with no army in an attempt to avert a potential crisis between them.

ACT 2

SCENE 1

Enter THIERRY, BRUNEHAUT, BAWDBERT, LACURE
[*and* Attendants].

Thierry. You are here in a sanctuary, and that viper —
  Who, since he hath forgot to be a son,
  I much disdain to think of as a brother —
  Had better in despite of all the gods
  To have razed their temples and spurned down their
    altars   5
  Than in his impious abuse of you
  To have called on my just anger.
Brunehaut.   Princely son,
  And in this worthy of so near a name,
  I have in the relation of my wrongs
  Been modest, and no word my tongue delivered   10
  T'express my insupportable injuries
  But gave my heart a wound; nor has my grief
  Being from what I suffer but that he,

SCENE 1] *Q1* (Act. 2. Scoe. 1). 0.1. SD] *Dyce; Enter Thierry, Brunhalt, Bawdber, Lecure. &c. Q1.* 8. of so near a] *conj Dyce;* of a nearer *1711;* of a neere *Q1.*

2.1.0.] Generally considered to be a Massinger scene. Weber adds the setting: '*Paris. An Apartment in the palace*'; Dyce adds the setting: '*Before the palace of* THIERRY'. It might be either, but there is no particular reason why this should be an outdoor scene.
  7. *called on*] incited, brought about.
  8. *so ... name*] Q1 reads 'a neere', which could be modernized to 'a nearer'. Yet, as Dyce wonders, 'What name could be nearer than that of son?' Cf. 1.2.68.
  9. *relation*] report.
  10. *modest*] free from exaggeration.
  13. *Being*] life, existence.
  that] from the fact that.

        Degenerate as he is, should be the actor
        Of my extremes and force me to divide   15
        The fires of brotherly affection,
        Which should make but one flame.
Thierry.   That part of his,
        As it deserves, shall burn no more if or
        The tears of orphans, widows or all such
        As dare acknowledge him to be their lord,   20
        Joined to your wrongs with his heart blood, have power
        To put it out, and you and these your servants —
        Who in our favours shall find cause to know,
        In that they left not you, how dear we hold them —
        Shall give Theodoret to understand   25
        His ignorance of the priceless jewel which
        He did possess in you, mother, in you,
        Of which I am more proud to be the owner
        Than if the absolute rule of all the world
        Were offered to this hand. Once more, you are
            welcome,   30

---

28. owner] *Seward;* doner *Q1.*

---

  14. *actor*] agent.
  15. *extremes*] extremities, hardships.
  15–17. *to divide ... flame*] As first pointed out by Theobald, the reference is to the enmity between Eteocles and Polynices, the sons of Oedipus and Jocasta, who had been doomed by their father to kill each other. The allusion is to the version of the myth – related both by Lucan (*Pharsalia* 1.549–52) and Statius (*Thebaid* 12.429ff.) – according to which the flames arising from their funeral pyre divided into two separate fires to signify their never-ending hatred. A similar image is to be found in *Rollo* 1.1.5–7: 'The fires of love, which the dead Duke believed / His equal care of both would have united, / Ambition hath divided.'
  16. *affection*] pronounced as four syllables.
  17–30. *That ... hand*] Theodoret's fire will be put out if the tears of either orphans, widows, or all the people who follow him as their King (joined with the blood of his heart to the wrong he has made you suffer) can extinguish it; and you and your servants – whom I will keep in high regard because they have not abandoned you – will make Theodoret understand how ignorant he was of what invaluable jewel he had in his hands when you were there with him. Owning that jewel now makes me prouder than if I could be the ruler of the entire world.
  18. *or*] either.
  23–4.] Thierry is probably supposed to look at Brunehaut's minions as he delivers these lines.

Which with all ceremony due to greatness
I would make known but that our just revenge
Admits not of delay.

Enter PROTALDI, *with soldiers.*

[*To* PROTALDI] Your hand, Lord General.
Brunehaut. Your favour and his merit — I may say —
   Have made him such, but I am jealous how   35
   Your subjects will receive it.
Thierry.   How! My subjects?
   What do you make of me? O heaven! My subjects?
   How base should I esteem the name of prince
   If that poor dust were anything before
   The whirlwind of my absolute command?   40
   Let them be happy and rest so contented:
   They pay the tribute of their hearts and knees
   To such a prince that not alone has power
   To keep his own but to increase it; that,
   Although he hath a body may add to   45
   The famed night-labour of strong Hercules,
   Yet is the master of a continence
   That so can temper it that I forbear
   Their daughters and their wives; whose hands, though strong,

---

33. SD1] *Turner; following* revenge *Dyce; following* general. *Q1*. SD2] *this edn; not in Q1.*

32. *but*] were it not.
33–5. *Your ... such*] Cf. Grimeston, sig. D4ʳ: 'Thierry ... prepares an army against Theodebert and employs this Protade in the principal charge.'
33. *Lord General*] commander-in-chief.
35. *jealous*] doubtful, fearful.
43. *alone*] only.
46. *night-labour*] sexual exertion.
Hercules] the Roman equivalent of the Greek mythological hero Heracles, son of Jupiter and the mortal Alcmene, famous for his superhuman strength and his adventurous achievements, especially the accomplishing of the seemingly impossible Twelve Labours. The specific reference here is to the myth of Hercules' prowess with the fifty daughters of Thespius, the king of Thespiae in Boeotia. One version of the story relates that Hercules had sexual intercourse with each of Thespius' daughters for each of the fifty nights that he spent as a guest at his house; in an alternative version, Hercules had sexual intercourse with all of them in a single night.

    As yet have never drawn by unjust mean 50
    Their proper wealth into my treasury —
    But I grow glorious. And let them beware
    That in their least repining at my pleasures
    They change not a mild prince — for, if provoked,
    I dare and will be so — into a tyrant. 55

    [*While* THIERRY *and* PROTALDI *confer privately,*
    BRUNEHAUT, BAWDBERT *and* LACURE *talk aside.*]

Brunehaut. You see there's hope that we shall rule again
    And your fall'n fortunes rise.
Bawdbert.   I hope your highness
    Is pleased that I shall still hold my place with you,
    For I have been so long used to provide you
    Fresh bits of flesh since mine grew stale that surely, 60
    If cashiered now, I shall prove a bad cater
    In the fish-market of cold chastity.
Lacure. For me, I am your own, nor since I first
    Knew what it was to serve you have remembered
    I had a soul but such a one whose essence 65
    Depended wholly on your highness's pleasure,
    And therefore, madam —
Brunehaut.   Rest assured you are
    Such instruments we must not lose.
Lacure and Bawdbert.   Our service. [*They bow.*]

55.1–2. SD] *this edn; Apart to* LECURE *and* BAWDBER. *Weber; not in Q1.* 57. fall'n] *1711;* falne *Q1.* 66. highness's] *Colman;* Highnesse *Q1.* 68. SD] *this edn; not in Q1.*

---

    50. *mean*] means.
    51. *proper*] own.
    52. *glorious*] vainglorious.
    53. *repining*] grumbling.
    61. *cashiered*] dismissed, laid aside.
    cater] caterer.
    62. *fish-market ... chastity*] 'Fish' was a slang term for the sexual organs or for a whore, while 'Fishmonger' was a slang term for a bawd (Williams, *Dictionary,* 1:490–6). The meaning of Bawdbert's words seems to be that it would be very difficult for him to move successfully from dealing with licentious women to having to do with chaste ones. It would be a whole different market.

Thierry. [To PROTALDI] You have viewed them, then.
    What's your opinion of 'em?
    In this dull time of peace we have prepared 'em   70
    Apt for the war. Ha?
Protaldi.   Sir, they have limbs
That promise strength sufficient, and rich armours,
The soldier's best loved wealth; more, it appears
They have been drilled, nay, very prettily drilled,
For many of them can discharge their muskets   75
Without the danger of throwing off their heads
Or being offensive to the standers-by
By sweating too much backwards; nay, I find
They know the right- and left-hand file, and may
With some impulsion no doubt be brought   80
To pass the ABC of war and come
Unto the hornbook.
Thierry.   Well, that care is yours,

---

69. SD] *this edn; not in Q1.*

---

69. *them*] i.e., the soldiers.

74. *drilled*] 'train[ed] or exercise[d] in military evolutions and the use of arms' (*OED* v.3 4a), with the secondary meaning of copulating, hence being trained in sexual activities (see Williams, *Dictionary*, 1:415).

75. *discharge ... muskets*] Muskets were 'a type of infantry gun with a long barrel, typically smooth-bored and firing a large calibre muzzle-loaded ball, usually aimed from the shoulder or mounted on a forked stand' (*OED* n.2), which are here referred to anachronistically, since muskets started appearing in the early sixteenth century. 'Musket', however, was also slang for the penis, so that 'discharge their muskets' also has the additional meaning of 'ejaculate' (Williams, *Dictionary*, 1.391).

76. *heads*] with a quibble on glandes.

78. *sweating ... backwards*] The bawdy overtones to this speech continue, as sweat is secondarily intended here as 'a sign of coital exertion' (Williams, *Dictionary*, 3:1343). There might be a reference to sodomitic intercourse in 'backwards'.

80. *impulsion*] incitement, pronounced as four syllables.

82. *hornbook*] a 'leaf of paper containing the alphabet (often with the addition of the ten digits, some elements of spelling, and the Lord's Prayer) protected by a thin plate of translucent horn, and mounted on a tablet of wood with a projecting piece for a handle' (*OED* n. a), used here metaphorically as a second step in military training. There may also be a second, bawdy meaning to 'hornbook', having to do with cuckoldry (see Williams, *Dictionary*, 2:681). Protaldi might be implying that the soldiers will quickly become

And see that you effect it.
Protaldi.   I am slow
    To promise much, but, if within ten days
    By precepts and examples — not drawn from   85
    Worm-eaten precedents of the Roman wars,
    But from mine own — I make them not transcend
    All that e'er yet bore arms, let it be said:
    'Protaldi brags', which would be unto me
    As hateful as to be esteemed a coward;   90
    For, sir, few captains know the way to win 'em
    And make the soldiers valiant. You shall see me
    Lie with them in their trenches, talk and drink,
    And be together drunk, and (what seems stranger)
    We'll sometimes wench together, which once practised   95
    (And with some other rare and hidden arts
    They being all made mine), I'll breathe into them
    Such fearless resolution and such fervour
    That, though I brought them to besiege a fort
    Whose walls were steeple-high and cannon-proof —   100
    Not to be undermined — they should fly up
    Like swallows, and, the parapet once won,

---

91. 'em] *F2;* him *Q1.*   92. see me] *Seward;* seeme *Q1.*   96. rare] *Seward;* care *Q1.*   arts] *Seward;* acts *Q1.*

---

cuckolds – probably because they will spend long stretches of time away from home and their wives. Cf. *Brother* 4.4.127–8, when Andrew comments on Brisac's offer of a larger grant of land to buy his silence after Andrew discovers that his wife Lily is Brisac's mistress: 'To bring me back from my grammar to my hornbook? / That is unpardonable.'

83–106. *I am ... necks*] This is probably the passage in which Protaldi's characterization as *miles gloriosus* comes most ridiculously to the fore.

83. *effect*] accomplish, take care of.

86. *Worm-eaten*] antiquated, outworn.

87. *transcend*] surpass, excel.

96. *rare ... arts*] Q1's readings 'care' and 'acts' are possible, but Seward's emendations are much better suited to Protaldi's bragging posture, and the implications of magic are stronger with 'arts' than with the more generic 'acts'; moreover, Turner points out that '[a]nother instance of "care" for "rare" ... occurs at [2.3.65]'.

100. *steeple-high*] high as a lofty tower.

102. *parapet*] a 'defence of earth or stone to conceal troops from the enemy's observation and fire; spec. (in permanent fortifications) a protection against missiles, raised on the top of a wall or rampart' (*OED* n. 1).

	For proof of their obedience, if I willed them,	
	They should leap down again and, what is more,	
	By some directions they should have from me,	105
	Not break their necks.	

Thierry. This is above belief.
Brunehaut. Sir, on my knowledge, though he hath spoke much,
   He's able to do more.
Lacure. [*Aside*] She means on her.
Brunehaut. And howsoever in his thankfulness,
   For some few favours done him by myself, 110
   He left Austrasia, not Theodoret,
   Though he was chiefly aimed at, could have laid
   With all his dukedom's power that shame upon him,
   Which in his barbarous malice to my honour
   He swore with threats to effect.
Thierry.   I cannot but 115
   Believe you, madam. [*To* PROTALDI] Thou art one degree
   Grown nearer to my heart, and I am proud
   To have in thee so glorious a plant
   Transported hither. In thy conduct we
   Go on assured of conquest. Our remove 120
   Shall be with the next sun.

Enter THEODORET, MEMBERGE, MARTEL [*and*] DE VITRY.

[*As they approach,* BRUNEHAUT *and her minions talk aside.*]

---

108. SD] Weber (subst); not in *Q1*.   116. SD] this edn; not in *Q1*.   121. SD2] this edn; Apart. Weber; not in *Q1*.   121–4. Shall ... me | 'Tis ... guilt | Hath ... now | Your ... us,] Seward; *Q1* lines Shall ... sunne. | Amazement ... hee. | We ... vndone. | Our ... defence. | If ... vs.

103. *willed*] gave orders to.
107. *spoke*] spoken.
109. *howsoever*] nevertheless, yet.
111. *not*] and not even.
112. *Though ... was*] even if he (i.e., Protaldi) had been.
115. *effect*] carry out.
118. *glorious*] pronounced as three syllables.
119. *conduct*] leadership.

Lacure.   Amazement leave me:
    'Tis he!
Bawdbert.   We are again undone.
Protaldi.   Our guilt
    Hath no assurance nor defence.
Bawdbert.   [*To* BRUNEHAUT] If now
    Your ever ready wit fail to protect us,
    We shall be all discovered.
Brunehaut.   Be not so   125
    In your amazement and your foolish fears:
    I am prepared for't.
Theodoret.   [*To* THIERRY] How! Not one poor welcome
    In answer of so long a journey made
    Only to see you, brother?
Thierry.   I have stood
    Silent thus long and am yet unresolved   130
    Whether to entertain thee on my sword
    As fits a parricide of a mother's honour
    Or whether, being a prince, I yet stand bound,
    Though thou art here condemned, to give thee hearing
    Before I execute. What foolish hope   135
    (Nay, pray you, forbear) or desperate madness rather —
    Unless thou com'st assured I stand in debt
    As far to all impiety as thyself —
    Has made thee bring thy neck unto the axe?
    Since, looking only here, it cannot but   140
    Draw fresh blood from thy seared-up conscience

---

123. SD] *this edn; not in Q1.*   127. SD] *this edn; not in Q1.*   129. you] *Seward;* your *Q1.*

---

121. *Amazement*] both bewilderment (*OED* n. 1) and fear (n. 3). Also at l. 126.
124. *ever*] always.
130. *unresolved*] undecided.
131. *entertain*] engage battle with.
on] with.
132. *parricide*] killer of a near relative.
136. *forbear*] This appears to be a command from Thierry in response to an attempt by Theodoret to get closer to him or to interrupt him.
141. *seared-up*] closed by means of cauterizing.
conscience] pronounced as three syllables.

SC I]   THIERRY AND THEODORET   85

  To make thee sensible of that horror which
  They ever bear about them that like Nero —
  'Like', said I? Thou art worse, since thou dar'st strive
  In her defame to murder thine alive.   145
Theodoret. That she, that long since had the boldness to
  Be a bad woman (though I wish some other
  Should so report her), could not want the cunning
  (Since they go hand in hand) to lay fair colours
  On her black crimes, I was resolved before,   150
  Nor make I doubt but that she hath empoisoned
  Your good opinion of me and so far
  Incensed your rage against me that too late
  I come to plead my innocence.
Brunehaut.   To excuse
  Thy impious scandals rather.
Protaldi.   Rather forced   155
  With fear to be compelled to come.
Thierry.   [*To* BRUNEHAUT *and* PROTALDI] Forbear.

---

143. Nero —] *Seward; Nero, Q1.* 144. art] *F2;* are *Q1.* 154–6. I ... excuse | Thy ... forced | With ... Forbear] *Dyce; Q1 lines* I ... innocence. | To ... rather. | Rather ... come. | Forbeare. 156. SD] *this edn; not in Q1.*

---

143. *Nero* —] Thierry stops mid-sentence, but he would probably have continued with something like 'conspire to kill their mothers'. Nero was Roman Emperor between 54 and 68 CE. He was considered one of the most vicious rulers in the history of ancient Rome, who had even had his mother Julia Agrippina murdered.
 145. *defame*] dishonour.
 thine] i.e., your mother.
 148. *want*] lack.
 149–50. *lay ... crimes*] The opposition between 'fair' and 'black' is far from unusual in early modern texts. Hall (9) points out that '"black" in Renaissance discourses is opposed not to "white" but to "beauty" or "fairness"'; more precisely, Karim-Cooper (11) argues that 'the terms "fair" and "white" are not always to be taken as interchangeable', inasmuch as '[p]aleness or whiteness is one thing as complexions go; however, fairness is quite another. It conveys a lustre that is comparable to silver ... to be "fair" is to be white and glistening, and to be thus is to be beautiful.' Such a glistening effect, adds Karim-Cooper (11), could also be obtained through cosmetics, and it is precisely from the domain of cosmetics that Theodoret's metaphor comes.
 150. *resolved*] determined, convinced.
 151. *empoisoned*] embittered, made hostile.
 153. *Incensed*] inflamed, excited.
 155. *scandals*] slanders.

Theodoret. This moves not me, and yet, had I not been
    Transported on my own integrity,
    I neither am so odious to my subjects
    Nor yet so barren of defence but that   160
    By force I could have justified my guilt
    Had I been faulty; but, since innocence
    Is to itself a hundred thousand guards
    And that there is no son — but though he owe
    That name to an ill mother — but stands bound   165
    Rather to take away with his own danger
    From the number of her faults than for his own
    Security to add unto them: this,
    This hath made me to prevent th'expense
    Of blood on both sides, the injuries, the rapes   170
    (Pages that ever wait upon the war),
    The account of all which, since you are the cause —
    Believe it — would have been required from you.
    Rather I say to offer up my daughter,
    Who living only could revenge my death,   175
    With my heart blood, a sacrifice to your anger
    Than that you should draw on your head more curses
    Than yet you have deserved.
Thierry.   [*Aside*] I do begin

---

178. SD] *Weber (subst); not in Q1.*

157–73.] Your threats have no effect on me. Yet, if I had not been brought here by my own moral rectitude, I could have easily justified my guilt – if any – since my subjects, who do not hate me, would have defended me from any attack of yours. That being said, innocence is a sufficient protection for itself, and every son – even though he has a despicable mother – is bound to detract from her defects at his own peril rather than add more of them for the sake of his own safety: this is the reason why I have decided not to wage war against you and spare all the blood and violence that would have resulted from it and for which you, my brother, would have been accountable as the ultimate instigator of the conflict.
    157. *moves*] affects, stirs.
    158. *Transported*] carried away by emotion.
    162. *faulty*] guilty of wrongdoing.
    164. *that*] given that.
    but though] even though.
    165. *ill*] evil.
    171. *Pages*] boy attendants.
    172. *account*] responsibility.

>
> To feel an alteration in my nature
> And in his full-sailed confidence a shower 180
> Of gentle rain, that, falling on the fire
> Of my hot rage, hath quenched it. Ha! I would
> Once more speak roughly to him, and I will.
> Yet there is something whispers to me that
> I have said too much. [*To* THEODORET] How is my
> heart divided 185
> Between the duty of a son and love
> Due to a brother! Yet I am swayed here
> And must ask of you how 'tis possible
> You can affect me, that have learned to hate
> Where you should pay all love.
>
> *Theodoret.*   Which, joined with duty, 190
> Upon my knees I should be proud to tender,
> Had she not used herself so many swords
> To cut those bonds that tied me to it.
>
> *Thierry.*   Fie!
> No more of that.
>
> *Theodoret.*   Alas, it is a theme
> I take no pleasure to discourse of. Would 195
> It could as soon be buried to the world
> As it should die to me; nay, more, I wish
> (Next to my part of heaven) that she would spend
> The last part of her life so here that all
> Indifferent judges might condemn me for 200
> A most malicious slanderer, nay, text it
> Upon my forehead. [*To* BRUNEHAUT] If you hate me,
> mother,

---

185. SD] *this edn; not in Q1*.   193–4. To ... Fie! | No ... theme] *Seward; Q1 lines* To ... it. | Fie, ... that. | Alas .... theame.   201. text] *Colman;* texde *Q1*.   202. SD] *this edn; not in Q1*.

---

187. *swayed*] influenced, prevailed upon.
189. *affect*] love.
190. *pay*] give, render.
  joined] were it joined.
200. *Indifferent*] impartial.
201. *text*] to 'inscribe, write, or print in a text-hand or in capital or large letters. Also *figurative*' (*OED* v. 1a).

88   THIERRY AND THEODORET   [ACT 2

  Put me to such a shame, pray you do; believe it:
  There is no glory that may fall upon me
  Can equal the delight I should receive   205
  In that disgrace, provided the repeal
  Of your long-banished virtues and good name
  Ushered me to it.   [*She weeps.*]
Thierry.   See, she shows herself
  An easy mother, which her tears confirm.
Theodoret. 'Tis a good sign, the comfortablest rain 210
  I ever saw.
Thierry. [*To* BRUNEHAUT *and* THEODORET] Embrace.
       [*They embrace.*] Why, this is well.
  May never more but love in you, and duty
  On your part, rise between you.
Bawdbert. [*Aside to* PROTALDI] Do you hear, Lord General?
  Does not your new-stamped honour on the sudden
  Begin to grow sick?
Protaldi.   [*Aside to him*] Yes, I find it fit 215
  That, putting off my armour, I should think of
  Some honest hospital to retire to.
Bawdbert.   [*Aside to him*] Sure,
  Although I am a bawd, yet, being a lord,
  They cannot whip me for't.
      [*Aside to* LACURE] What's your opinion?
Lacure. [*Aside to him*] The beadle will resolve you, for I
  cannot: 220
  There is something that more near concerns myself

---

208. SD] *this edn; not in Q1.*   211. SD1] *this edn; not in Q1.*   SD2] *this edn;* THEODORET *embraces* BRUNHALT. *Dyce; not in Q1.*   213. SD] *this edn; Apart. Turner; not in Q1.*   215. SD] *this edn; not in Q1.*   217. SD] *this edn; not in Q1.*   217–18. Some ... Sure, | Although ... lord] *Seward; Q1 lines* Some ... to. | Sure ... Lord.   219. SD] *this edn; not in Q1.*   220. SD] *this edn; not in Q1.*

---

 203. *pray*] i.e., I pray.
 210. *comfortablest*] the most comforting, reassuring, pleasing.
 212. *you*] i.e., Brunehaut.
 213. *your*] i.e., Theodoret's.
 217. *hospital*] hospice.
 220. *beadle*] minor parish officer, often in charge of inflicting corporal punishment on petty offenders.
 221. *near*] closely.

SC I]   THIERRY AND THEODORET   89

    That calls upon me.
Martel.   [*Aside to* DE VITRY] Note but yonder scarabs,
    That lived upon the dung of her base pleasures,
    How from the fear that she may yet prove honest
    Hang down their wicked heads.
de Vitry.   [*Aside to him*] What is that to me?   225
    Though they and all the polecats of the court
    Were trussed together, I perceive not how
    It can advantage me a cardecu
    To help to keep me honest.   *A horn* [*sounded within*].
                    Enter a Post.

Thierry.   How! From whence?
Post. These letters will resolve your grace.
                      [*Gives him the letters.*]
Thierry.   What speak they?   230
                      Reads.

---

222. SD] *this edn; Apart. Turner; not in Q1.*   225. SD] *this edn; not in Q1.*
229. SD1] *Dyce; A horne. Q1.*   230. SD] *Dyce (subst); not in Q1.*

222. *scarabs*] 'beetle[s] of any kind (chiefly referred to as supposed to be bred in and to feed upon dung)' (*OED* n. 1a).
226. *polecats*] sexually promiscuous women, whores.
228. *cardecu*] 'the *quart d'écu*, a French silver coin worth a quarter of the écu, or 15 sous tournois' (*OED* n.), which was first issued in the late sixteenth century by King Henri III. Cotgrave, *Dictionary* (3Tiiii^v) suggests that it was worth 18 pence (i.e., one and a half shillings, or 3/40 of a pound) in 1611, which is not particularly valuable. It appears to have been chosen just to invoke a foreign currency.
229–326. *How ... sure*] The last section of the scene is based on Grimeston, sig. D4^v: 'Thierry had remained long unmarried ... but ... he takes to wife Membergue, the daughter of Dataric, King of Spain, loving her with that honest affection that a man ought to love his wife. Brunehaut, jealous of this lawful love, fearing to be dispossessed of her authority and credit if a lawful wife possessed her husband's heart, she works by her charms, reducing Thierry to that extremity that he was not able to accompany with his wife ... as she loathed him of this poor princess.'
229. SD2. *Post*] 'any of a series of men stationed at suitable places along appointed post-roads, the duty of each being to ride with, or forward speedily to the next stage, the monarch's (and later also other) letters and dispatches, and to provide fresh horses for express messengers riding through' (*OED* n.3 1).
230. *resolve*] inform.

How all things meet to make me this day happy!
See, mother, brother, to your reconcilement
Another blessing almost equal to it
Is coming towards me: my contracted wife,
Ordella, daughter of wise Dataric, 235
The King of Aragon, is on our confines.
Then to arrive, at such a time when you
Are happily here to honour with your presence
Our long deferred but much wished nuptial,
Falls out above expression. Heaven be pleased 240
That I may use these blessings poured on me
With moderation.
Brunehaut.   [*Aside*] Hell and furies aid me,
That I may have power to avert the plagues
That press upon me.
Thierry.   'Two-days' journey', sayst thou?
We will set forth to meet her. In the meantime, 245
See all things be prepared to entertain her.
Nay, let me have your companies: there's a forest
In the midway shall yield us hunting sport
To ease our travel. I'll not have a brow
But shall wear mirth upon it; therefore, clear them. 250
We'll wash away all sorrow in glad feasts,
And the war we meant to men we'll make on beasts.
      Exeunt all but BRUNEHAUT, BAWDBERT, PROTALDI
                              and LACURE.
Brunehaut. [*To her minions*] Oh, that I had the magic to
    transform you

---

241. blessings] *Q2;* blessing *Q1.*   242. SD] *Weber (subst); not in Q1.*   244. thou?] *1711;* thou. *Q1.*   252. meant] *1711;* meane *Q1.*   252.1–2. SD] *Weber (subst);Exeunt omnes,praeter Brun.Bawdber,Portaldy,Lecure.Q1.*   253. SD] *this edn; not in Q1.*

---

  236. *confines*] borders.
  239. *nuptial*] pronounced as three syllables. A different scansion of the line is possible in which 'deferrèd' has three syllables, 'wishèd' has two, and 'nuptial' has two: 'Our long deferrèd but much wishèd nuptial'.
  240. *Falls ... expression*] turns out so felicitously that I cannot find words to express my joy.
  248. *shall*] that shall.
  249. *travel*] with the common pun on 'travail'.

>   Into the shape of such that your own hounds
>   Might tear you piecemeal. Are you so stupid?   255
>   No word of comfort? Have I fed you moths
>   From my excess of moisture, with such cost,
>   And can you yield no other retribution
>   But to devour your maker? Pander, sponge,
>   Empoisoner, all grown barren?
> *Protaldi.*   You yourself   260
>   That are our mover, and for whom alone
>   We live, have failed yourself in giving way
>   To the reconcilement of your sons.
> *Lacure.*   Which if
>   You had prevented or would teach us how
>   They might again be severed, we could easily   265

---

256. moths] *Dyce;* mothers *Q1.*

---

256. *moths*] I have accepted Dyce's emendation, as 'moths' seems to me more appropriate than 'mothers', especially in light of 1.2.102 (see above). Richard Dutton (pers. comm.), however, suggests that 'mother may be plausible': 'here there is no metrical argument for the change, and I would suggest there is a strong thematic argument for keeping mothers: she is mocking her minions, suggesting that she has fed them so much of her excess moisture that they have become womanish (i.e., mothers, though "barren" ones). It is all of course deeply ironic, coming from an actual mother who plots against both her sons.'

256–7. *fed ... moisture*] According to the theory of humours, the early moderns assumed that the human body contained four fluids: blood, yellow bile, black bile, and phlegm. These humours were believed to correspond to the four elements – air, fire, earth, and water – and to the qualities of cold, hot, dry, and wet. These fluids were thought to be mixed in different amounts in each individual, thus determining their personality, but they were also related to sex: men were said to have a propensity to be hot and dry; women were assumed to have a tendency to be cold and moist. Women were believed to be characterized by a shamefully excessive production of fluids that caused them to be regarded as 'leaky vessels'; the shame derived from the belief that women were unable to control their own bodies. They were also totally different from men insofar as they produced menstrual blood and breastmilk. As Kenny (5) points out, 'all bodily fluids were considered fungible, and therefore, menstrual blood and breastmilk were the same substance. The woman's "superfluous blood" helped nurture a fetus during gestation', and 'menses provided sustenance to an infant in the form of breastmilk'.

259–60. *Pander ... Empoisoner*] i.e., Bawdbert, Protaldi, and Lacure.

260. *barren*] unresponsive.

262. *failed*] disappointed.

  Remove all other hindrances that stop
  The passage of your pleasures.
Bawdbert.   And for me,
  If I fail in my office to provide you
  Fresh delicates, hang me.
Brunehaut.   Oh, you are dull and find not
  The cause of my vexation. Their reconcilement   270
  Is a mock castle built upon the sand
  By children, which, when I am pleased to o'erthrow,
  I can with ease spurn down.
Lacure.   If so, from whence
  Grows your affliction?
Brunehaut.   My grief comes along
  With the new queen, in whose grace all my power   275
  Must suffer shipwreck. For me now,
  That hitherto have kept the first, to know
  A second place or yield the least precedence
  To any other's death. To have my sleeps
  Less inquired after, or my rising up   280
  Saluted with less reverence, or my gates
  Empty of suitors, or the King's great favours
  To pass through any hand but mine, or he
  Himself to be directed by another
  Would be to me — Do you understand me yet?   285
  No means to prevent this?
Protaldi.   Fame gives her out
  To be a woman of a chastity
  Not to be wrought upon, and therefore, madam,
  For me, though I have pleased you, to attempt her

---

285. me —] *Seward;* me: *Q1.* me yet?] *Colman;* me, yet *Q1.*

269. *Fresh delicates*] new handsome young men to sleep with.
276.] The line is two syllables short. A longer midline pause may be intended.
278. *precedence*] pronounced 'precèdence'.
279. *other's*] i.e., other is.
279–81. *To have ... reverence*] Cf. *HMF* 3.1.55–6: 'my sleeps are inquired after, / My rising up saluted with respect'. The model seems to be Sidney, *Arcadia*, 3.2: 'my sleeps were inquired after, and my wakings never unsaluted'.
288. *wrought upon*] influenced, prevailed upon.

	Were to no purpose.	
Brunehaut.	Tush, some other way.	290
Bawdbert.	Faith, I know none else; all my bringing up	
	Aimed at no other learning.	
Lacure.	Give me leave.	
	If my art fail me not, I have thought on	
	A speeding project.	
Brunehaut.	What is't? But effect it,	
	And thou shalt be my Aesculapius:	295
	Thy image shall be set up in pure gold,	
	To which I will fall down and worship it.	
Lacure. The lady is fair?		
Brunehaut.	Exceeding fair.	
Lacure.	And young?	
Brunehaut. Some fifteen at the most.		
Lacure.	And loves the King	
	With equal ardour?	
Brunehaut.	More, she dotes on him.	300
Lacure. Well then, what think you if I make a drink		
	Which, given unto him on the bridal night,	
	Shall for five days so rob his faculties	
	Of all ability to pay that duty	
	Which new-made wives expect that she shall swear	305
	She is not matched to a man?	
Protaldi.	'Twere rare.	
Lacure.	And then,	
	If she have any part of woman in her,	
	She'll or fly out or at least give occasion	
	Of such a breach which ne'er can be made up,	

---

297. I will] *Seward;* I'le *Q1.* 299–300. Some ... King | With ... him] *Weber;* *Q1 lines* Some ... most. | And ... ardor | More, ... him.

---

290. *Tush*] a mild expletive expressing impatience.
294. *speeding*] decisive.
295. *Aesculapius*] the Roman god of medicine and healing, equivalent to Asclepius in Greek mythology.
298. *fair*] beautiful.
304. *duty*] sexual obligation.
306. *rare*] exceptional.
308. *or fly*] either fly.
308–9. *occasion / Of*] grounds for.

        Since he, that to all else did never fail   310
        Of as much as could be performed by man,
        Proves only ice to her.
Brunehaut.   'Tis excellent.
Bawdbert. [*Aside*] The physician
        Helps ever at a dead lift, a fine calling,
        That can both raise and take down. Out upon thee!   315
Brunehaut. For this one service I am ever thine.
        Prepare it; I will give it him myself. —
        For you, Protaldi,   [*Kisses him.*]
        By this kiss and our promised sport at night,
        I do conjure you to bear up, not minding   320
        The opposition of Theodoret
        Or any of his followers. Whatsoe'er
        You are, yet appear valiant and make good
        The opinion that is had of you. For myself,
        In the new queen's remove being made secure,   325
        Fear not: I'll make the future building sure.   *Exeunt.*

---

313. SD] *Turner; not in Q1.* 317–19. Prepare ... myself. | For ... Protaldi, | By ... night] *Dyce; Q1 lines* Prepare ... *Protaldye,* | By ... night. 317. I will] *Dyce;* Ile *Q1.* 318. SD] *this edn; not in Q1.* 320. I] *Seward; not in Q1.*

---

314. *at ... lift*] i.e., at a 'juncture in which one can do no more, an extremity' (*OED* dead lift n. 2), with a bawdy quibble on the image of a flaccid penis.
    315. *raise ... down*] provoke or abate an erection.
    Out ... thee] Curses on you!
    317–18.] Q1's lineation might work if the first 'it' is elided to ''t', if 'will' is elided to ''ll' (this is already indicated in Q1: 'ile') and if the vocative ('Protaldi') is considered extrametrical (which is not unusual in Fletcher, though less so in Massinger, to whom this scene is generally attributed). However, the lineation proposed by Dyce, which I have accepted, has the advantage of creating a perfect pentameter (317) plus a half-line that can be justified on the grounds of intervening stage business that calls for a real pause, that is, a prolonged, passionate kiss between Brunehaut and Protaldi.
    319. *sport*] sexual intercourse.
    320. *conjure*] entreat; pronounced 'conjùre'.
    bear up] keep up your spirits.
    321. *opposition*] pronounced as five syllables.
    325–6. *secure ... sure*] a rhyme Massinger employs in *SJVOB* too: 'And let this Prince of Orange seat him sure, / Or he shall fall when he is most secure' (2.1.748–9).

[SCENE 2]

Wind horns. Enter THEODORET [*and*] THIERRY.

Theodoret. This stag stood well, and cunningly.
Thierry.   My horse,
   I am sure, has found it, for her sides are blooded
   From flank to shoulder. Where's the troop?

Enter MARTEL.

Theodoret.   Passed homeward,
   Weary and tired as we are. — Now, Martel,
   Have you remembered what we thought of?
Martel.   Yes,   5
   Sir, I have sniggled him, and, if there be

SCENE 2] *Weber; not in Q1.* 0.1. SD] *Colman; Q1 lines* Wind hornes. | Enter Theodoret, Trierry. 2–6. I ... blooded | From ... homeward, | Weary ... Martel, | Have ... Yes, | Sir, ... be] *this edn; Q1 lines* I ... are | Blooded ... troope? | Past ... are, | Now ... of? | Yes ... be. 5. thought] *Q2; though Q1.*

2.2.0.] Generally considered to be a Fletcher scene. Weber adds the setting: '*A forest*'. It is plausible to assume that 'some portable properties such as weapons or hunting horns', together with 'items of costume ... associated with the hunt or the woods' (Dessen, *Recovering*, 59), would have been used to signal to the audience that the scene was set in the forest, though it is impossible to be sure, because the text offers no indication as to the use of such objects.
   1. *stood well*] remained firm, kept its ground without budging.
   3. *Passed homeward*] They left for home.
   6. *sniggled*] Sniggling is the 'action or practice of fishing for eels by means of a baited hook or needle thrust into their holes or haunts' (*OED* n. 1). Walton: 'And because you that are but a young angler know not what sniggling is, I will now teach it to you ... observing your time in a warm day, when the water is lowest, [you] may take a hook tied to a strong line or to a string about a yard long, and then into one of these holes, or between any boards about a mill, or under any great stone or plank, or any place where you think an eel may hide or shelter herself, there with the help of a short stick put in your bait, but leisurely and as far as you may conveniently. And it is scarce to be doubted but that, if there be an eel within the sight of it, the eel will bite instantly and as certainly gorge it; and you need not doubt to have him, if you pull him not out of the hole too quickly, but pull him out by degrees, for he, lying folded double in his hole, will, with the help of his tail, break all unless you give him time to be wearied with pulling and so get him out by degrees, not pulling too hard' (194–5).

    Any desert in his blood beside the itch
    Or manly heat but what decoctions,
    Leeches and cullises have crammed into him,
    Your lordship shall know perfect.
Thierry.   What is that?   10
    May not I know too?
Theodoret.   Yes, sir. To that end
    We cast the project.
Thierry.   What is't?
Martel.   A desire, sir,
    Upon the gilded flag your grace's favour
    Has stuck up for a General, and to inform you,
    For this hour he shall pass the test, what valour,   15
    Staid judgement, soul or safe discretion
    Your mother's wandering eyes and your obedience
    Have flung upon us, to assure your knowledge
    He can be, dare be, shall be, must be nothing —
    Load him with piles of honours, set him off   20
    With all the cunning foils that may deceive us —

10–12. Your ... that? | May ... end | We ... sir,] *Colman; Q1 lines* Your ... perfect. | Whats ... too? | Yes Sir, | To ... project. | What ist? | A ... Sir. 10. What is] *Colman;* Whats *Q1.*

---

 8. *manly heat*] According to the theory of the four humours men were thought to have a propensity to be hot and dry; see 2.1.256–7.
  what] that which.
  decoctions] 'liquor[s] in which a substance, usually animal or vegetable, has been boiled, and in which the principles thus extracted are dissolved; *spec.* as a medicinal agent' (*OED* n. 3); pronounced as four syllables.
 9. *Leeches*] physicians.
  cullises] OED defines 'cullis' as a 'strong broth, made of meat, fowl, etc., boiled and strained; used especially as a nourishing food for sick persons' (n.1 a).
 10. *perfect*] perfectly.
 13. *gilded*] adorned or embellished so as to seem attractive (*OED* adj. 3).
 16. *Staid*] sober, steady.
  discretion] pronounced as four syllables.
 17. *wandering*] roving, restless.
 20. *set him off*] set him in relief.
 21. *cunning*] skilfully made.
  foils] A foil is 'a thin leaf of some metal placed under a precious stone to increase its brilliancy or under some transparent substance to give it the appearance of a precious stone' (*OED* n.1 5a).

SC 2]   THIERRY AND THEODORET   97

  But a poor, cold, unspirited, unmannered,
  Unhonest, unaffected, undone fool
  And most unheard-of coward, a mere lump
  Made to load beds withal and, like a nightmare,   25
  Ride ladies that forget to say their prayers;
  One that dares only be diseased and in debt,
  Whose body mews more plasters every month
  Than women do old faces.
Thierry.   No more. I know him.
  I now repent my error. Take your time   30
  And try him home, ever thus far reserved
  You tie your anger up.
Martel.   I lost it else, sir.
Thierry. Bring me his sword fair taken, without violence,
  For that will best declare him.
Theodoret.   That's the thing.
Thierry. [*To* MARTEL] And my best horse is thine.
Martel.   Your grace's servant.   35
         Exit [MARTEL].
Theodoret. You'll hunt no more, sir?
Thierry.   Not today, the weather
  Is grown too warm; besides, the dogs are spent.
  We'll take a cooler morning. Let's to horse

---

23. undone fool] *1711*; vndone, foole *Q1*. 35. SD] *this edn; not in Q1*. 35.1. SD] *this edn; Exit. Q1*.

---

 22. *unspirited*] spiritless.
 23. *Unhonest*] dishonest
 unaffected] untouched, unmoved.
 undone] ruined.
 25–6. *like ... ladies*] See 1.1.168. Williams (*Dictionary*, 2.852) detects a sexual innuendo in 'Ride'.
 28. *mews*] changes, sheds as if plumage.
 31. *home*] fully, effectively.
 31–2. *ever ... up*] as long as you do not get carried away in your anger.
 32. *lost*] would lose.
 else] otherwise.
 33. *fair*] fairly.
 34. *declare*] expose.

98   THIERRY AND THEODORET   [ACT 2

    And hollo in the troop.
                    Exeunt [THIERRY *and* THEODORET].
                                    Wind horns.

                    Enter two [Keepers].
1 Keeper.   Ay, marry, trainer,
    This woman gives indeed: these are the angels   40
    That are the keepers' saints.
2 Keeper.   I like a woman

---

39. SD1–2] *this edn; Q1 lines Exeunt. Wind hornes.* SD3] *this edn; Enter 2 Huntsmen. Q1; Dyce, Strachey, and Turner have a new scene start here.* trainer] *conj Coleridge;* Twainer *Q1.*

---

39. *hollo*] call.
    SD3] There is no need to mark a new scene here as Dyce, Strachey, and Turner do, even though the stage is briefly clear after Thierry and Theodoret's exit. In what is to date the most rigorous analysis of scene division in Shakespeare's plays, James E. Hirsh argues that '[t]he continuity of a play is not broken, and hence a scene division does not occur, even if the stage is technically cleared for a moment, if either the exiting or the entering characters express awareness of the other group' (211), which is exactly what occurs here. The Keepers' reply to Protaldi's question as to the King's whereabouts – 'he's newly mounted, / And, as we take it, ridden home' (48–9) – clearly indicates that the Keepers have seen (or heard) the King and his brother depart from the hunting area in which they all are. Moreover, line 39 is an iambic pentameter with a double ending shared between Thierry and 1 Keeper, which also evidently presupposes that no scene break is intended here.
    39–46. *Ay ... else*] The bawdy exchange between the Keepers is reminiscent of that between the Woodmen about Arethus, Gallatea, and Megra in *Phil* 4.2.
    39. *marry*] indeed, a mild interjection. It was originally an invocation of the name of the Virgin Mary, but it had lost that meaning by the time this play was written.
    trainer] The emendation was first suggested by Coleridge (lxxxiv), but his suggestion has never been incorporated into any previous editions of the text. If Coleridge is right, this use of 'trainer' in the sense of 'a person who trains animals to obey orders or to perform particular tasks or functions' predates the first recorded instance (1659) in *OED* (n. 1c).
    40. *angels*] with a pun on the gold coins that owed their name to the figure of the archangel Michael killing a dragon depicted on them, whose value oscillated between a third and half of a pound.
    41–3. *I ... proportion*] While discussing their sale of the deer's dowsets (i.e., testicles), the Keepers 'hint at a connection between her purchase and her continuing sexual viability' (Williams, *Dictionary*, 1:410). The bawdy quibble continues over the next few lines.

	That handles the deer's dowsets with discretion	
	And pays us by proportion.	
1 Keeper.	'Tis no treason	
	To think this good old lady has a stump yet	
	That may require a coral.	
2 Keeper.	And the bells too;	45
	She has lost a friend of me else.	

Enter PROTALDI.

But here's the clerk.
No more, for fear a th' bell-ropes.
Protaldi. How now, keepers?
Saw you the King?
1 Keeper. Yes, sir, he's newly mounted,
And, as we take it, ridden home.
Protaldi. Farewell, then.

Exeunt Keepers.

Enter MARTEL [*again, disguised*].

---

46. SD] *Weber; following line 45.1 Q1.*   49.1. SD] *Seward; Exit Keepers. Q1.*
49.2. SD] *this edn; Enter* Martell *disguised. Turner;* Enter Martell. *Q1.*

44–5. *this ... too*] The coral was a toy, originally 'made of polished coral, given to infants to assist them in cutting their teeth' (*OED* coral n. 3). Sometimes coral had bells attached to them. Since 'coral' could also be used to signify the penis, here Fletcher takes advantage of the 'bells' in order 'to quibble on testicles' (Williams, *Dictionary*, 1:306). 'Stump' means the 'part of a broken tooth left in the gum' (*OED* n.1 3c). Williams suggests that the 'joke depends on the vagina as a lower mouth', but it could also be a reference to oral intercourse.

46. *clerk*] The word here probably has a double meaning. On the one hand, Protaldi is Brunehaut's clerk because he is one of her subordinates, but 'clerk' also means 'clerk in holy orders', which fits with the Keepers' mention of the 'bell-ropes' in the ensuing line. The Keepers stop talking because they fear being discovered by Protaldi as they talk bawdily about Brunehaut: Protaldi, Brunehaut's clerk, might ring the bells, i.e., inform Brunehaut and have them punished, perhaps by pulling their testicles (another potential quip on 'bell-ropes'). Alternatively, they might be afraid that the clerk Protaldi might order them to ring bells (i.e., do heavy work) as punishment.

47. *a*] of.
bell-ropes] 'the rope[s] by which a bell is rung, i.e., either those in a belfry, or those which hang from the bell-levers in a room or chamber' (*OED*). This predates the earliest use recorded in *OED* by seventeen years.

Martel. My honoured lord, fortune has made me happy 50
    To meet with such a man of men to side me.
Protaldi. How, sir?
    I know ye not, nor what your fortune means.
Martel. Few words shall serve: I am betrayèd, sir,
    Innocent and honest; malice and violence 55
    Are both against me, basely and foully laid for.
    For my life, sir, danger is now about me,
    Now in my throat, sir.
Protaldi.   Where, sir?
Martel.   Nay, I fear not,
    And, let it now pour down in storms upon me,
    I have met a noble guard.
Protaldi.   Your meaning, sir? 60
    For I have present business.
Martel.   O my lord,
    Your honour cannot leave a gentleman —
    At least a fair design of this brave nature,
    To which your worth is wedded, your profession
    Hatched in and made one piece — in such a peril. 65
    There are but six, my lord.
Protaldi.   What six?

---

50. SP *Martel*] *1711; not in Q1.* 52–3. How, sir? | I ... means] *Turner; Q1 lines* How ... not, | Nor ... meanes. 66–8. There ... villains, | Sworn ... sir, | What ... present?] *Colman; Q1 lines* There ... What six? | Six villaines ... mee. | Six? | Alas ... present.

    50–125.] This sequence bears resemblances with the exchange between Oswald and the disguised Kent in *KL* 2.2.11–33: '*Oswald.* Why dost thou use me thus? I know thee not. *Kent.* Fellow, I know thee. *Oswald.* What dost thou know me for? *Kent.* A knave ...; a lily-livered, action-taking knave, ... one that wouldst be a bawd in way of good service and art nothing but the composition of a knave, beggar, coward, pander ...; one whom I will beat into clamorous whining if thou deniest the least syllable of thy addition. *Oswald.* Why, what a monstrous fellow art thou, thus to rail on one that is neither known of thee, nor knows thee! *Kent.* ... Draw, you rogue ... *Oswald.* Away, I have nothing to do with thee.'
    57. *about*] around.
    65. *Hatched in*] inlaid.
    66–108.] As noted by Wiggins (#1848), 'Martel's ruse to expose Protaldi's cowardice by confronting him with a progressively diminishing number of imaginary assailants is an inversion of Falstaff's escalating sequence of buckram men.' Cf. *1H4* 2.4.186–215.

Martel.   Six villains,
  Sworn and in pay to kill me.
Protaldi.   Six?
Martel.   Alas, sir,
  What can six do or six score now you are present?
  Your name will blow 'em off. Say they have shot too,
  Who dare present a piece? Your valour's proof, sir.   70
Protaldi. No, I'll assure you, sir, nor my discretion
  Against a multitude. 'Tis true I dare fight
  Enough, and well enough, and long enough,
  But wisdom, sir, and weight of what is on me —
  In which I am no more mine own nor yours, sir,   75
  Nor, as I take it, any single danger
  But what concerns my place — tells me directly
  (Beside my person) my fair reputation,
  If I thrust into crowds and seek occasions,
  Suffers opinion. Six? Why, Hercules   80
  Avoided two, man. Yet, not to give example,
  But only for your present danger's sake, sir,
  Were there but four, sir, I cared not if I killed 'em:
  They will serve to set my sword.
Martel.   There are but four, sir.
  I did mistake them, but four such as Europe,   85
  Excepting your great valour —
Protaldi.   Well considered,
  I will not meddle with 'em. Four in honour
  Are equal with fourscore; besides, they are people

---

81. two, man] *Colman;* two men *Q2;* two man *Q1*. 85. them] *Q2;* vm *Q1*.
86. valour —] *Colman;* valour. *Q1*.

---

  68. *six score*] one hundred and twenty.
  69. *shot*] firearms.
  70. *present a piece*] point a handgun.
    proof] impenetrable, invulnerable.
  80. *Suffers opinion*] will be damaged by common, vulgar opinion.
    Hercules] See 2.1.46.
  84. *set*] whet.
  88. *fourscore*] eighty.

　　　　　Only directed by their fury.
Martel.　　　　　　　　　　So much nobler
　　Shall be your way of justice.
Protaldi.　　　　　　　　　That I find not.　　　　90
Martel. You will not leave me thus?
Protaldi.　　　　　　　　I would not leave you,
　　But look you, sir: men of my place and business
　　Must not be questioned thus.
Martel.　　　　　　　　You cannot pass, sir,
　　Now they have seen me with you, without danger.
　　They are here, sir, within hearing. Take but two.　95
Protaldi. Let the law take 'em. Take a tree, sir — I
　　Will take my horse — that you may keep with safety
　　If they have brought no handsaws. Within this hour
　　I'll send you rescue and a toil to take 'em.
Martel. You shall not go so poorly. Stay but one, sir.　100
Protaldi. I have been so hampered with these rescues,
　　So hewed and tortured that the truth is, sir,
　　I have mainly vowed against 'em. Yet, for your sake,
　　If, as you say, there be but one, I'll stay
　　And see fair play a both sides.
Martel.　　　　　　　　There is no more, sir,　105

89–93. Only ... nobler | Shall ... not. | You ... leave you, | But ... business | Must ... sir,] *Dyce; Q1 lines* Only ... fury. | So ... Iustice. | That ... not. | You ... thus? | I ... Sir, | Men ... not | Be ... thus. | You ... Sir.　96–7. Let ... I | Will ... safety] *Dyce; Q1 lines* Let ... Sir, | Ile ... safety.　96–7. I | Will] *Dyce;* Ile *(on line 97) Q1.*　100. Stay but] *Q1;* Stay! But *Colman.*　105–12. And see ... sir, | And, as ... him! | Go ... sir, | The ... me? | Yes, for ... coward | And upstart ... puppy | That ... patience. | Yes, this ... you,] *Dyce; Q1 lines* And ... sides. | There is no | More ... two. | Fie... eares. | Yes: | This ... kingdome. | Do ... me? | Yes for ... foole, | A knaue ... bawd, | Beast, ... bite. | The ... patience. | Yes, | This ... you.

---

90. *way of justice*] administration of justice. Cf. *Corinth* 2.3.145–7: 'If all the art I have or power can do it, / He shall be found, and such a way of justice / Inflicted on him'; *LC* 2.1.134–6: 'This is he apprehends whores in the way of justice, and lodges 'em in his own house in the way of profit.'
　99. *toil*] snare, net.
　100. *poorly*] abjectly, mean-spiritedly.
Stay] Stop.
　105. *a*] on.

And, as I doubt, a base one too.
Protaldi.   Fie on him!
    Go lug him out by the ears.
Martel.   [*Wrings him by the ears.*] Yes, this is he, sir,
    The basest in the kingdom.
Protaldi.   Do you know me?
Martel. Yes, for a general fool, a knave, a coward
    And upstart stallion bawd, beast, barking puppy   110
    That dares not bite.
Protaldi.   The best man best knows patience.
Martel. Yes, this way, sir. Now draw your sword and right
        you,
    Or render it to me, for one you shall do.
Protaldi. If wearing it may do you any honour,
    I shall be glad to grace you. There it is, sir.   115
                    [*Gives him the sword.*]
Martel. Now get you home, and tell your lady mistress
    She has shot up a sweet mushroom. Quit your place too,
    And say you are counselled well; thou wilt be beaten else
    By thine own lanceprisadoes when they know thee,

---

106. too] *Q2;* two *Q1.* 107. SD] *this edn; Seizing him by the ears. Dyce; Seizes him. Weber.* 112. your] *Q2;* you *Q1.* 115.1. SD] *Dyce (subst); not in Q1.*

---

  109. *general*] punning on Protaldi's rank.
  110. *stallion bawd*] male bawd (Williams, *Dictionary*, 3:1305).
  112. *this way*] Some editors add an SD here – '*Kicks him*' (Seward, Colman, Weber) or '*Kicking him*' (Dyce, Strachey, Turner) – but the text does not justify such an insertion. In fact, the final exchange of the scene (ll. 124–5) suggests that Martel is still holding Protaldi by the ears at that point, so that Martel's 'this way, sir' here would appear to signal that he drags Protaldi by the ears rather than kicking him. Other options are available – Martel may push Protaldi, tweak him by the nose (cf. 2.3.89), or even draw his sword and challenge him to do the same – but they seem to me less likely.
    right you] do justice to yourself.
  114–15.] Compare Bessus' words to Bacurius in *KNoK* 3.2.144–6: 'It is a pretty hilt, and if your lordship take an affection to it, with all my heart I present it to you, for a new year's gift.'
  117. *mushroom*] upstart.
  119. *lanceprisadoes*] lance-corporals, low-grade non-commissioned officers.

That tuns of oil of roses will not cure thee. 120
Go, get you to your foining work at court,
And learn to sweat again and eat dry mutton.
An armour like a frost will search your bones
And make you roar, you rogue. Not a reply,
For, if you do, your ears go off.
Protaldi.   Still patience.   *Exeunt.*   125

[SCENE 3]

Loud music, a banquet set out.

Enter THIERRY, ORDELLA, BRUNEHAUT, THEODORET,
LACURE, BAWDBERT [*and* Attendants].

---

125. SD] *Q1; Exeunt severally.* Dyce.

SCENE 3] *Weber;* SCENE IV *Dyce; not in Q1.* 0.1. SD] *Weber (subst); Enter Trierry, Ordella, Brunhalt, Theodoret, Lecure, Bawdber. &c. Q1.*

---

120. *That*] so much that.
tuns] large casks or barrels, usually for liquids or for various provisions (*OED* n. 1a).
oil of roses] used at the time for treating a variety of physical ailments, including 'the ache in the back' (Vicary, 2M4^r) and 'the weakness of the back' (Williams, *Physical Rarities*, C2^r); Martel assumes that Protaldi will be beaten on the back because he will try to escape, coward that he is (see also 2.3.36–9). Cf. Beaumont, *Pestle*, in which Luce advises Humphrey, who has just been beaten by Jasper, to use 'A little oil of roses and a feather / To 'noint thy back withal' (2.1.245–6) in order 'To cure your beaten bones' (243).
121. *foining work*] sexual activity (Williams, *Dictionary*, 2:522).
122–4. *sweat ... roar*] Sweating and dry mutton were the regimen typically prescribed for treating syphilis, while bone ache was one of the most common symptoms (Williams, *Dictionary*, 1:384–6, 2:522, 1:129). Martel's mention of the 'armour' – the coldness of which ('frost') sharply contrasts with the heat that would make Protaldi 'sweat' – implies that he believes militarism to be the only cure for Protaldi's disease.

2.3.0.] Generally considered to be a Massinger scene. Weber adds the setting: '*Paris. A hall in the palace*'.
0.1. SD Loud music] The musicians would probably have been located in a 'music room' on the same level as the upper stage.
a banquet set out] 'For the larger-scale banquets, for the seated banquets scenes at least, an audience would see before them the table covered almost certainly with a cloth, having been brought in ... with a number of trenchers, dishes, bowls or cups and pots upon it, appropriate to the requirements of

Thierry. It is your place, and, though in all things else
    You may and ever shall command me, yet
    In this I'll be obeyed.
Ordella.   Sir, the consent
    That made me yours shall never teach me to
    Repent I am so, yet be you but pleased   5
    To give me leave to say so much: the honour
    You offer me were better given to her
    To whom you owe the power of giving.
Thierry.   Mother,
    You hear this and rejoice in such a blessing,
    That pays to you so large a share of duty —   10
    But fie! No more! [*To* ORDELLA] For as you hold a place
    Nearer my heart than she, you must sit nearest
    To all those graces that are in the power
    Of majesty to bestow.   [*They sit.*]
Brunehaut.   [*Aside*] Which I'll provide
    Shall be short-lived. — Lacure!
Lacure.   [*Aside to her*] I have it ready.   15
Brunehaut. [*Aside to him*] 'Tis well. — Wait on our cup.
Lacure.   You honour me.
Thierry. We are dull. No object to provoke mirth?

10. duty —] *Weber;* duty, *Q1.* 11. SD] *this edn; not in Q1.* 14. SD1] *this edn; not in Q1.* SD2] *Weber (subst); not in Q1.* 15. SD] *Turner (subst); not in Q1.* 16. SD] *Turner (subst); not in Q1.* 17. We ... mirth?] *Dyce; Q1 lines* We ... dull, | No ... mirth.

---

the play's action. There may have been need for lighting in the form of tapers on the table, along with a number of diapered or plain napkins corresponding to the number of characters important enough to warrant them. The distribution of the items upon the table could be in ordered rows along the table's upstage edges in scenes of formal nature, or generally dispersed ready for the actors, as guests, to take them up if needed in the course of stage business. The fact that food would be eaten, if eaten it was, with the fingers and cut with a personal knife, as was still the practice in real life, explains the lack of modern cutlery upon the table' (Meads, 56).

  1. *place*] i.e., place at the table. Thierry is possibly letting Ordella sit at the head of the table – an unusual honour for a lady, even a queen (which would certainly outrage Brunehaut).
  7. *her*] i.e., Brunehaut.
  14. *provide*] take measures to ensure.
  17.] Arranged in this way, the line becomes headless (i.e., a line with a missing unstressed syllable before the first stressed one), with a double ending.
    dull] sad, gloomy.

Theodoret. Martel,
    If you remember, sir, will grace your feast
    With something that will yield matter of mirth   20
    Fit for no common view.
Thierry.   Touching Protaldi?
Theodoret. You have it.
Brunehaut.   (*Aside*) What of him? I fear his baseness,
    In spite of all the titles that my favours
    Have clothed him with, will make discovery
    Of what is yet concealed.

            Enter MARTEL [*with* PROTALDI's *sword*].

Theodoret.   [*To* THIERRY] Look, sir, he has it.   25
    Nay, we shall have peace when so great a soldier
    As the renowned Protaldi will give up
    His sword rather than use it.
Brunehaut.   (*Aside*) 'Twas thy plot,
    Which I will turn on thy own head.
Thierry.   Pray you, speak:
    How won you him to part from't?
Martel.   Won him, sir?   30
    He would have yielded it upon his knees
    Before he would have hazarded the exchange
    Of a fillip of the forehead. Had you willed me,
    I durst have undertook he should have sent you
    His nose, provided that the loss of it   35
    Might have saved the rest of his face. He is, sir,
    The most unutterable coward that e'er nature
    Blessed with hard shoulders, which were only given him

---

24. with] *Seward;* which *Q1.*   25. SD1] *Weber; Enter Martell. Q1.*   SD2] *this edn; not in Q1.*

---

21. *Touching*] regarding.
25. *he*] i.e., Martel.
30. *won*] persuaded.
33. *fillip of*] flip on.
    willed] commanded.
37. *unutterable*] unspeakable.

	To the ruin of bastinadoes.	

Thierry.   Possible?
Theodoret. [*Aside*] Observe but how she frets!
Martel.   Why, believe it.   40
   But that I know the shame of this disgrace
   Will make the beast to live with such and never
   Presume to come more among men, I'll hazard
   My life upon it that a boy of twelve
   Should scourge him hither like a parish-top   45
   And make him dance before you.
Brunehaut.   Slave, thou liest!
   Thou dar'st as well speak treason in the hearing
   Of those that have the power to punish it
   As the least syllable of this before him,
   But 'tis thy hate to me.
Martel.   Nay, pray you, madam,   50
   I have no ears to hear you, though a foot
   To let you understand what he is.
Brunehaut.   Villain.
Theodoret. [*To* MARTEL] You are too violent.

                    Enter PROTALDI.

Protaldi.   [*Aside*] The worst that can come
   Is blanketing, for beating and such virtues
   I have been long acquainted with.
Martel.   Oh, strange!   55
Bawdbert. Behold the man you talk of.
Brunehaut.   Give me leave.

---

40. SD] *this edn; not in Q1.* 53. SD1] *this edn; not in Q1.* SP *Protaldi*] *1711; not in Q1.* SD3] *Dyce; not in Q1.* 56. you] *Q2;* yon *Q1.*

---

39. *To ... of*] for ruin by.
bastinadoes] beating with a stick, esp. on the soles of the feet.
40. *frets*] chafes, worries.
42. *such*] i.e., other beasts.
45. *parish-top*] 'a spinning top kept for the amusement of parishioners' (*OED* parish n. C2).
54. *blanketing*] the 'punishment of tossing in a blanket' (*OED* n. 3), which was regarded as suitable for cowards.
55. *strange*] incredible.

108   THIERRY AND THEODORET   [ACT 2

    [*To* PROTALDI] Or free thyself —
            [*Aside to him*] think in what place you are —
    From the foul imputation that is laid
    Upon thy valour — [*Aside to him*] be bold: I'll protect
      you —
    Or here I vow — [*Aside to him*] deny it or forswear it —   60
    These honours which thou wearst unworthily —
    [*Aside to him*] Which be but impudent enough and
      keep them —
    Shall be torn from thee with thy eyes.
Protaldi.   [*Aside to her*] I have it! —
    My valour? Is there any here beneath
    The style of king dares question it?
Thierry.   This is rare.   65
Protaldi. Which of my actions, which have still been noble,
    Has rendered me suspected?
Thierry.   Nay, Martel,
    You must not fall off.
Martel.   Oh, sir, fear it not.
    [*To* PROTALDI] Do you know this sword?
Protaldi.   Yes.
Martel.   Pray you, on what terms
    Did you part with it?
Protaldi.   'Part with it', say you?
Martel.   So.   70

---

57. SD1] *this edn; not in Q1.* SD2] *this edn; not in Q1.* 59. SD] *this edn; not in Q1.* 60. SD] *this edn; not in Q1.* 62. SD] *this edn; not in Q1.* 63. SD] *this edn; aside Turner; not in Q1.* 65. rare] *Q1c*; care *Q1u.* 69. SD] *this edn; not in Q1.* 70. Did ... so] *this edn; Turner lines* Did ... you? | So; *Q1 lines* Did ... it: | Part ... you? | So.

---

  63. *I have it!*] This statement recalls the typical '*habeo*' (i.e., I've got it! I've found a solution!) of the *callidus servus* of Latin comedy (e.g., Terence, *Andria* 344, 498), subtly reminding the audience that Protaldi is primarily a comic character. Cf. *Shrew* 1.1.188 ('I have it, Tranio!'); *Ham* (Q2) 4.7.154 ('I ha't!'); *Oth* 1.3.402 ('I have't, it is engendered!')
  65. *style*] title.
  rare] exceptional.
  66. *still*] always.
  67–8. *Nay ... fall off*] Thierry seems to respond to some movement by Martel. He perhaps steps either back or aside ('fall off'), and Thierry interprets this as springing from Martel's intention no longer to confront Protaldi.

Thierry. [*To* PROTALDI] Nay, study not an answer; confess
  freely.
Protaldi. Oh, I remember't now: at the stag's fall,
  As we today were hunting, a poor fellow —
  And, now I view you better, I may say,
  Much of your pitch — this silly wretch I spoke of,   75
  With his petition falling at my feet
  (Which much against my will he kissed), desired
  That as a special means for his preferment
  I would vouchsafe to let him use my sword
  To cut off the stag's head.
Brunehaut.   Will you hear that?   80
Bawdbert. [*Aside*] This lie bears a similitude of truth.
Protaldi. I, ever courteous (a great weakness in me),
  Granted his humble suit.
Martel.   Oh, impudence!
Thierry. This change is excellent.
Martel.   [*To* PROTALDI] A word with you:
  Deny it not. I was that man disguised.   85
  You know my temper and — as you respect
  A daily cudgelling for one whole year
  Without a second pulling by the ears
  Or tweaks by the nose, or the most precious balm
  You used of patience (patience, do you mark me?) —   90
  Confess before these kings with what base fear
  Thou didst deliver it.
Protaldi.   Oh, I shall burst,

---

71. SD] *this edn; not in Q1.* 72. fall] *1711;* falls *Q1.* 81. SD] *this edn; not in Q1.* 84. SD] *this edn; not in Q1.*

---

71. *study ... answer*] Look for an appropriate answer in your mind.
72. *fall*] death, killing.
75. *pitch*] stature.
79. *vouchsafe*] grant.
80. *Will ... that*] These words may be addressed either to Thierry directly or to all the characters on stage.
82. *ever*] always.
86. *temper*] temperament, disposition, frame of mind.
92–101. *Oh ... head*] Cf. *KL* 2.2.63–8: '*Oswald.* This ancient ruffian, sir, whose life I have spared at suit of his grey beard – *Kent.* Thou whoreson zed, thou unnecessary letter! – My lord, if you will give me leave, I will tread this unbolted villain into mortar and daub the walls of a jakes with him.'

110   THIERRY AND THEODORET   [ACT 2

    And, if I have not instant liberty
    To tear this fellow limb by limb, the wrong
    Will break my heart, although Herculean,   95
    And somewhat bigger. There's my gage.
                   [*Throws a glove on the ground.*]
                [*To* THIERRY] Pray you, here
    Let me redeem my credit.
Thierry.   Ha ha! Forbear.
Martel. Pray you, let me take it up, and, if I do not
    Against all odds of armour and of weapons
    With this make him confess it on his knees,   100
    Cut off my head.
Protaldi.   No, that is my office.
Bawdbert.   Fie!
    You take the hangman's place!
Ordella.   [*To* THIERRY] Nay, good my lord,
    Let me atone this difference. Do not suffer
    Our bridal night to be the Centaurs' feast.

---

96. SD1] *this edn; not in Q1.* SD2] *this edn; not in Q1.* 101–2. Cut ... Fie! | You ... lord,] *Colman; Q1 lines* Cut ... head. | No, ... office. | Fie ... place. | Nay ... Lord.   102. SD] *this edn; not in Q1.*

---

  96. *gage*] 'a pledge (usually a glove thrown on the ground) of a person's appearance to do battle in support of his assertions' (*OED* n.1 2).
  96–7. *Pray ... credit*] 'For Protald[i] knew he might safely ask what could not be granted, to fight in the court as Brun[e]ha[u]lt had before hinted to him' (Seward).
  97. *Ha ha*] For the metrical use of 'ha ha' and 'ha ha ha', see Steggle, 28–9.
  99.] This suggests that Protaldi has come onstage fully armed and attired as his new office of Lord General requires.
  100. *With this*] probably pointing at Protaldi's sword in his own hands.
  103. *atone ... difference*] compose this quarrel.
  104. *Centaurs' feast*] The allusion is to Greek mythology, namely to the feast to celebrate the wedding of Pirithous, King of the Lapiths (a group of legendary people based in Thessaly), with Hippodamia. The Centaurs, mythological creatures with the upper body of a human and the lower body and legs of a horse, were invited. Under the influence of wine, to which they were not accustomed, one of them attempted to abduct the bride. The other Centaurs followed suit, trying to seize women and boys. A bloody war ensued, which ended with the Centaurs' defeat and banishment from Thessaly.

SC 3]   THIERRY AND THEODORET   111

[*To* PROTALDI] You are a knight, and bound by oath to
       grant   105
    All just suits unto ladies: for my sake,
    Forget your supposed wrong.
Protaldi.   Well, let him thank you:
    For your sake he shall live, perhaps a day
    And maybe, on submission, longer.
Theodoret.   Nay,
    Martel, you must be patient.
Martel.   I am yours,   110
    And this slave shall be once more mine.
Thierry.   Sit all! [*They sit.*]
    One health, and so to bed, for I too long
    Defer my choicest delicates.
Brunehaut.   [*Aside*] Which, if poison
    Have any power, thou shalt like Tantalus
    Behold and never taste. [*Aside to* LACURE] Be careful.
Lacure.   [*Aside to her*] Fear not.   115
Brunehaut. Though it be rare in our sex, yet for once

---

105. SD] *this edn; not in Q1.*   107. you] *Q2;* yon *Q1.*   109–10. And ... Nay,
| Martel ... yours,] *Colman; Q1 lines* And ... longer, | Nay, ... patient. | I
am yours.   111. SD] *this edn; not in Q1.*   113. SD] *Weber; not in Q1.*
115. SD1] *Turner (subst); not in Q1.*   SD2] *Turner (subst); not in Q1.*

---

105. *knight*] Cf. Grimeston, sig. D3ʳ: 'This old bitch [i.e., Brunehaut] ...
advanced him [i.e., Protaldi] beyond duty or desert.'
    109. *on submission*] i.e., if he submits to me.
    109–10. *Nay ... patient*] Theodoret's words suggest that Martel must have
threatened Protaldi in some way after the latter's sneering remarks, so that
Theodoret needs to restrain him from reacting violently.
    113. *choicest delicates*] most exquisite delights (i.e., sexual intercourse with
Ordella).
    poison] 'a drink prepared for a special purpose; a medicinal draught; a
potion' (*OED* n. 2).
    114. *Tantalus*] a Greek mythological figure guilty of various offences
against the gods, including the theft of nectar and ambrosia from their table.
Relegated to the underworld, he was condemned to suffer hunger and thirst
for eternity, immersed up to his neck in a lake, the water of which receded
at every attempt of his to drink it, and tied to a tree full of fruit, the branches
of which overhung his head, only to be immediately blown away by the wind
as soon as he raised his arm to reach them. Tantalus was the father of Niobe,
which might make this aside an oblique response to Theodoret's earlier
exhortation to Brunehaut to 'live like Niobe' (see 1.1.125).

    I will begin a health.
Thierry.   Let it come freely.
Brunehaut. Lacure, the cup. — [*He gives her a cup of wine.*]
                          Here, to the son we hope
    This night shall be an embryon.   [*Drinks.*]
Thierry.   You have named
    A blessing that I most desired. I pledge you. —   120
        [LACURE *gives him a cup of drugged wine.*]
    Give me a larger cup: that is too little
    Unto so great a good.
Brunehaut.   Nay, then you wrong me.
    Follow as I began.
Thierry.   Well, as you please.   [*Drinks.*]
Brunehaut. [*Aside to* LACURE] Is't done?
Lacure.   [*Aside to her*] Unto your wish, I warrant you,
    For this night I durst trust him with my mother.   125
Thierry. So, 'tis gone round. [*To* Attendants] Lights!
                                      [*They rise.*]
Brunehaut.   [*To* ORDELLA] Pray you, use my service.
Ordella. 'Tis that which I shall ever owe you, madam,
    And must have none from you; pray you, pardon me.
Thierry. Good rest to all.
Theodoret.   And to you pleasant labour. —
    Martel, your company. — Madam, goodnight.   130
       Exeunt all but BRUNEHAUT, PROTALDI, LACURE
                                  and BAWDBERT.
Brunehaut. [*To* PROTALDI] Nay, you have cause to blush,
    but I will hide it,
    And, what's more, I forgive you. Is't not pity

---

118. SD] *this edn; not in Q1*.   119. SD] *Dyce; not in Q1*.   120.1. SD] *this edn; not in Q1*.   122. good] *Seward;* god *Q1*.   123. SD] *Dyce; not in Q1*.   124. SD1] *Turner (subst); not in Q1*. SD2] *Turner (subst); not in Q1*.   126. SD1] *this edn; not in Q1*. SD2] *Dyce; not in Q1*. SD3] *this edn; not in Q1*.   130.1-2. SD] *Weber;* Exeunt all, but Brunhalt, Protal. Lecure, Bawdber. *Q1*.   131. SD] *this edn; not in Q1*.

    118. we] to whom we.
    119. shall ... embryon] will enable him to conceive a child.
    126. 'tis ... round] We have all drunk.
    129. pleasant labour] sexual exertion.

SC 3]   THIERRY AND THEODORET   113

  That thou, that art the first to enter combat
  With any woman and, what is more, o'ercome her
  (In which she is best pleased), should be so fearful   135
  To meet a man?
Protaldi.   Why, would you have me lose
  That blood that is dedicated to your service
  In any other quarrel?
Brunehaut.   No, reserve it,
  As I will study to preserve thy credit.
  [*To* BAWDBERT] You, sirrah, be't your care to find out
    one   140
  That is poor though valiant, that at any rate
  Will, to redeem my servant's reputation,
  Receive a public baffling.
Bawdbert.   Would your highness
  Were pleased to inform me better of your purpose.
Brunehaut. Why, one, sir, that would thus be boxed or kicked.   145
         [*Strikes and kicks him.*]
  Do you apprehend me now?
Bawdbert.   I feel you, madam.
  The man that shall receive this from my lord
  Shall have a thousand crowns.
Brunehaut.   He shall.
Bawdbert.   Besides,
  His day of bastinadoing passed o'er,
  He shall not lose your grace nor your good favour.   150
Brunehaut. That shall make way to it.
Bawdbert.   [*To* PROTALDI] It must be a man

140. SD] *this edn; not in Q1.* 145.1. SD] *Dyce; not in Q1.* 145–6. Why ... kicked. | Do ... madam] *Colman; Q1 lines* Why ... boxed, | Or ...now? | I ... Madam. 148. SP *Brunehaut*] *Seward; Prot. Q1.* 151. SD] *this edn; not in Q1.*

---

  133. *combat*] with the secondary meaning of sexual intercourse (Williams, *Dictionary,* 1:276).
  134. *o'ercome*] an allusion to coitus (Williams, *Dictionary,* 1:280).
  137. *That blood*] i.e., the blood needed for erections.
  140. *sirrah*] term of address used for servants or social inferiors.
  143. *baffling*] humiliation.
  Would] I wish.
  146. *apprehend*] understand.
  149. *bastinadoing*] the action of giving bastinadoes (see 2.3.39).

	Of credit in the court that is to be	

      Of credit in the court that is to be
      The foil unto your valour.
Protaldi.   True, it should.
Bawdbert. And, if he have place there, 'tis not the worse.
Brunehaut. 'Tis much the better.
Bawdbert.   If he be a lord,   155
      'Twill be the greater grace.
Brunehaut.   Thou art in the right.
Bawdbert. [*To* PROTALDI] Why then, behold that valiant
      man and lord
      That for your sake will take a cudgelling,
      For — be assured — when it is spread abroad
      That you have dealt with me, they'll give you out   160
      For one of the Nine Worthies.
Brunehaut.   Out, you pander!
      Why, to beat thee is only exercise
      For such as do affect it. Lose not time
      In vain replies but do it. [*To* PROTALDI] Come, my
      solace,
      Let us to bed, and, our desires once quenched,   165
      We'll there determine of Theodoret's death,
      For he's the engine used to ruin us. —
      Yet one word more: Lacure, art thou assured

---

157. SD] *this edn; not in Q1.*   164. SD] *this edn; not in Q1.*   168. word] *1711;* worke *Q1.*

---

  157. *behold*] Bawdbert here either points to himself or makes it clear to the others on stage that he refers to himself through other kinds of body language.
  159. *abroad*] openly, publicly.
  160. *dealt*] fought.
  give ... out] report you.
  161. *Nine Worthies*] a group of nine characters drawn from history, the Bible, and legend, who were regarded as constituting the supreme embodiment of the chivalric ideals established in the Middle Ages. Still popular in the Renaissance, this group usually included three pagan generals (Hector, Alexander the Great, and Julius Caesar), three Old Testament heroes (David, Joshua, and Judas Maccabeus), and three Christian warriors (King Arthur, Charlemagne, and Godfrey of Bouillon).
  163. *affect*] like to practise (*OED* v.1 3).
  167. *engine*] agent, instrument.

    The potion will work?
Lacure.   My life upon it.
Brunehaut. Come, my Protaldi, then; glut me with   170
    Those best delights of man that are denied
    To her that does expect them, being a bride.   *Exeunt.*

---

170. then; glut] *Dyce (subst);* thou then glut *Seward;* then glut *Q1.*   172. SD] *Q1c; not in Q1u.*

---

169. *potion*] pronounced as three syllables.
170–2. *Come ... bride*] 'The villains take an erotic delight in their "stealing joy" plot', as 'the sexual energy of the wedding night is siphoned off into illicit pleasures' (Blamires, 212–13).

Act 3

Scene 1

Enter THIERRY *and* ORDELLA, *as from bed.*

Thierry. Sure, I have drunk the blood of elephants;
 The tears of mandrake and the marble dew,
 Mixed in my draught, have quenched my natural heat

SCENE 1] *Q1* (Act. 3. Scoe. 1).

3.1.0.] I assign this scene to Field. Weber adds the setting: '*An apartment in the same*', i.e., in the same palace.

0.1. SD *as from bed*] As can be inferred by several other comparable though more detailed SDs of the period, Thierry and Ordella are probably wearing their night clothes, which would readily convey to the audience the information that they have just got out of bed (Dessen, *Elizabethan*, 40–3; Dessen, *Recovering*, 136).

1. *blood of elephants*] As Theobald and Sympson first pointed out, the source for this is probably Pliny the Elder, 8.12: 'the elephant's blood is exceeding cold, and therefore the dragons be wonderful desirous thereof to refresh and cool themselves therewith during the parching and hot season of the year. And to this purpose they lie under the water, waiting their time to take the elephants at a vantage when they are drinking, where they catch fast hold first of their trunk, and they have not so soon clasped and entangled it with their tail, but they set their venomous teeth in the elephant's ear (the only part of all their body which they cannot reach unto with their trunk) and so bite it hard. Now, these dragons are so big withal that they be able to receive all the elephant's blood. Thus are they sucked dry until they fall down dead, and the dragons again, drunken with their blood, are squized under them, and die both together.'

2. *tears*] 'gums that exude from plants in tear-shaped or globular beads, which then become solid or resinous' (*OED* n.1 3).

mandrake] a plant with strong narcotic properties, also known as mandragora.

marble dew] 'an imaginary antiaphrodisiac' (*OED* 'marble' n. and adj. C2). Cf. *Guardian* 3.1.19–22: 'And kill this lecherous itch with drinking water, / ... / Then bathe myself, night by night, in marble dew / And use no soap but camphor balls.'

3. *quenched*] extinguished by cooling.

natural heat] 'the inherent heat of the body' (*OED* 'natural', adj., C2).

116

SC I]   THIERRY AND THEODORET   117

    And left no spark of fire but in mine eyes,
    With which I may behold my miseries.   5
    Ye wretched flames, which play upon my sight,
    Turn inward, make me all one piece, though earth;
    My tears shall overwhelm you else too.
Ordella. What moves my lord to this strange sadness?
    If any late discernèd want in me   10
    Give cause to your repentance, care and duty
    Shall find a painful way to recompense.
Thierry. Are you yet frozen, veins? Feel you a breath
    Whose temperate heat would make the north star reel,
    Her icy pillars thawed, and do you not melt?   15
    [*To* ORDELLA] Draw nearer, yet nearer,
    That from thy barren kiss thou mayst confess

---

16. SD] *this edn; not in Q1.*   17. thy] *Q1;* my *Turner.*

6–7.] 'Thierry complains that he has lost his natural heat in every part of him, except his eyes, which enable him to behold his miseries; he wishes, therefore, either to be entirely himself again or to become totally insensible, to be all one piece, though that piece should be cold clay only' (Mason). Besides, in the old physiology, earth was regarded as the heaviest of the four elements, combining the properties of coldness and dryness, and thus it was associated with dullness of nature.

    10. *late*] lately.
    11. *repentance*] regret of having married me.
    12. *recompense*] compensate.
    13–15.] Thierry addresses his own body, probably staring at his own arms lifted up, before talking to Ordella.
    14. *temperate*] 'Thierry is speaking of Ordella's breath, the heat of which *even when* temperate would make, etc' (Dyce).
    north star] Pole Star.
    15. *icy pillars*] As a fixed star, the Pole Star was believed to be attached to a crystal sphere supported by props commonly labelled 'pillars' (*OED* n. 3) and made of ice.
    16.] Thierry's words should probably prompt Ordella's gradual movement towards him, but it is also possible that she remains still, confused by her husband's ravings. Whether she moves or not, though, either the intervening stage business or Ordella's hesitation may stand as the reason behind the shortness of the line.
    17. *thy*] Turner proposes 'my', arguing that 'Thierry is the cold one, and his kiss, not really Ordella's, is barren. Q1's "thy" could have arisen from misreading or confusion with the immediately following "thou".' Turner's interpretation is possible, but the emendation is unnecessary, given that the line can be also construed as signifying that it is in fact Ordella's kiss that is barren, because it does not elicit any warmth in Thierry.

I have not heat enough to make a blush.
Ordella. Speak nearer to my understanding, like a husband.
Thierry. How should he speak the language of a husband   20
   Who wants the tongue and organs of his voice?
Ordella. It is a phrase will part with the same ease
   From you with that you now deliver.
Thierry.   Bind not
   His ears up with so dull a charm who hath
   No other sense left open. Why should thy words   25
   Find more restraint than thy free-speaking actions,
   Thy close embraces and thy midnight sighs,
   The silent orators to slow desire?
Ordella. Strive not to win content from ignorance,
   Which must be lost in knowledge. Heaven can witness   30
   My farthest hope of good reached at your pleasure,
   Which seeing alone may in your look be read.
   Add not a doubtful comment to a text
   That in itself's direct and easy.
Thierry. Oh, thou hast drunk the juice of hemlock too!   35
   Or did upbraided nature make this pair
   To show she had not quite forgot her first
   Justly praised workmanship, the first chaste couple,

23–5. From ... not | His ... hath | No ... words] *Dyce; Q1 lines* From ... deliuer. | Bind ... charme, | Who ... words. 32. your] *Q1c;* you *Q1u.*

22. *will*] that will.
23. *that you*] that which you.
24. *dull*] soothing (see Crystal and Crystal, 141, a meaning not listed in *OED*).
29–30. *Strive ... knowledge*] 'Do not endeavour to deprive me of that contentment which I now feel in my ignorance of the cause of your happiness by a disclosure which could deprive me of that content' (Weber).
35. *hemlock*] a poisonous plant also used medicinally as a powerful sedative.
36. *this pair*] i.e., Thierry and Ordella.
38. *the ... couple*] i.e., Adam and Eve before the fall. As Blamires (213) points out, '[t]his notion of an asexual Adam and Eve goes back to patristic exegesis, but also reflects Renaissance debates about sin and sexuality. The matter of Edenic sex – if, when, how – was a particular concern for Protestant divines looking to counter what they felt was an unhealthy and hypocritical Catholic privileging of virginity and celibacy.'

SC I]   THIERRY AND THEODORET   119

    Before the want of joy taught guilty sight
    A way through shame and sorrow to delight?   40
    Say, may we mix, as in their innocence
    When turtles kissed, to confirm happiness,
    Not to beget it?
Ordella.   I know no bar.
Thierry. Should I believe thee? Yet thy pulse beats, woman,
    And says the name of wife did promise thee   45
    The blessed reward of duty to thy mother,
    Who gave so often witness of her joy
    When she did boast thy likeness to her husband.
Ordella. 'Tis true
    That to bring forth a second to yourself   50
    Was only worthy of my virgin loss,
    And should I prize you less unpatterned, sir,
    Than being exemplified? Is't not more honour
    To be possessor of unequalled virtue
    Than what is paralleled? Give me belief: 55
    The name of mother knows no way of good
    More than the end in me. Who weds for lust
    Is oft a widow. When I married you,
    I lost the name of maid to gain a title
    Above the wish of change, which that part can   60
    Only maintain is still the same in man,

49–50. 'Tis true | That ... yourself] *Dyce; Q1 lines* 'Tis ... your selfe.

---

    39. *want of joy*] the lack of happiness that followed Adam and Eve's eating of the forbidden fruit of the Tree of Knowledge.
    41. *mix*] get close together, be intimate.
    41–2. *as ... When*] as when in their innocence.
    42. *turtles*] turtle-doves.
    43. *beget*] engender.
    bar] obstacle.
    48. *thy ... husband*] It was often argued in the early modern period that the father was uniquely responsible for passing on the physical traits and personality of the child, the mother being viewed as only furnishing the material substances from which the body of the child was shaped.
    50. *a ... yourself*] See 3.1.48.
    51. *only*] the only thing.
    52. *unpatterned*] unparalleled.
    53. *exemplified*] imitated in your offspring's physical resemblance to you.
    57. *the end*] its result, its purpose.
    61. *is still*] that is always.

   His virtue and his calm society,
   Which no grey hairs can threaten to dissolve
   Nor wrinkles bury.
Thierry. Confine thyself to silence, lest thou take   65
   That part of reason from me is only left
   To give persuasion to me I am a man,
   Or say thou hast never seen the rivers haste
   With gladsome speed to meet the amorous sea.
Ordella. Ne'er but to praise the coolness of their streams.   70
Thierry. Nor viewed the kids, taught by their lustful fires,
   Pursue each other through the wanton lawns
   And liked the sport.
Ordella. As it made way unto their envied rest
   With weary knots binding their harmless eyes.   75
Thierry. Nor do you know the reason why the dove,
   One of the pair your hands wont hourly feed,
   So often clipped and kissed her happy mate?
Ordella. Unless it were to welcome his wished sight
   Whose absence only gave her mourning voice.   80
Thierry. And you could dove-like to a single object
   Bind your loose spirits? To one, nay, such a one
   Whom only eyes and ears must flatter good,
   Your surer sense made useless? Nay, myself,
   As in my all of good already known?   85

---

70. Ne'er] *conj Heath;* We are *Q1.*   84. Nay, myself] *Seward (subst);* my selfe, nay *Q1.*

---

 66. *is*] that is.
 69. *gladsome*] cheering, pleasant.
  70. *Ne'er*] Q1's 'We are' is possible, but Heath's emendation (first accepted by Dyce) seems more suitable to the context, as Ordella reflects on past events and actions and repeats Thierry's own 'never' (l. 68).
 71. *kids*] the young of a goat.
 77. *wont*] were accustomed to.
 78. *clipped*] embraced.
  81–5.] And could your free nature remain bound, like doves are said to do, to one single person? To someone who can only be gratified by sight and hearing, since I am no longer able to enjoy sexual pleasure? To me, whom you already know in all my good qualities and nature (and there is therefore nothing else for you to discover if we cannot consummate our marriage)?
 81. *dove-like*] Doves were believed to be monogamous and faithful.
 85. *my all of*] all my.

Ordella. Let proof plead for me: let me be mewed up
    Where never eye may reach me but your own,
    And, when I shall repent but in my looks,
    If sigh —
Thierry. Or shed a tear that's warm?
Ordella.   But in your sadness.   90
Thierry. Or, when you hear the birds call for their mates,
    Ask if it be Saint Valentine, their coupling day?
Ordella. If anything may make a thought suspected
    Of knowing any happiness but you,
    Divorce me by the title of most falsehood.   95
Thierry. Oh, who would know a wife that might have such a
        friend?
    Posterity henceforth lose the name of blessing
    And leave the earth inhabited to people heaven.

         Enter THEODORET, BRUNEHAUT, MARTEL [*and*]
                     PROTALDI.

88–9. And ... looks, | If sigh] *Dyce; Q1 lines* And ... sigh. 89. sigh
—] *Colman;* sigh, *Q1.* 93. thought] *Q2;* though *Q1.* 96–8. Oh ... friend?
| Posterity ... blessing, | And ... heaven] *Q1; Cotgrave lines* Oh who | Would
... friend? | Posterity ... blessing, | And ... heaven.; *Colman lines* Oh, ... wife
| That ... Posterity | Henceforth ... leave | The ... heaven.

---

  86. *mewed up*] confined, shut away.
  88. *but*] only.
  95. *most falsehood*] 'This expression ... seems odd and may be a mistake for "most false", "most falsest", or something similar' (Turner).
  96–8.] I have preserved Q1's lineation rather than following Colman's emendation (adopted by successive editors up to Turner). Colman's lineation produces four lines: a trimeter and three pentameters, at least one of which does not scan particularly well ('Henceforth lose the name of blessing and leave'). Not completely satisfied with Colman's solution, Turner ('Introduction', 372) comments that this 'passage seems to have been left in metrical disrepair'. Yet Q1's lineation is in my view defensible, in that it produces three hexameters. Hexameters are not infrequent in the canon of Fletcher and his collaborators, and Field in this play seems to be particularly fond of using them. Here, Thierry is rejoicing at Ordella's virtue and at her unexpectedly enthusiastic reaction to the prospect of a platonic marriage, and the three lines of hexameter contribute to bestowing a sense of grandeur and magniloquence to his words, as well as foregrounding this passage through a bold and unmistakably perceptible metrical variation.
  96. *know*] with the secondary meaning of having sexual intercourse with.
  98. *inhabited*] uninhabited.

Martel. All happiness to Thierry and Ordella!
Thierry. 'Tis a desire but borrowed from me. My happiness 100
  Shall be the period of all good men's wishes,
  Which friends, nay, dying fathers shall bequeath,
  And in my one give all. Is there a duty
  Belongs to any power of mine or love
  To any virtue I have right to? Here, place it here. 105
  Ordella's name shall only bear command,
  Rule, title, sovereignty.
Brunehaut. What passion sways my son?
Thierry. O mother, she has doubled every good
  The travail of your blood made possible 110
  To my glad being.
Protaldi. [*Aside*] He should have done little to her, he is so
  light-hearted.
Thierry. Brother, friends, if honour unto shame,
  If wealth to want enlarge the present sense,
  My joys are unbounded. Instead of question 115
  Let it be envy not to bring a present
  To the high offering of our mirth. Banquets and masques
  Keep waking our delights, mocking night's malice,

107–8.] *Q1; one line in Turner.*   110. travail] *Q1;* travel *F2.*   112. SD] *Weber; not in Q1.*   He ... light-hearted] *conj Dyce; Q1 lines* He ... done | Little ... light harted.   114. enlarge] *F2;* in large *Q1.*   116. to] *Seward; not in Q1.*   117. mirth. Banquets] *Seward (subst);* mirth, banquets *Q1.*

---

  101. *period*] termination.
  104. *Belongs*] that belongs.
  105.] *Here ... here*] Here Thierry probably indicates Ordella.
  112.] I have accepted Dyce's suggestion that 'Perhaps this speech ... was meant to form a single line of verse'. The line becomes an iambic pentameter with a double ending if 'have' and 'is' are elided.
    he ... light-hearted] i.e., yet he is so high-spirited.
  113–17. *if ... mirth*] '"If the accession of honour to a person condemned to shame; if the accession of wealth to want enlarge their feelings, their joys are unbounded." He considers himself as relieved both from a sense of his own inability or poverty, as he calls it, and a sense of shame also, by Ordella's temperance. "Instead of question" means instead of questioning whether I am happy or not, let it be considered as malice not to congratulate me on it' (Weber).
  117. *masques*] courtly dramatic entertainments that were extremely popular in the Jacobean and the Caroline periods.

SC I]   THIERRY AND THEODORET   123

 Whose dark brow would fright pleasure from us. Our
  court
 Be but one stage of revels, and each eye   120
 The scene where our content moves.
Theodoret.   There shall want
 Nothing to express our shares in your delight, sir.
Martel. Till now I ne'er repented the estate
 Of widower.
Thierry. Music, why art thou so
 Slow-voiced? — It stays thy presence, my Ordella. 125
 This chamber is a sphere too narrow for
 Thy all-moving virtue. — Make way. Free way, I say!
 Who must alone her sex's want supply
 Had need to have a room both large and high.
Martel. [*To* THEODORET] This passion's above utterance.
Theodoret.   Nay, credulity. 130
   Exeunt all but THIERRY *and* BRUNEHAUT.
Brunehaut. Why, son, what mean you?
 Are you a man?
Thierry.   No, mother, I am no man.
 Were I a man, how could I be thus happy?
Brunehaut. How can a wife be author of this joy, then?
Thierry. That, being no man, I am married to no woman. 135
 The best of men in full ability
 Can only hope to satisfy a wife,

119–20. Whose ... court | Be ... eye] *Colman; Q1 lines* Whose ... vs, | Our ... eye.   124–7. Of ... so | Slow-voiced? ... Ordella. | This ... for | Thy ... say] *Colman; Q1 lines* Of widower. | Musique ... presence | My ... spheare | Too ... vertue. | Make ... say.   130. SD] *this edn; Apart.* Turner; *not in Q1.*   130.1. SD] *Seward (subst); Exit all but Thierry, Brunhalt. Q1.*   131–3. Why ... you? | Are ... man. | Were ... happy?] *Dyce; Q1 lines* Why ... man? | No ... man, | How ... happy?.

---

 120. *but*] nothing but.
 121. *want*] lack.
 123. *repented*] regretted, been sorry for.
 127. *all-moving*] affecting everyone with emotion.
 128. *alone*] by herself.
 130. *credulity*] belief.
 135. *no woman*] an almost god-like being that is superior to all other women.

    And, for that hope ridiculous, I in my want
    And such defective poverty, that to her bed
    From my first cradle brought no strength but thought, 140
    Have met a temperance beyond hers that rocked me,
    Necessity being her bar. Where this
    Is so much senseless of my deprived fire,
    She knows it not a loss by her desire.
Brunehaut. It is beyond my admiration. 145
Thierry. Beyond your sex's faith.
    The unripe virgins of our age to hear't
    Will dream themselves to women and convert
    The example to a miracle.
Brunehaut. Alas, 'tis your defect moves my amazement, 150
    But what ill can be separate from ambition?
    Cruel Theodoret!
Thierry.   What of my brother?
Brunehaut. That to his name your barrenness adds rule;
    Who, loving the effect, would not be strange
    In favouring the cause. Look on the profit, 155
    And gain will quickly point the mischief out.
Thierry. The name of father to what I possess
    Is shame and care.
Brunehaut. Were we begot to single happiness,
    I grant you, but from such a wife, such virtue, 160
    To get an heir what hermit would not find
    Deserving argument to break his vow,
    Even in his age, of chastity?
Thierry. You teach a deaf man language.

---

163. age, of] *Dyce;* age of *Q1.*

 141. *hers ... me*] that of my mother who rocked me in my cradle as a baby.
 142. *Necessity ... bar*] given that her (i.e., Brunehaut's) temperance was limited by the sheer fact of being a mother (and so, by definition, sexually active).
 Where] whereas.
 143. *senseless of*] insensitive to.
 145. *admiration*] pronounced as five syllables.
 152. *Cruel*] pronounced as two syllables.
 154. *strange*] uncomplying, unwilling.
 159. *begot*] engendered.
 163. *age*] old age.

Brunehaut. The cause found out, the malady may cease. 165
    Have you heard of one Lefort?
Thierry. A learned astronomer, great magician,
    Who lives hard by, retired.
Brunehaut. Repair to him with the just hour and place
    Of your nativity. Fools are amazed at fate. 170
    Griefs, but concealed, are never desperate.
Thierry. You have timely wakened me, nor shall I sleep
    Without the satisfaction of his art.
Brunehaut. Wisdom prepares you to't.

                      Exit THIERRY.

           Enter LACURE.

                Lacure, met happily.
Lacure. The ground answers your purpose, the conveyance 175
    Being secure and easy, falling just
    Behind the state set for Theodoret.
Brunehaut. 'Tis well.
    Your trust invites you to a second charge.
    You know Lefort's cell? 180
Lacure. Who constellated your fair birth.

---

166. Lefort] *Seward (subst); Forts Q1.*   174. SD1] *Dyce; following* his art *Q1.* SD2] *Weber; following* his art *Q1.*   178–9. 'Tis well. | Your ... charge] *Weber; Q1 lines* 'Tis ... charge.

---

    167. *astronomer*] astrologer.
    magician] pronounced as four syllables.
    169. *Repair*] go.
    just] exact.
    171. *but*] unless.
    desperate] pronounced as three syllables.
    173. *satisfaction*] 'solution, answer, esp. to a difficulty' (*OED* n. 6a), but also 'information that answers a person's demands or needs' (6b).
    175. *conveyance*] secret passage.
    176. *falling*] 'of an object which is raised and lowered on a hinge ...: to drop to a lower position' (*OED* v. 6b). The reference is to the stage trapdoor. See 3.2.119.1. SD.
    177. *state*] chair of state, throne.
    179. *charge*] task, duty.
    180. *cell*] 'a dwelling consisting of a single chamber inhabited by a hermit or anchorite' (*OED* n.1 1a).
    181. *constellated ... birth*] cast the nativity or horoscope of your son.

126   THIERRY AND THEODORET   [ACT 3

Brunehaut. Enough, I see thou knowst him. Where's
 Bawdbert?
Lacure. I left him careful of the project cast
 To raise Protaldi's credit.
Brunehaut. A sore that must be plastered, in whose wound   185
 Others shall find their graves think themselves sound.
 Your ear and quickest apprehension!   *Exeunt.*

[SCENE 2]

Enter BAWDBERT *and a* Servant.

Bawdbert. This man of war will advance.
Servant. His hour's upon the stroke.
Bawdbert. Wind him back as you favour my ears: I love no
 noise in my head. My brains have hitherto been employed
 in silent businesses.   5

Enter DE VITRY.

Servant. The gentleman is within your reach, sir.
Bawdbert. Give ground whilst I drill my wits to the encounter.
                                            Exit [Servant].
 De Vitry, I take it.
de Vitry. All that's left of him.

SCENE 2] *Dyce; not in Q1.* 2. SP *Servant*] *Dyce; Lecure Q1.* 3–5. Wind ...
businesses] *Weber; Q1 lines as verse:* Wind ... eares, | I ... haue hitherto |
Bin ... businesses. 3. love] *Q1;* have *Q2.* 6. SP *Servant*] *Dyce; Lecure Q1.*
7.1. SD] *Turner; Exit. Q1, following line 6.*

---

186. *think*] who think.
187. *apprehension*] understanding; pronounced as five syllables.

3.2.0.] I assign this scene to Field. Dyce adds the setting: '*The presence
chamber in the palace of* THIERRY'.
 1. *man of war*] fighting man, soldier.
 2. *upon ... stroke*] on the point of striking.
 3. *Wind ... back*] Make him turn back. The image is that of turning back
an analogue clock.
 7. *Give ground*] retire.
 drill] 'train or instruct as with military rigour and exactness' (*OED* v. 5).
 8. *take it*] assume.

Bawdbert. Is there another parcel of you? If it be at pawn, I   10
  will gladly redeem it to make you wholly mine.
de Vitry. You seek too hard a pennyworth.
Bawdbert. You do ill to keep such distance. Your parts have
  been long known to me, howsoever you please to forget
  acquaintance.   15
de Vitry. I must confess I have been subject to lewd company.
Bawdbert. Thanks for your good remembrance. You have been
  a soldier, de Vitry, and borne arms.
de Vitry. A couple of unprofitable ones that have only served
  to get me a stomach to my dinner.   20
Bawdbert. Much good may it do you, sir.
de Vitry. You should have heard me say I had dined first. I
  have built on an unwholesome ground, raised up a house
  before I knew a tenant, marched to meet weariness,
  fought to find want and hunger.   25
Bawdbert. It is time you put up your sword and run away for
  meat, sir; nay, if I had not withdrawn ere now, I might
  have kept the fast with you, but, since the way to thrive
  is never late, what is the nearest course to profit, think
  you?   30
de Vitry. It may be your worship will say bawdry.
Bawdbert. True sense, bawdry.
de Vitry. Why, is there five kinds of 'em? I never knew but one.

10–11. Is ... mine] *Weber; Q1 lines as verse:* Is ... pawne | I ... mine.   13–15. You ... acquaintance] *Weber; Q1 lines as verse:* You ... knowne | To ... acquaintance.   13. do] *Seward;* to *Q1.*   17–18. Thanks ... arms] *Weber; Q1 lines as verse:* Thankes ... remembrance, | You ... armes.   24. marched] *Seward;* matcht *Q1.*   26. away] *Q2;* a way *Q1.*   28. the fast] *Colman;* fast *Seward;* thee; fast *Q2;* the; fast *Q1.*   33. there] *Q2;* their *Q1.*

---

  10. *parcel*] portion.
  12. *a pennyworth*] something the value of which is only one penny.
  16. *lewd*] base, wicked.
  20. *stomach*] appetite.
  25. *want*] poverty.
  26. *put up*] sheathe.
  27. *ere*] before.
  31. *bawdry*] the practice of a bawd.

128   THIERRY AND THEODORET   [ACT 3

Bawdbert. I'll show you a new way of prostitution. Fall back.
Further yet. Further. There is fifty crowns. Do but as much   35
to Protaldi, the Queen's favourite, they are doubled.
                                      [*Gives him money.*]
de Vitry. But thus much?
Bawdbert. Give him but an affront as he comes to thy presence and in his drawing make way like a true bawd to his
valour, the sum's thy own. If you take a scratch in the   40
arm or so, every drop of blood weighs down a ducat.
de Vitry. After that rate, I and my friends would beggar the
kingdom. Sir, you have made me blush to see my want,
whose cure is such a cheap and easy purchase. This is
male bawdry, belike.   45

Enter PROTALDI [*and*] *a* Lady [*stopping some way from*
BAWDBERT *and* DE VITRY].

36.1. SD] *Dyce (subst);not in Q1.*   38. thy] *this edn;* the *Q1.*   40. sum's] *1711;*
son's *Q1.*   45.1–2. SD] *this edn; Enter* PROTALDY *and a* Lady. *Dyce; Enter
Protaldy, a Lady, and Reuellers. Q1.*

34–5. *Fall ... Further*] Bawdbert probably lightly pushes de Vitry at this
point to simulate what he is expected to do later with Protaldi, but this is
not the only possibility; for example, Bawdbert might also invite de Vitry to
step back only with gestures, without actually touching him.
   39. *drawing*] i.e., of the sword.
   41. *ducat*] 'a gold coin of a type minted by the Republic of Venice from
the 13th cent., and until the 19th cent. used widely in trade and commerce
throughout Europe, the eastern Mediterranean, and further afield; any of
various gold coins minted elsewhere, esp. those produced to the same standards as the Venetian coin for the purposes of facilitating international trade'
(*OED* n. 1a).
   42. *After*] at.
   43. *want*] poverty.
   44. *purchase*] gain.
   45. *belike*] probably.
   45.1–2. SD] Q1 reads '*Enter Protaldy, a Lady, and Reuellers*', but the Revellers do not enter until later (93.1–2. SD). As Dyce first argued, 'that portion
of this stage-direction was merely intended to warn the actors who played
the Revellers to be ready for their entrance, when Thierry ... should command
them in'. In addition, Turner ('Introduction', 369–70) points out that '[i]t is
difficult to see how the compositor could have been guilty of placing a direction forty lines early'; it seems more likely to posit either 'an authorial error
during revision' or 'a scribal rationalization of a marginal direction whose
exact location was unclear'.

Bawdbert. See? You shall not be long earning your wages: your
    work's before your eyes.
de Vitry. Leave it to my handling; I'll fall upon't instantly.
Bawdbert. [*Aside*] What opinion will the managing of this
    affair bring to my wisdom? My invention tickles with   50
    apprehension on't.
Protaldi. These are the joys of marriage, lady,
    Whose sights are able to dissolve virginity.
    Speak freely: do you not envy the bride's felicity?
Lady. How should I, being partner of 't?
Protaldi.   What you   55
    Enjoy is but the banquet's view; the taste
    Stands from your palate. If he impart by day
    So much of his content, think what night gave!
              [DE VITRY *and* BAWDBERT *approach them.*]
de Vitry. Will you have a relish of wit, lady?

---

46. be long] *F2;* belong *Q1.*   49. SD] *Dyce; not in Q1.*   49–51. What ...
on't] *Weber; Q1 lines as verse:* What ... affaire | Bring ... tickles | With ...
on't.   55–8. How ... you | Enjoy ... taste | Stands ... day | So ...
gave] *Seward; Q1 lines* How ... of 't? | What ... view, | The ... impart | By
... gaue?   58.1. SD] *this edn; not in Q1.*

---

49. *opinion*] reputation.
51. *apprehension*] anticipation.
52–4.] I have kept Q1's lineation here. Line 52 is a decasyllabic line if
'marriage' is trisyllabic; in addition, as Richard Dutton (pers. comm.) points
out, 'having "lady" (... or any vocative, for that matter) at the end of a line
is a very standard way of hinging a sentence of two halves'; besides, line
53 is a pentameter with double ending if 'virginity' is read 'virgin'ty'; line
54 is a pentameter with double ending if 'do you' is elided to 'd'you', if 'the
bride' is slurred to 'th'bride', and 'felicity' is read 'felic'ty'. At the same time,
as Dutton (pers. comm.) again suggests, it is also possible that 'the author
was trying to do something fancy ... with the four-syllable quasi-rhymes
of "virginity" and "felicity"' and that he was accordingly deliberately going
'extra-metrical for effect with those four-syllable words'. Cf. 3.1.96–8. Be
that as it may, Protaldi's words reinforce our sense of what an oleaginous
creature he is.
52. *These ... marriage*] The irony of Protaldi's comment is heightened by
his words echoing Amintor's question 'Are these the joys of marriage?' (*MT*
2.1.215) upon learning of Evadne's affair with the King, which deprives his
marriage of the joys of sexual consummation.
56. *but*] only.
57. *Stands from*] is far from.
impart] shares, distributes.

Bawdbert. [*Aside to* PROTALDI] This is the man. 60
Lady. If it be not dear, sir.
de Vitry. If you affect cheapness, how can you prize this sullied
    ware so much? Mine is fresh, my own, not retailed.
Protaldi. You are saucy, sirrah.
de Vitry. The fitter to be in the dish with such dry stockfish 65
    as you are. [PROTALDI *strikes him.*] How, strike?
Bawdbert. Remember the condition as you look for payment.
de Vitry. That box was left out of the bargain. [*Strikes*
    PROTALDI.]
Protaldi. Help! Help! Help! 70
Bawdbert. Plague of the scrivener's running hand! What a
    blow is this to my reputation!

    Enter THIERRY, THEODORET, BRUNEHAUT, ORDELLA,
    MEMBERGE, MARTEL [*with* Attendants *and* Guards].

Thierry. What villain dares this outrage?
de Vitry. Hear me, sir. [*Pointing to* BAWDBERT] This creature
    hired me with fifty crowns in hand to let Protaldi have 75

---

60. SD] *Turner; not in Q1.* 66. SD] *Weber; not in Q1.* 68–9. SD] *Dyce; Gives him a box on the ear. Weber; not in Q1.* 71–2. Plague ... reputation] *Weber; Q1 lines as verse:* Plague ... hand, | What ... reputation. 71.1–2. SD] *Dyce; Enter Thierry, Theodoret, Brunhalt, Ordella, Memberge, Martell. Q1.* 74. SD] *this edn; not in Q1.*

---

  61. *dear*] expensive.
  62–3. *sullied ware*] soiled goods.
  63. *not retailed*] The meaning would appear to be 'sold on' or 'second-hand', but this is not recorded in *OED*. Perhaps what de Vitry implies is that his 'ware' is unique because it is not sold anywhere and is accordingly impossible for anyone to buy.
  64. *saucy*] insolent.
  65. *stockfish*] 'a name for cod and other gadoid fish cured by splitting open and drying hard in the air without salt' (*OED* n. 1a), often used to address people contemptuously.
  67.] I have not marked Bawdbert's line as an aside to de Vitry because after Protaldi strikes de Vitry, the Lady is likely to move away from the fight (she might even exit here), so that there is no need for secrecy on Bawdbert's part (both Protaldi and de Vitry know what is happening).
  68. *box*] blow.
  71. *Plague ... hand*] 'Plague on the scrivener for leaving out, in his hurry, the blow' (Mason).
  73. *outrage*] violent clamour, outcry.

SC 2]   THIERRY AND THEODORET   131

    the better of me at single rapier on a made quarrel. He,
    mistaking the weapon, lays me over the chops with his
    club-fist, for which I was bold to teach him the art of
    memory.
All. Ha ha ha ha!   80
        [BRUNEHAUT, PROTALDI, BAWDBERT *and* DE VITRY
                do not laugh.]
Theodoret. Your General, mother, will display himself
    Spite of our peace, I see.
Thierry. Forbear these civil jars. — Fie, Protaldi!
    So open in your projects?
           [*To* DE VITRY] Avoid our presence, sirrah.
de Vitry. Willingly. If you have any more wages to earn, you   85
    see I can take pains.
Theodoret. There's somewhat for thy labour, more than was
    promised. Ha ha ha!
                  [*Exit* DE VITRY.]
Bawdbert. [*Aside*] Where could I wish myself now? In the Isle
    of Dogs, so I might scape scratching, for I see by her cat's   90
    eyes I shall be clawed fearfully.
Thierry. We'll hear no more on't. Music drown all sadness.
                        Soft music.

---

80. SP *All*] this edn; Thi. Theod. Martell, &c. Dyce; Omnes Q1. 80.1–2. SD] this edn; not in Q1. 84. SD] this edn; not in Q1. 85–6. Willingly … pains] Weber; Q1 lines as verse: Willingly … earne, | You … paines. 88.1. SD] Dyce; not in Q1. 89. SD] Dyce; not in Q1. 89–91. Where … fearfully] Weber; Q1 lines as verse: Where … dogs, | So … eyes | I … fearefully.

---

76. *rapier*] 'a long, thin, sharp-pointed sword designed chiefly for thrusting' (*OED* n. 1a).
    made] 'brought about by contrivance, arranged' (*OED* adj. 4).
77. *over the chops*] upon the jaws.
78. *club-fist*] 'a large clenched fist that can deal a heavy blow' (*OED* n.)
81. *display himself*] show off.
82. *Spite*] in spite.
84. *sirrah*] extrametrical.
89–90. *Isle of Dogs*] a peninsula in the River Thames, here mentioned chiefly with reference to the traditional antipathy between cats and dogs. If Brunehaut is a cat, the only place in which Bawdbert could be safe would be an island inhabited by dogs.
    90. *scape*] escape
    her] i.e., Brunehaut's.
92. *Music … sadness*] the cue for the musicians to start playing.

[*To* Attendant] Command the revellers in.
                              [*Exit* Attendant.]
  [*Aside*] At what a rate I'd purchase
My mother's absence, to give my spleen full liberty!
[THIERRY *and* THEODORET *sit, each in his chair of state.*]
  [*Enter* Revellers. *As they begin to dance,* BRUNEHAUT
       and PROTALDI *talk aside.*]
Brunehaut. Speak not a thought's delay: it names thy ruin.   95
Protaldi. I had thought my life had borne more value with
    you.
Brunehaut. Thy loss carries mine with't; let that secure thee.
  The vault is ready, and the door conveys to't
  Falls just behind his chair. The blow once given,
  Thou art unseen.   100
Protaldi. I cannot feel more than I fear, I'm sure.
Brunehaut. Be gone, and let them laugh their own destruction.
                              [PROTALDI] *withdraws.*
Thierry. [*Aside to* THEODORET] You will add unto her rage.
Theodoret.   'Foot, I shall burst

---

93. SD1] *this edn; not in Q1.* SD2] *Dyce (subst); not in Q1.* SD3] *Turner; not in Q1.* I'd] *conj Mason;* I do *Q1.*   94.1. SD] *Strachey (subst); not in Q1.*   94.2–3. SD] *this edn; Enter* Revellers. *Turner; Enter several* Revellers. *Dyce; not in Q1. Weber has* Apart to PROTALDYE. *at line 91.*   98. conveys] *Q2;* conuyes *Q1.*   102.1. SD] *Colman; following line 99 Q1.*   103–6. You ... burst | Unless .... sir? | You ... invite | More ... pleasure] *Colman; Q1 lines* You ... rage. | Foote ... ha. | Me ... could | Haue ... willingnesse, | In .... pleasure.   103. SD] *Turner (subst); not in Q1.*

94. *spleen*] considered to be the seat of laughter or mirth.
96. *borne*] had.
97.] a headless line with an epic caesura. This stress pattern skilfully foregrounds the link between 'Thy' and 'mine', and thus the reciprocal dependence between Brunehaut and Protaldi.
99. *Falls*] See 3.1.176 and 3.2.119.1. SD.
  his] i.e., Theodoret's.
102. *them*] i.e., Thierry and Theodoret.
103. *'Foot*] a corruption of '(by) God's foot', a strong oath, referring to the feet of Jesus, nailed to the cross. Interestingly, all the oaths focusing on the body of Christ used in the play are in sections attributed to Field. See 5.1.52, 60, 85, 136, 161, 191, 201, 222 ("Foot'); 5.1.110 ("Heart'); 5.1.124 ('Zounds'). Three oaths are uttered by 2 Soldier ("Foot' three times), two by de Vitry ("Heart' and "Swounds'), Protaldi ("Foot' twice), and 1 Soldier ("Foot' twice), one by 4 Soldier ("Foot') and Theodoret ("Foot').

SC 2]   THIERRY AND THEODORET   133

    Unless I vent myself. Ha ha ha!
                  [1 Reveller *offers* BRUNEHAUT *to dance*.]
Brunehaut.   Me, sir?
    You never could have found a time to invite   105
    More willingness in my dispose to pleasure.
                  [2 Reveller *offers* MEMBERGE *to dance*.]
Memberge. Would you would please to make some other
    choice.
2 Reveller. 'Tis a disgrace would dwell upon me, lady,
    Should you refuse.
Memberge. Your reason conquers. [*Aside*] My grandmother's
    looks   110
    Have turned all air to earth in me. They sit
    Upon my heart like night charms, black and heavy.

                       The dance.

Thierry. [*To* THEODORET] You are too much libertine.
Theodoret. The fortune of the fool persuades my laughter

---

104. SD] *this edn; To one of the* Revellers. *Dyce; not in Q1.* 106.1. SD] *this edn; To another of the* Revellers. *Dyce; not in Q1.* 108. SP 2 *Reveller*] *Turner; Reuel. Q1.* 110. SD] *Weber; not in Q1.* 112.1. SD] *Q1; They dance F2.* 113. SD] *this edn; not in Q1.*

---

  104. *Ha ha ha*] See 2.3.97.
  106. *dispose*] disposition.
  107. *Would*] I wish.
  111. *turned ... earth*] Memberge's words draw upon the theory of the four humours (see 2.1.256–7). The element of air (warm and moist) corresponded to blood and was accordingly associated with a sanguine, enthusiastic attitude, while earth (cold and dry) corresponded to black bile, and thus to a melancholy temperament. Brunehaut's evil looks have completely dampened Memberge's enthusiasm for the wedding feast.
  sit] weigh.
  113. *too ... libertine*] excessively unrestrained. To understand why Theodoret's behaviour is particularly improper it is necessary to consider the early modern physiology of laughter. As Paster (124) argues, for the early moderns 'laughter operates indiscriminately but predictably on the body of the laugher, without regard for the social coordinates of age, rank, and especially gender by which hierarchical difference is constructed'; consequently, laughter 'threatens to destabilize ... the hierarchical differences of rank and station ... because it threatens the bodily control that is construed ... as a central attribute of male privilege'.
  114. *the fool*] i.e., Protaldi.
  persuades] urges.

More than his cowardice. Was ever rat	115
Ta'en by the tail thus? Ha ha ha!	

Thierry. Forbear, I say.
Protaldi. (*Behind the state*) No eye looks this way. I will wink
   and strike,
   Lest I betray myself.
             Stabs THEODORET [*and sinks into the vault*].

Theodoret. Ha? Did you not see one near me?	120

Thierry. How! Near you? Why do you look so pale, brother? —
   Treason! Treason!   [THEODORET *dies.*]
Memberge. Oh, my presage! — Father!
Ordella. Brother!

Martel. Prince! Noble Prince!	125

Thierry. [*To* Guards] Make the gates sure, search into every
   angle

119.1. SD] *this edn; Stabs* THEODORET, *and disappears. Weber; stabs Theodoret. Q1.*   122. SD] *Weber; not in Q1.*   126. SD] *this edn; not in Q1.*

115–16. *Was ... thus*] Ironically, Theodoret is stabbed in the back immediately after imagining Protaldi as a rat taken by the tail.
   118. *wink*] close my eyes.
   119.1. SD] The most expedient and effective way for Protaldi to disappear quickly from the crime scene would have been by using a trapdoor immediately behind Theodoret's 'state'. That the scene was performed in this way is suggested by Brunehaut's words at l. 186 ('Protaldi, rise'). The use of the verb 'fall' at 3.1.176 and 3.2.99 might seem problematic in this sense, but it chimes with what is known regarding the trapdoor on the Blackfriars stage. As O'Connell argues, the evidence drawn from Blackfriars plays 'indicates that the trapdoor opened from beneath the stage, rather than from onstage' and that it 'probably opened down' (83), which agrees with the use of the verb 'fall' used in *Thierry and Theodoret*; besides, play-texts primarily devised for the Blackfriars have characters much more frequently 'sink' and 'rise' (the verb used by Brunehaut) rather than 'descend' and 'ascend' to indicate entrances and exits thought the trapdoor (82). Moreover, O'Connell contends that the Blackfriars trapdoor 'was equipped with a lift device or a similar flexible ascent system' (85), and that 'most ascensions in [Blackfriars plays] take place in silence, without the noise of thunder or trumpets' (86). Accordingly, a trapdoor exit for Protaldi after murdering Theodoret could have been performed silently and spookily on the Blackfriars stage – only visible to the audience when Protaldi suddenly looms over Theodoret and stabs him: a kind of magician's trick performed mysteriously in killing Theodoret, with Brunehaut then taking pleasure in revealing how it was done.
   123. *presage*] presentiment (not mentioned earlier in the play, as the 'suspicion' at l. 142 below).

SC 2]   THIERRY AND THEODORET   135

    And corner of the court.
                              [*Exeunt* Guards.]
                    Oh, my shame! — Mother,
    Your son is slain, Theodoret, noble Theodoret,
    Here in my arms, too weak a sanctuary
    'Gainst treachery and murder!
                    [*Enter* Guards *again*.]
                    [*To* Guards] Say, is the traitor taken?   130
1 Guard. No man has passed the chamber; on my life, sir.
Thierry. [*To* MARTEL *and* Guards] Set present fire unto the
    place, that all
    Unseen may perish in this mischief. Who
    Moves slow to it shall add unto the flame.
Brunehaut. What mean you? Give me your private hearing.   135
Thierry. Persuasion is a partner in the crime.
    I will renounce my claim unto a mother
    If you make offer on't.
Brunehaut. Ere a torch can take flame, I will produce
    The author of the fact.   140
Thierry. [*To* MARTEL *and* Guards] Withdraw but for your
    lights.
Memberge. Oh, my too true suspicion!
                    Exeunt [*all but* THIERRY *and* BRUNEHAUT.]
Thierry. Speak. Where's the engine to this horrid act?

---

127. SD] *this edn; not in Q1.*   130. SD1] *this edn; not in Q1.*   SD2] *this edn;
not in Q1.*   132. SD] *this edn; not in Q1.*   place] *Q1;* palace *Turner.*   132–
4. Set ... all | Unseen ... Who | Moves ... flame] *Dyce; Q1 lines* Set ... vnseene
| May ... to't, | Shall ... flame.   134. to it] *Dyce;* to't *Q1.*   141. SD] *this
edn; not in Q1.*   142.1. SD] *Weber;* Exeunt Martell, Memberge. *Q1.*

128.] Theodoret's name is both times pronounced as three syllables.
    132. *place*] Turner emends to 'palace', because 'Thierry means the entire
building'. This is true; yet that emendation causes more problems than it
solves by creating metrical difficulties that cannot be overcome by any
reshuffling in the lineation whatsoever. Q1's reading makes sense and enables
a scansion with three full lines of pentameter if 'to't' is expanded to 'to it'
(l. 134), following Dyce.
    138. *make offer on't*] attempt it, i.e., try to justify the killing.
    141. *Withdraw ... lights*] 'Withdraw but to procure the torches' (Dyce).
    143. *engine to*] agent of.

Brunehaut. Here, you do behold her, upon whom
 Make good your causeless rage. The deed was done 145
 By my incitement, not yet repented.
Thierry. Whither did nature start when you conceived
 A birth so unlike woman? Say, what part
 Did not consent to make a son of him,
 Reserved itself within you to his ruin? 150
Brunehaut. Ha ha! A son of mine? Do not dissever
 Thy father's dust, shaking his quiet urn,
 To which thy breath would send so foul an issue.
 My son? Thy brother?
Thierry.   Was not Theodoret
 My brother, or is thy tongue confederate with 155
 Thy heart to speak and do only things monstrous?
Brunehaut. Hear me, and thou shalt make thine own belief.
 Thy still-with-sorrow-mentioned father lived
 Three careful years in hope of wishèd heirs
 When I conceived. Being from his jealous fear 160
 Enjoined to quiet home, one fatal day,
 Transported with my pleasure to the chase,
 I forced command and in pursuit of game

144–6. Here, ... whom | Make ... done | By ... repented] *Weber; Q1 lines* Here ... good | Your ... incitement, | Not ... repented. 154–6. Was ... Theodoret | My ... with | Thy ... monstrous] *Seward; Q1 lines* Was ... tongue | Confederate ... do | Only ... monstrous. 160. conceived.] *Turner (subst);* conceiude, *Q1*.

---

146. *incitement*] pronounced as four syllables.
151. *Ha ha*] See 2.3.97.
153. *To ... issue*] 'by ascribing to him so foul an issue' (Seward).
158–76.] Cf. Grimeston, sig. D4[r]: 'This lewd woman persuades Thierry that Theodebert was a bastard, the son of a gardener, and that he had lawful cause to make war against him as a usurper of that which belonged unto him by right.' But also see Flavigny, G3[r]: 'She [i.e., Brunehaut], full of rage and spite, had recourse to Thierry, whom she set up against her eldest by claiming that Theodebert was a changeling taken from a gardener at a time when his mother had no hope of ever conceiving children; also adding that he [i.e., Theodoret] had defrauded him [i.e., Thierry] of the treasures of his father that he had seized at his death' (my translation).
158. *lived*] had lived.
159. *careful*] full of care.
161. *Enjoined to*] commanded to stay at.
163. *forced command*] overruled my husband's orders.
game] quarry, prey.

SC 2]   THIERRY AND THEODORET   137

  Fell from my horse, lost both my child and hopes.
  Despair, which only in his love saw life   165
  Worthy of being, from a gardener's arms
  Snatched this unlucky brat and called it mine.
  When the next year repaid my loss with thee
  But in thy wrongs preserved my misery,
  Which that I might diminish though not end,   170
  My sighs and wet eyes from thy father's will
  Bequeathed this largest part of his dominions
  Of France unto thee and only left Austrasia
  Unto that changeling, whose life affords
  Too much of ill 'gainst me to prove my words   175
  And call him stranger.   [*Weeps.*]
Thierry. Come, do not weep. I must, nay, do believe you,
  And in my father's satisfaction count it
  Merit, not wrong or loss.
Brunehaut.   You do but flatter:
  There is anger yet flames in your eyes.   180
Thierry. See, I will quench it and confess that you
  Have suffered double travail for me.
Brunehaut. You will not fire the house, then?
Thierry. Rather reward the author, who gave cause
  Of knowing such a secret. My oath and duty   185
  Shall be assurance on't.
Brunehaut.   Protaldi, rise,
  Good faithful servant.

---

172. Bequeathed] *conj Mason;* Bequeathe *Q1.*   173–4. Of ... Austrasia | Unto ... affords] *Seward; Q1 lines* Of ... left | Austracia ... affoords.   176. SD] *this edn; not in Q1.*   179–80. Merit, ... flatter: | There ... eyes] *Colman; Q1 lines* Merit ... losse: | You ... flames | In ... eyes.   180. There is] *Dyce;* there's *Q1.*   186–90. Shall ... rise, | Good ... hardly | He ... had | A ... hand. | Sir, ... service] *Weber; Q1 lines* Protaldye? ... sweare | Fell ... seruice.

 165. *his*] my husband's.
 167. *brat*] child, but with the implication of contempt or insignificance.
 174. *affords*] provides.
 176. *stranger*] 'a person not of one's kin' (*OED* n. 6).
 180. *flames*] that glows like flame.
 182. *travail*] labour (pronounced as three syllables).

Enter PROTALDI [*again, rising from the vault*].

[*To* THIERRY] Heaven knows how hardly
He was drawn to this attempt.
Thierry. [*Aside*] Protaldi? He had
A gardener's fate, I'll swear, fell by thy hand.
[*To* PROTALDI] Sir, we do owe unto you for this service. 190
Brunehaut. [*Aside to* PROTALDI] Why lookst thou so
dejected?

Enter MARTEL [*again, with* Guards].

Protaldi. [*Aside to her*] I want a little shift, lady, nothing else.
Martel. The fires are ready. Please it your grace withdraw
Whilst we perform your pleasure.
Thierry. Reserve them for the body. Since he had 195
The fate to live and die a prince, he shall
Not lose the title in his funeral.
Exit [THIERRY, *with* BRUNEHAUT *and* PROTALDI].
Martel. His fate to live a prince? — Thou old impiety,

---

187. SD1] *this edn;* PROTALDYE *rises from the Trap-door. Weber; Enter Protaldye. following* attempt. *Q1.* SD2] *this edn; not in Q1.* 188. SD] Turner; *not in Q1.* 190. SD] *this edn; not in Q1.* 191. SD] *this edn; not in Q1.* 191.1. SD] *this edn; Enter* Martell [*attended*]. *Turner; Re-enter* MARTELL *and* Attendants. *Dyce; Enter Martell. Q1.* 192. SD] *this edn; not in Q1.* 195-7. Reserve ... had | The ... shall | Not ... funeral] *this edn; Q1 lines* Reserue ... fate | To ... lose | The ... funerall. 197.1. SD] *Dyce; Exit. Q1.* 198-9. His ... impiety, | Made ... body] *Seward; Q1 lines* His ... Prince, | Thou ... mischief, | Take ... body. *Turner marks Martel's words* 'Thou ... mischief' *as an aside*.

---

187. SD1] See 3.2.119.1. SD.

188-9. *He ... hand*] 'That is, he [i.e., Theodoret] had the fate deserving of so low a person who fell by thy hand' (Weber).

192. *shift*] This could mean an 'entertaining or humorous device; a jest' (*OED* n. 3c), but, according to Farmer and Henley (6:174), 'to do a shift' was a common expression for 'to evacuate'. Unfortunately, they do not provide a temporal reference for this meaning, but it would make sense for the coward Protaldi to have been so scared of the potential consequences of stabbing Theodoret as to need to relieve himself.

196-7.] Emending the lineation in this way produces a rhyming couplet made up of two perfectly decasyllabic lines. The shall–funeral rhyme is attested in *A&C* 5.2.357-89: 'Our army shall / In solemn show attend this funeral'.

198-9. *Thou ... mischef*] Martel is thinking of Brunehaut, who he clearly mistrusts. Turner marks this as an aside, but there are other possibilities for

Made up by lust and mischief. [*To* Guards] Take up
the body.
Exeunt with the body of THEODORET.

[SCENE 3]

Enter LACURE [*disguised as* LEFORT] *and a* Servant.

Lacure. Dost think Lefort's sure enough?
Servant. As bonds can make him. I have turned his eyes to
the east and left him gaping after the morning star: his
head is a mere astrolabe; his eyes stand for the poles, the
gag in his mouth being the Coachman; his five teeth have 5
the nearest resemblance to Charles's Wain.
Lacure. Thou hast cast a figure which shall raise thee. Direct
my hair a little, [*The* Servant *does so.*] and in my likeness
to him read a fortune suiting thy largest hopes.

199. SD] *this edn; not in Q1.* 199.1. SD] *Seward; Exeunt with the body of Theod. Q1.*

SCENE 3] *Dyce;* SCENE II *Weber; not in* Q1. 0.1. SD] *Dyce (subst); Enter* LECURE, *disguised as an Astrologer, and a Servant. Weber; Enter Lecure, and a seruant. Q1.* 8. SD] *this edn; not in Q1.*

the delivery of these lines. Martel's utterance, for instance, would be very
effective if he yelled it at Brunehaut immediately after her exit.

3.3.0.] I assign this scene to Field. Weber adds the setting: '*A mean hut*',
though he considers this to be 3.2 rather than 3.3. Dyce adds the setting: '*A
room in the dwelling of* LE FORTE'.
  1. *sure*] unable to escape.
  2. *bonds*] shackles, chains.
  3. *gaping after*] longing for.
    morning star] 'the planet Venus when visible in the east before sunrise'
(*OED*).
  4. *astrolabe*] 'any of various portable instruments formerly used for
making astronomical measurements, esp. the altitudes of celestial objects,
typically taking the form of a graduated metal disc with rotating parts and
a sighting arm' (*OED* n.).
  5. *Coachman*] a constellation lying near Ursa Major (i.e., Charles's Wain,
see below), more commonly known as Auriga, the brightest star of which is
Capella. This meaning is unrecorded in *OED*.
  6. *Charles's Wain*] 'the asterism comprising the seven bright stars in Ursa
Major; known also as The Plough' (*OED*).
  7. *cast a figure*] set up a diagram of the aspects of the astrological houses.
    Direct] put in order.

Servant. You are so far 'bove likeness you are the same. If you 10
love mirth, persuade him from himself. 'Tis but an
astronomer out of the way, and lying will bear the better
place for't.
Lacure. I have profitabler use in hand. Haste to the Queen,
and tell her how you left me changed. 15
            Exit Servant.
Who would not serve this virtuous active Queen?
She, that loves mischief 'bove the man that does it
(And him above her pleasure), yet knows no heaven
 else.

      Enter THIERRY.

Thierry. How well this loneness suits the art I seek,
Discovering secret and succeeding fate, 20
Knowledge that puts all lower happiness on
With a remiss and careless hand.
[*To* LACURE] Fair peace unto your meditations, father.
Lacure. The same to you you bring, sir.
Thierry. Drawn by your much famed skill, I come to know 25
Whether the man who owes this character
Shall e'er have issue.   [*Gives him a scroll.*]
Lacure. A resolution falling with most ease
Of any doubt you could have named. [*Reads the scroll.*]
         He is a prince

10–13. You ... for't] *Turner; Q1 lines as verse:* You ... same, | If ... himselfe | 'Tis ... way, | And ... for't. 14–15. I ... changed] *Turner; Q1 lines as verse:* I ... Queene? | And ... changed. 19. loneness] *Seward;* loanes *Q1.* 23. SD] *this edn; not in Q1.* 27. SD] *Dyce (subst); not in Q1.* 29. SD] *this edn; not in Q1.*

---

 11. *persuade ... himself*] convince Lefort he is not himself.
 12. *astronomer*] astrologer.
 bear] have, be endowed with.
 20. *succeeding*] subsequent.
 21. *puts ... on*] takes upon.
 22. *remiss*] lax, negligent.
 24. *you bring*] that you bring.
 26. *owes*] owns.
 27. *issue*] offspring.
 28. *resolution*] solution.

SC 3]   THIERRY AND THEODORET   141

    Whose fortune you inquire.
Thierry.   He is nobly born.   30
Lacure. He had a dukedom lately fall'n unto him
    By one called brother, who has left a daughter.
Thierry. The question is of heirs, not lands.
Lacure.   Heirs? Yes,
    He shall have heirs.
Thierry.   Begotten of his body?
    Why lookst thou pale? Thou canst not suffer in   35
    His want.
Lacure.   Nor thou. I neither can nor will
    Give farther knowledge to thee.
Thierry. Thou must: I am the man myself,
    Thy sovereign, who must owe unto thy wisdom
    In the concealing of my barren shame.   40
Lacure. Your grace doth wrong your stars. If this be yours,
    You may have children.
Thierry. Speak it again.
Lacure.   You may have fruitful issue.
Thierry. By whom? When? How?
Lacure. It was the fatal means first struck my blood   45
    With the cold hand of wonder when I read it
    Printed upon your birth.
Thierry. Can there be any way unsmooth has end
    So fair and good?
Lacure. We that behold the sad aspects of heaven,   50
    Leading sense-blinded men, feel grief enough
    To know, though not to speak, their miseries.

---

31. fall'n] *1711; falne Q1.*   33–6. The ... yes, | He ... body? | Why ... in | His ... will] *Turner; Q1 lines* The ... lands. | Heires, ... heires. | Begotten ... pale? | Thou ... want.   33. Heirs?] *Colman;* Heires, *Q1.*   47–9. Printed ... birth. | Can ... end | So ... good] *Q1; Turner lines* Printed ... any | Way ... good.

---

  34. *Begotten*] engendered.
  36. *want*] deficiency.
  45. *first struck*] that first struck.
  47. *Printed ... birth*] written in your horoscope.
  48. *unsmooth*] rough, violent.
  50–2.] 'We that are learned in the sad aspects of heaven, which lead men sense-blinded to their fate, have grief enough to know and not to declare the miseries of men' (Seward).

Thierry. Sorrow must lose a name where mine finds life,
   If not in thee, at least ease pain with speed,
   Which must know no cure else.   55
Lacure. Then thus:
   The first of females which your eye shall meet
   Before the sun next rise coming from out
   The temple of Diana being slain,
   You live father of many sons.   60
Thierry. Callst thou this sadness? Can I beget a son
   Deserving less than to give recompense
   Unto so poor a loss? — Whate'er thou art,
   Rest peaceable, blessed creature, born to be
   Mother of princes, whose grave shall be more fruitful   65
   Than others' marriage beds.
                              [*Exit* LACURE.]
                    Methinks his art
   Should give her form and happy figure to me.

---

53. a] *Q1;* her *Mason.* 59–60. The ... slain, | You ... sons] *Weber; Q1 lives The ... live | Father ... sonnes.* 66. SD] *this edn; following line 64 Dyce; following line 59 Colman, Weber; not in Q1.*

53.] Sorrow must 'lose its being where mine, i.e., my name, finds life by my gaining heirs to it' (Seward). Believing that '[t]here is an antithesis intended between her name and mine', Mason attractively emends to 'Sorrow must lose her name'. His suggestion, however, seems unnecessary and has not been accepted into the text.

54–5. *If ... else*] 'If it be not in your power to point out a remedy to my calamity, put me out of pain by telling me so speedily, as you are my only resource' (Mason).

57–60.] Cf. *MadL* 3.6.22–31: '*Cleanthe.* I'th morning, / But very early, will the Princess visit / The temple of the goddess, being troubled / With strange things that distract her. From the oracle, / Being strongly too in love, she will demand / The goddess's pleasure and a man to cure her. / That oracle you give: describe my brother – / You know him perfectly. *Priestess.* I have seen him often. / *Cleanthe.* And charge her take the next man she shall meet with / When she comes out.'

59. *Diana*] the virgin goddess of the countryside, hunters, crossroads, and the Moon, also considered a protectress of childbirth.

61. *beget*] engender.

66. SD] Lacure exits furtively, and Thierry does not notice his departure until after he has gone away.

66–7. *his art ... to me*] Cf. *Rollo* 4.2.239–40: 'Why, he will show you him in his magic glass / If you entreat him.'

67. *form*] visible aspect, shape.

I long to see my happiness. He is gone.
As I remember, he named my brother's daughter.
Were it my mother, 'twere a gainful death   70
Could give Ordella's virtue living breath.   [*Exit.*]

---

71. SD] *Colman; Exeunt. Q1.*

71. *Could*] the one that could.

ACT 4

SCENE I

Enter THIERRY *and* MARTEL.

Martel. Your grace is early stirring.
Thierry.   How can he sleep
  Whose happiness is laid up in an hour
  He knows comes stealing toward him? O Martel!
  Is't possible the longing bride, whose wishes
  Outruns her fears, can on that day she is married   5
  Consume in slumbers? Or his arms rust in ease
  That hears the charge and sees the honoured purchase
  Ready to gild his valour? Mine is more,
  A power above these passions: this day France —
  France, that in want of issue withers with us   10
  And like an agèd river runs his head
  Into forgotten ways — again I ransom
  And his fair course turn right; this day Thierry,
  The son of France, whose manly powers like prisoners

SCENE 1] *Q1* (Act. 4. Scoe. 1).

4.1.0.] Generally held to be a Fletcher scene. Weber adds the setting: '*Before the temple of Diana*'. As first noticed by Koeppel (36), the sequence in which Thierry and Martel wait outside the temple for the first woman to come out is redolent of the tale of Jephthah's daughter (Judg. 11:30–39) – and is absent from Grimeston/de Serres. See Introduction, 20–2.
  1. *stirring*] out of bed.
  2. *laid up*] stored up.
  3. *stealing*] moving secretly or stealthily.
  5. *Outruns*] See 1.1.6.
  6. *Consume*] waste away.
  6–7. *his ... charge*] can the arms of him who hears the charge rust in ease?
  7. *purchase*] gain.
  11. *runs ... head*] directs its course.
  14. *son*] Fletcher seems here to be exploiting the common pun on the homophones 'son' and 'sun' in light of the traditional English association of

144

SC 1]   THIERRY AND THEODORET   145

    Have been tied up and fettered, by one death   15
    Gives life to thousand ages; this day beauty,
    The envy of the world, pleasure, the glory,
    Content above the world, desire beyond it
    Are made mine own and useful.
Martel.   Happy woman
    That dies to do these things.
Thierry.   But ten times happier   20
    That lives to do the greater. O Martel,
    The gods have heard me now, and those that scorned me,
    Mothers of many children and blessed fathers
    That see their issues like the stars unnumbered
    (Their comfort more than them), shall in my praises   25
    Now teach their infants songs, and tell their ages
    From such a son of mine or such a queen
    That chaste Ordella brings me. Blessèd marriage,
    The chain that links two holy loves together,
    And in thee marriage, more than blessed Ordella,   30
    That comes so near the sacrament itself
    The priests doubt whether purer.
Martel.   Sir, y'are lost.
Thierry. Ay, prithee, let me be so.
Martel.   The day wears,
    And those that have been offering early prayers

---

16. Gives] *1711;* Give *Q1.*   22. heard] *Q2;* hard *Q1.*   32. y'are] *Q2;* year' *Q1.*   33. Ay, prithee] *this edn;* I prithee *Q1.*

---

kingship with the imagery of the sun. The pun may have even acquired additional meaning by virtue of the play's French setting. Even though Louis XIV would not be officially declared 'Le Roi Soleil' until 1662, the first king to add the sun to the French monarchical emblem was Charles VI (1380–1422) in 1385. Louis XI (1461–83) coined the sun crown in 1475, which was still in circulation at the time of Louis XIV. Charles IX (1560–74), Henri III (1574–89), Henri IV (1589–1610), and Louis XIII (1610–43) all associated themselves in some way with the sun. See Mousnier, 109–10.
    21. *the greater*] the greater thing, i.e., generate Thierry's offspring.
    26. *tell*] calculate.
    30. *in*] with.
    32. *whether purer*] whether Ordella is purer than marriage itself.
    33. *Ay, prithee*] yes, I pray you.
    wears] passes on.

Are now retiring homeward.
Thierry.   Stand and mark, then.   35
Martel. Is it the first must suffer?
Thierry.   The first woman.
Martel. What hand shall do it, sir?
Thierry.   This hand, Martel,
    For who less dare presume to give the gods
    An incense of this offering?
Martel.   Would I were she,
    For such a way to die and such a blessing   40
    Can never crown my parting.

            Enter two men passing over.

Thierry.   What are those?
Martel. Men, men, sir, men.
Thierry.   The plagues of men light on 'em:
    They cross my hopes like hares.

            Enter a Priest [*passing over*].

                              Who's that?
Martel.   A priest, sir.
Thierry. Would he were gelt.
Martel.   May not these rascals serve, sir,
    Well hanged and quartered?
Thierry.   No.

            Enter ORDELLA, *veiled.*

Martel.   Here comes a woman.   45

---

43. SD] *Colman (subst); placed here Dyce; Enter a Priest. following* Who's that *Q1.*   45. SD] *this edn; Enter Ordella, vail'd. following* Here comes a woman *Q1.*

---

   35. *mark*] observe.
   36. *must*] who must.
   41. *parting*] death.
   SD passing over] Various versions of this SD appear 'in roughly a quarter of the extant plays of the period from 1580 to 1642' (Thomson, '"*Pass over the stage*"', 33), indicating that 'the character should enter through one door, cross to the opposite door, and exit through that door' (Ichikawa, 91).
   44. *gelt*] castrated.

Thierry. Stand and behold her, then.
Martel.   I think a fair one.
Thierry. Move not whilst I prepare her. May her peace
    (Like his whose innocence the gods are pleased with
    And, offering at their altars, gives his soul,
    Far purer than those fires) pull heaven upon her. —   50
    You holy powers, no human spot dwell in her,
    No love of anything but you and goodness
    Tie her to earth; fear be a stranger to her,
    And all weak blood's affections but thy hope
    Let her bequeath to women. Hear me, heaven: 55
    Give her a spirit masculine and noble,
    Fit for yourselves to ask and me to offer.
    Oh, let her meet my blow, dote on her death,
    And, as a wanton vine bows to the pruner
    That by his cutting off more may increase,   60
    So let her fall to raise me fruit. [*To* ORDELLA] Hail, woman,
    The happiest and the best — if thy dull will
    Do not abuse thy fortune — France e'er found yet.
Ordella. She is more than dull, sir, less and worse than woman,
    That may inherit such an infinite   65
    As you propound, a greatness so near goodness,
    And brings a will to rob her.
Thierry.   Tell me this, then:
    Was there e'er woman yet, or may be found,
    That for fair fame, unspotted memory,
    For virtue's sake and only for itself's sake   70
    Has or dare make a story?
Ordella.   Many dead, sir;

---

61. SD] *this edn; not in Q1.*

---

46. *fair*] beautiful.
51. *spot*] moral stain.
58. *dote on*] love.
59. *wanton*] luxuriant.
62. *dull*] obtuse, inapprehensive.
65. *infinite*] i.e., infinite glory.
71. *make a story*] become the subject of a narrative that will be recorded by historians.

Living I think as many.
Thierry.   Say the kingdom
   May from a woman's will receive a blessing,
   The King and kingdom, not a private safety,
   A general blessing, lady?
Ordella.   A general curse   75
   Light on her heart denies it.
Thierry.   Full of honour
   And such examples as the former ages
   Were but dim shadows of and empty figures?
Ordella. You strangely stir me, sir, and, were my weakness
   In any other flesh but modest woman's,   80
   You should not ask more questions. May I do it?
Thierry. You may, and, which is more, you must.
Ordella.   I joy in't,
   Above a moderate gladness. Sir, you promise
   It shall be honest?
Thierry.   As ever time discovered.
Ordella. Let it be what it may, then, what it dare: 85
   I have a mind will hazard it.
Thierry.   But hark ye,
   What may that woman merit makes this blessing?
Ordella. Only her duty, sir.
Thierry. 'Tis terrible.
Ordella.   'Tis so much the more noble.
Thierry. 'Tis full of fearful shadows.
Ordella.   So is sleep, sir,   90
   Or anything that's merely ours and mortal;
   We were begotten gods else. But those fears,

88–9. Only ... sir. | 'Tis ... noble.] *Leech; Turner lines* Only ... terrible | 'Tis ... noble; *Q1 lines* Only ... sir. | 'Tis terrible. | 'Tis .... noble.

---

76. *her ... denies*] the heart of her who denies.
79. *strangely stir*] excite extremely.
86. *will*] that will.
hark] listen.
87. *makes*] who makes.
89. *'Tis terrible*] As is the case with 1.1.170, this is a 'squinting' or 'amphibious' half-line. The lineation in this edition has been chosen to highlight the repeated pattern of Thierry starting a line and Ordella completing it (ll. 89 and 90).

                Feeling but once the fires of nobler thoughts,
                Fly, like the shapes of clouds we form, to nothing.
Thierry. Suppose it death.
Ordella.   I do.
Thierry.   And endless parting   95
                With all we can call ours, with all our sweetness,
                With youth, strength, pleasure, people, time, nay,
                    reason,
                For in the silent grave no conversation,
                No joyful tread of friends, no voice of lovers,
                No careful father's counsel, nothing's heard,   100
                Nor nothing is, but all oblivion,
                Dust and an endless darkness. And dare you, woman,
                Desire this place?
Ordella.   'Tis of all sleeps the sweetest:
                Children begin it to us, strong men seek it,
                And kings from height of all their painted glories   105
                Fall, like spent exhalations, to this centre;
                And those are fools that fear it or imagine

---

96. with all] *Q1c;* withall *Q1u.*   100. heard] *Cotgrave;* hard *Q1.*

98–101. *For ... is*] Cf. Eccles. 9:10: 'for there is neither work nor invention, nor knowledge, nor wisdom in the grave whither thou goest' (Lamb, 402n99).

100. *careful*] full of care or concern.

104–11.] Cf. *Lieut* 3.6.1–8: 'Let no man fear to die: we love to sleep all, / And death is but the sounder sleep; all ages / And all hours call us; 'tis so common, easy, / That little children tread those paths before us; / We are not sick, nor our souls pressed with sorrows, / Nor go we out like tedious tales, forgotten; / High, high we come, and hearty, to our funerals, / And, as the sun that sets, in blood let's fall'; *MadL* 2.1.1–2, 8–12 "Tis but to die: dogs do it, ducks with dabbling; / Birds sing away their souls, and babies sleep 'em. / ... / Besides, no brother, father, kindred there / Can hinder us; all languages are alike too. / There love is everlasting, ever young, / Free from diseases, ages, jealousies. / Bawds, beldams, painters, purgers die: 'tis nothing.'

104. *begin ... us*] provide us with an example by dying before us.

105. *painted glories*] feigned praises.

106. *Fall ... exhalations*] Cf. *H8* 3.2.225–7: 'I shall fall / Like a bright exhalation in the evening, / And no man see me more'; *SJVOB* 4.3.20–2: 'Must all these glories vanish into darkness / And Barnavelt pass with them and glide away / Like a spent exhalation?'

exhalations] meteors, shooting stars, which were believed to be formed by vapours exhaled from the earth under the influence of the sun, which would then fall back to earth.

   A few unhandsome pleasures or life's profits
   Can recompense this place, and mad that stays it
   Till age blow out their lights or rotten humours   110
   Bring 'em dispersed to the earth.
Thierry.   Then you can suffer?
Ordella. As willingly as say it.
Thierry.   Martel, a wonder!
   Here is a woman that dares die! [*To her*] Yet tell me,
   Are you a wife?
Ordella.   I am, sir.
Thierry.   And have children?
   [*To* MARTEL] She sighs and weeps.
Ordella.   Oh, none, sir.
Thierry.   Dare you venture,   115
   For a poor barren praise you ne'er shall hear,
   To part with these sweet hopes?
Ordella.   With all but heaven,
   And yet die full of children: he that reads me
   When I am ashes is my son in wishes,
   And those chaste dames that keep my memory,   120
   Singing my yearly requiems, are my daughters.
Thierry. Then there is nothing wanting but my knowledge;
   And what I must do, lady.
Ordella.   You are the King, sir,
   And what you do I'll suffer, and that blessing

---

113. SD] *this edn; not in Q1.*   115. SD] *this edn; not in Q1.*

---

 108. *unhandsome*] inconvenient.
 109. *recompense*] compensate, make up for.
 stays it] holds back.
 110. *their*] of those who try to avoid death.
 rotten humours] According to the theory of the four humours (see 2.1.256–7), as humans aged, the natural heat of their bodies would gradually decrease, thus making the physiological functions of bodily maintenance work less efficiently and compromising the necessary balance and the integrity of the humours on which good health was thought to be predicated.
 111. *'em*] those who try to avoid death.
 119. *ashes*] 'Ordella is completely de-personalized: from the partly sentient, intuitively compliant "vine," she becomes "ashes," then an adorned "tomb" – a place of worship – and next a fertile land or Nature, a much-inclusive abstraction' (Galant, 219).
 122. *wanting*] missing.

	That you desire the gods shower on the kingdom.	125

Thierry. Thus much before I strike, then, for I must kill you.
    The gods have willed it so. Thou'rt made the blessing
    Must make France young again and me a man.
    Keep up your strength still nobly.
Ordella.   Fear me not.
Thierry. And meet death like a measure.
Ordella.   I am steadfast.   130
Thierry. Thou shalt be sainted, woman, and thy tomb
    Cut out in crystal, pure and good as thou art,
    And on it shall be graven, every age,
    Succeeding peers of France, that rise by thy fall,
    Till thou liest there like old and fruitful nature.   135
    Dar'st thou behold thy happiness?
Ordella.   I dare, sir.
                               Pulls off her veil.
Thierry. Ha?   *Lets fall his sword.*
Martel. O sir, you must not do it!
Thierry.   No, I dare not.
    There is an angel keeps that paradise,
    A fiery angel, friend; O virtue, virtue,   140
    Ever and endless virtue!
Ordella.   Strike, sir, strike!   [*Kneels.*]
    And, if in my poor death fair France may merit,

---

127. Thou'rt] *Seward;* They'r *Q1.*   133. graven, every] *Seward;* grauen euery *Q1.*   135. Till] *Seward;* Tell *Q1.*   141. SD] *Dyce; not in Q1.*

---

   127. *willed it*] commanded.
   130. *measure*] 'solemn, stately dance, with slow and measured steps' (Dyce).
   133–5. *on ... nature*] 'on thy tomb shall be engraved from age to age the succeeding kings of France as acknowledging their being all derived from thee, till thou liest there like nature, the fruitful mother of all things' (Seward).
   137. *Ha?*] Thierry's bafflement and dismay at discovering Ordella under the veil is aptly captured by this monosyllabic interjection occupying an entire line on its own. He is temporarily shocked into silence.
   139–40. *There ... angel*] The allusion is to the cherubim that God placed east of the Garden of Eden with a flaming sword to prevent anyone going back (Gen. 3:24).
   139. *keeps*] that keeps.
   142. *merit*] 'become entitled to reward, gratitude, or commendation' (*OED* v. 3).

                Give me a thousand blows, be killing me
                A thousand days.
Thierry.   First let the earth be barren
                And man no more remembered. Rise, Ordella,
                                                [*She rises.*]   145
                The nearest to thy maker, and the purest
                That ever dull flesh showed us. — Oh, my heartstrings!
                                                        Exit.
Martel. I see you full of wonder. Therefore, noblest
                And truest amongst women, I will tell you
                The end of this strange accident.
Ordella.   Amazement   150
                Has so much won upon my heart that truly
                I feel myself unfit to hear. O sir,
                My lord has slighted me.
Martel.   Oh, no, sweet lady.
Ordella. Robbed me of such a glory by his pity
                And most unprovident respect.
Martel.   Dear lady,   155
                It was not meant to you.
Ordella.   Elsewhere the day is,
                And hours distinguish time, time runs to ages,
                And ages end the world, I had been spoken.
Martel. I'll tell you what it was if but your patience

145.1. SD] *Turner; Raises her. Dyce; not in Q1.* 151. won] *Colman;* woue *Q1;* wove *Q2.* 159. SP *Martel*] *1711; Deui. Q1.*

---

146. *thy maker*] God.
147. *dull*] insensible, inert.
heartstrings] in early modern anatomical thought, nerves or tendons supposed to brace and support the heart. This structure was conceived of as the source of an individual's most intense emotions or feelings. The snapping of these strings, under the pressure of excessive grief, would produce a 'broken heart'.
147.1. SD Exit] 'It is another mark of Fletcher's dramatic sense that he gives Thierry only a four-line response and allows him to rush off the stage' (Squier, 111).
150. *end*] final cause, purpose.
accident] event, occurrence.
155. *unprovident*] improvident.
156. *is*] exists.
159. *but*] only.

	Will give me hearing.	
Ordella.	If I have transgressed,	160
	Forgive me, sir.	
Martel.	Your noble lord was counselled,	

    Grieving the barrenness between you both
(And all the kingdom with him), to seek out
A man that knew the secrets of the gods.
He went, found such a one and had this answer,   165
That, if he would have issue, on this morning
(For this hour was prefixed him) he should kill
The first he met, being female, from the temple,
And then he should have children. The mistake
Is now too perfect, lady.
Ordella.   Still 'tis I, sir,   170
For may this work be done by common women?
Durst any but myself, that knew the blessing
And felt the benefit, assume this dying?
In any other 't had been lost, and nothing,
A curse and not a blessing. I was figured,   175
And shall a little fondness bar my purchase?
Martel. Where should he then seek children?
Ordella.   Where they are:
In wombs ordained for issues, in those beauties
That bless a marriage bed and makes it proceed

---

179. *proceed*] *Q1*; breed *Colman*; proud *conj Theobald*; procreant *Seward*.

---

    163. *And ... him*] i.e., grieving with him. As Blamires observes, 'There is a sense of "double-time" here ... – the royal couple's barrenness seems public knowledge (4.1.22; 4.1.162) but in the previous scene, set on the day before, Thierry demands "the concealing of my barren shame" (3.3.40).'
    166. *issue*] offspring.
    167. *prefixed him*] determined beforehand for him.
    170. *perfect*] certain.
    171.] suggesting Ordella's awareness of her own exceptionality, a slightly discordant note in her overall portrayal as the perfect woman and wife.
    173. *assume*] undertake.
    175. *figured*] astrologically revealed to be the person to sacrifice.
    176. *fondness*] foolishness, folly.
    bar] prevent.
    purchase] gain.
    178. *ordained*] designed, intended.
    179. *proceed*] 'Editors have found difficulty with the reading, but "proceed" is acceptable as meaning "prosper" (*OED* v. [4f]) or "give rise to" (compare 7b)' (Turner).

|With kisses that conceive and fruitful pleasures; 180
Mine, like a grave, buries those loyal hopes,
And to a grave it covets.

Martel.   You are too good,
Too excellent, too honest! Rob not us
And those that shall hereafter seek example
Of such inestimable worthies in woman, 185
Your lord of such obedience, all of honour,
In coveting a cruelty is not yours,
A will short of your wisdom. Make not error
A tombstone of your virtues, whose fair life
Deserves a constellation: your lord dare not, 190
He cannot, ought not, must not run this hazard;
He makes a separation nature shakes at,
The gods deny, and everlasting justice
Shrinks back and sheathes her sword at.

Ordella.   All's but talk, sir.
I find to what I am reserved and needful, 195
And, though my lord's compassion makes me poor
And leaves me in my best use, yet a strength
Above mine own or his dull fondness finds me:
The gods have given it to me.   *Draws a knife.*

Martel.   Self-destruction?

185. worthies] *Q1;* worthiness *Turner.*

---

182. *to ... covets*] desires to die.

185. *worthies*] Turner emends to 'worthiness' on the grounds that even though '"Worthies" ... makes sense ... it throws a false accent on "woman"'. His emendation turns the line into 'a hexameter or a pentameter in which the first three syllables are slurred'. There is no need, however, to make the change. 'Worthy' is here used in the sense of 'distinguished, eminent, or renowned person, esp. one of courage or noble character' (*OED* n. 1a), possibly with the hint that Martel is imagining a list of Nine (female) Worthies to match the male ones (see 2.3.161). The line remains hypermetrical, but it is possible emphatically to linger on 'worthies' to make it last three beats rather than two, so that no false accent falls on 'woman'. That way, the line can either be a hexameter or a pentameter if 'inestimable' is so slurred as to make it three syllables rather than five ('inest'mabl').

195. *to ... needful*] for what I have been set apart and to what I am indispensable.

197. *leaves ... use*] 'neglects putting me to the use I am most fit for, the best use I can be employed in' (Colman).

198. *dull fondness*] foolish, excessive affection.

	Now all good angels bless thee! O sweet lady,	200
	You are abused. This is a way to shame you,	
	And with you all that knows you, all that loves you,	
	To ruin all you build. Would you be famous?	
	Is that your end?	
Ordella.	I would be what I should be.	
Martel.	Live, and confirm the gods then, live, and be loaden	205
	With more than olives bear, or fruitful autumn.	
	This way you kill your merit, kill your cause	
	And him you would raise life to; where or how	
	Got you these bloody thoughts? What devil durst	
	Look on that angel face, and tempt? Do you know	210
	What 'tis to die thus, how you strike the stars	
	And all good things above? Do you feel	
	What follows a self-blood, whither you venture,	
	And to what punishment? Excellent lady,	
	Be not thus cozened, do not fool yourself.	215
	The priest was never his own sacrifice,	
	But he that thought his hell here.	
Ordella.	[*Giving the knife to* MARTEL] I am counselled.	
Martel.	And I am glad on't; lie I know you dare not.	
Ordella.	I never have done yet.	
Martel.	Pray, take my comfort. —	
	Was this a soul to lose? Two more such women	220
	Would save their sex. See, she repents and prays.	
	Oh, hear her, hear her: if there be a faith	

217. SD] *this edn; not in Q1.*

---

201. *abused*] deceived
202. *knows*] See 1.1.6.
loves] See 1.1.6.
203. *Would you*] would you like to.
206. *olives*] olive trees.
211. *thus*] i.e., by committing suicide.
213. *self-blood*] suicide (the only instance recorded in *OED*).
whither] to what place.
215. *cozened*] deceived.
217. SD] Ordella might theoretically simply sheathe the knife, but that she in fact gives it to Martel is suggested by l. 230, when he declares that he will show the knife to the people at court to spy Brunehaut's reaction. See also 4.2.139. SD.
220–3.] Martel is addressing the gods.

Able to reach your mercies, she hath sent it.
Ordella. Now, good Martel, confirm me.
Martel. I will, lady,
And every hour advise you, for I doubt 225
Whether this plot be heaven's or hell's your mother,
And I will find it if it be in mankind
To search the centre of it. In the meantime,
I'll give you out for dead, and by yourself,
And show the instrument, so shall I find 230
A joy that will betray her.
Ordella. Do what's fittest,
And I will follow you.
Martel. Then ever live
Both able to engross all love, and give. *Exeunt.*

[SCENE 2]

Enter BRUNEHAUT [*and*] PROTALDI.

Brunehaut. I am in labour
To be delivered of that burdenous project
I have so long gone with.

---

226. or ... mother] *Colman;* or hells; your mother *Q1.*

SCENE 2] *Weber; not in Q1.*

---

224. *confirm*] encourage, strengthen spiritually.
226. *hell's your mother*] hell is Brunehaut, Ordella's acquired mother. The punctuation in Q1 is confusing, as there is a break after 'hells' (i.e., 'hells; your mother'), but it is difficult to construe a meaningful sentence by keeping that break. Removing the semicolon and interpreting Q1's 'hells' as a genitive appears to be the only reasonable alternative.
227. *in mankind*] in the power of human beings.
229. *give ... for*] report you.
by yourself] by means of suicide.
230. *the instrument*] i.e., the knife.
231. *A ... her*] a joyful response to this sad news that will expose her guilt.

4.2.0.] Generally held to be a Massinger scene. Weber adds the setting: '*An apartment in the palace*'.
1–3.] 'The birth she is referring to is the completion of the plan to eliminate Ordella. The daughter-in-law's death is [Brunehaut]'s progeny' (Galant, 223).

SC 2]   THIERRY AND THEODORET   157

      Enter LACURE.

      Ha! Here's the midwife. —
Or life or death?
Lacure.   If in the supposition
 Of her death (in whose life you die) you ask me, 5
 I think you are safe.
Brunehaut.   Is she dead?
Lacure.   I have used
 All means to make her so. I saw him waiting
 At the temple door and used such art within
 That only she of all her sex was first
 Given up unto his fury.
Brunehaut.   Which if love 10
 Or fear made him forbear to execute
 The vengeance he determined, his fond pity
 Shall draw it on himself; for, were there left
 Not any man but he to serve my pleasures
 Or from me to receive commands (which are 15
 The joys for which I love life), he should be
 Removed, and I alone left to be queen
 O'er any part of goodness that's left in me.
Lacure. If you are so resolved, I have provided
 A means to ship him hence. Look upon this, 20
      [*Shows a handkerchief.*]
 But touch it sparingly, for this, once used
 (Say but to dry a tear), will keep the eyelid
 From closing until death perform that office.
Brunehaut. Give't me. [*Takes it.*] — [*To them*] I may have
 use of't, and on you
 I'll make the first experiment if one sigh 25

---

3. SD] *Turner; following* midwife! *Dyce; following* death? *Q1*. 20.1. SD] *Dyce (subst); not in Q1*. 24. SD1] *Dyce (subst); not in Q1*. SD2] *this edn; not in Q1*.

---

 4. *Or ... death*] Is it life or is it death?
 7. *him*] i.e., Thierry.
 10. *his*] i.e., Thierry's.
 12. *fond*] foolish.
 19. *resolved*] determined.
 20. *ship ... hence*] get rid of him.
 22. *keep*] prevent.
 23. *perform ... office*] i.e., closes the victim's eyes.

	Or heavy look beget the least suspicion	
	Childish compassion can thaw the ice	
	Of your so long congealed and flinty hardness.	
	'Slight, go on constant, or I shall!	
Protaldi.	Best lady,	
	We have no faculties which are not yours.	30
Lacure. Nor will be anything without you.		
Brunehaut.	Be so,	
	And we will stand or fall together, for,	
	Since we have gone so far that death must stay	
	The journey which we wish should never end,	
	And innocent or guilty we must die,	35
	When we do so, let's know the reason why.	

   Enter THIERRY *and* Courtiers [*stopping some way
    from the characters already on stage*].

Lacure. The King.
Thierry.   [*To* Courtiers] We'll be alone.
            [*Exeunt* Courtiers.]
Protaldi.   I would I had
 A convoy too to bring me safely off,
 For rage, although it be allayed with sorrow,

36.1–2. SD] *this edn; Enter Thierry, and Courtiers. Q1.* 37. SD1] *this edn; not in Q1.* SD2] *Dyce; not in Q1.* 38. safely] *conj Dyce;* safe *Q1*.

---

 26. *suspicion*] suspicion that.
 27. *compassion*] pronounced as four syllables.
 29. *'Slight*] a corruption of 'by God's light', a mild oath.
 go ... constant] keep being steadfast in your attachment to our cause.
 33. *stay*] bring to a halt.
 37. *would*] wish.
 38. *convoy*] guard, escort, in particular 'a military vessel or fleet accompanying a merchant ship, passenger vessel' (*OED* n. 4b).
 safely] I have accepted Dyce's conjecture, which results in a pristine line of iambic pentameter and chimes with Massinger's use of the phrase 'safely off' in his other writings. Cf. *Proph* 4.4.91: 'fetch them safely off'; *CustCount* 2.2.31: 'they brought them safely off'; *Bondman* 5.2.87: 'Guard him safely off too'; *Renegado* 2.5.25: 'bear her safely off'. One could also mention *Renegado* 3.5.93: 'We'll bring you safe off', and 5.3.169: 'Bear him safe off' as counter-arguments, but in both cases these sentences are part of full pentameters.
 off] away from land.

SC 2]   THIERRY AND THEODORET   159

  Appears so dreadful in him that I shake   40
  To look upon it.
Brunehaut.   Coward, I will meet it
  And know from whence 't has birth.
        [*Approaching* THIERRY] Son, kingly Thierry.
Thierry. Is cheating grown so common among men
  And thrives so well here that the gods endeavour
  To practise it above?
Brunehaut.   Your mother —
Thierry.   [*Not responding to her*] Ha!   45
  Or are they only careful to revenge,
  Not to reward? Or, when for our offences
  We study satisfaction, must the cure
  Be worse than the disease?
Brunehaut.   Will you not hear me?
Thierry. To lose th'ability to perform those duties   50
  For which I entertained the name of husband
  Asked more than common sorrow. But t'impose
  For the redress of that defect a torture,

---

42. 't has] *F2;* t'as *Q1*. SD] *this edn; not in Q1*. 45. SD] *this edn; not in Q1*. 45–6. To ... Ha! — | Or ... revenge,] *Seward; Q1 lines* To ... aboue! | Your mother. | Ha! ... reuenge. 47. our] *Seward;* your *Q1*.

---

47. *our offences*] the injuries that we suffer.
48. *study*] seek to achieve.
50–65.] The loss of my sexual functions, which prevented me from being a husband to all intents and purposes, called for extraordinary grief. But the fact that, to amend that weakness of mine, I had to go through the torture of having to kill the only woman for whom I felt that weakness as an actual fault requires more than tearing my hair, throwing myself on the ground, cursing, or praying. Such a sorrowful scene would be difficult to play even for an actor much more skilful than I am, because the cause of my grief is very intense, but my ability to express it is so ineffective that, even though the role is a good one, I am afraid that my weak performance will fail to impress the people, who will therefore refrain from pitying me. The strongly metatheatrical overtones of this sequence are typically Massingerian in their seeking to sharpen the audience's awareness of their being spectators of a performance. Massinger would go even further in developing the metatheatrical elements of his playwriting in his solo plays, most famously and effectively in *The Roman Actor*. For the possibility of Burbage as Thierry, see Introduction, 22–4.
50. *duties*] sexual obligations.
53. *redress*] amendment.

      In marking her to death for whom alone
      I felt that weakness as a want, requires   55
      More than the making the head bald! Or falling
            [*Tears his hair and throws himself on the ground.*]
      Thus flat upon the earth, or cursing that way,
      Or praying this! Oh, such a scene of grief,
      And so set down — the world the stage to act on —
      May challenge a tragedian better practised   60
      Than I am to express it, for my cause
      Of passion is so strong and my performance
      So weak that, though the part be good, I fear
      Th'ill acting of it will defraud it of
      The poor reward it may deserve, men's pity.   65
Brunehaut. I have given you way thus long. A king and, what
      Is more, my son, and yet a slave to that
      Which only triumphs over cowards, sorrow?
      For shame, look up.
Thierry.   Is't you? Look down on me
      And, if that you are capable to receive it,   70
      Let that return to you, that have brought forth
      One marked out only for it.
                [*Pointing to her minions*] What are these?
      Come they upon your privilege to tread on
      The tomb of my afflictions?
Protaldi.   No, not we, sir.
Thierry. How dare you, then, omit the ceremony   75
      Due to the funeral of all my hopes

56.1. SD] *Dyce; not in Q1.* 68. cowards, sorrow?] *Seward;* Cowards, sorrow; *1711;* cowards sorrow *Q1.* 72. SD] *this edn; not in Q1.*

---

  55. *want*] lack, deficiency.
  56. *making ... bald*] Pulling one's hair was a customary practice of mourning in ancient Greece. It functioned as a personal exhibition of grief by creating a visible sign of loss on the mourner's body.
  60. *tragedian*] tragic actor.
  63. *part*] role.
  70. *if that*] if.
  it] i.e., sorrow.
  71. *have ... forth*] gave birth to.
  72. *it*] i.e., sorrow.
  73. *upon ... privilege*] on the grounds of your special favour.

SC 2]   THIERRY AND THEODORET   161

    Or come unto the marriage of my sorrows
    But in such colours as may sort with them?
Protaldi. Alas, we will wear anything.
Brunehaut.   [*To* THIERRY] This is madness.
    Take but my counsel.
Thierry.   Yours? Dare you again,   80
    Though armed with the authority of a mother,
    Attempt the danger that will fall on you
    If such another syllable awake it?
    Go, and with yours be safe. I have such cause
    Of grief, nay, more, to love it, that I will not   85
    Have such as these be sharers in it.
Lacure.   [*Aside to* BRUNEHAUT] Madam.
Protaldi. [*Aside to her*] Another time were better.
Brunehaut.   [*Aside to them*] Do not stir,
    For I must be resolved, and will. Be statues.

              Enter MARTEL.

Thierry. [*To* MARTEL] Ay, thou art welcome, and upon my
        soul
    Thou art an honest man. — Do you see? He has tears   90
    To lend to him whom prodigal expense
    Of sorrow has made bankrupt of such treasure.
    [*To* MARTEL] Nay, thou dost well.
Martel.   I would it might excuse
    The ill I bring along.
Thierry.   Thou mak'st me smile
    In the height of my calamities, as if   95

---

79. SD] *this edn; not in Q1.*   86. SD] *Turner (subst); not in Q1.*   87. SD1] *this edn; not in Q1.*   SD2] *this edn; not in Q1.*   89. SD] *this edn; not in Q1.*   93. SD] *this edn; not in Q1.*

  78. *in ... them*] wearing black mourning clothes to match my sorrow.
  84. *yours*] i.e., your minions.
  86. *these*] i.e., your minions.
  87. *stir*] move.
  88. *statues*] i.e., still as statues.
  90-1. *He ... lend*] This seems to mean that Martel is weeping as he comes on stage. However, Thierry might conclude that Martel has tears to lend simply because his expression is very sad, on the brink of tears.
  94. *ill*] bad news.

>   There could be the addition of an atom
>   To the giant body of my miseries.
>   But try, for I will hear thee. — All sit down: 'tis death
>   To any that shall dare to interrupt him
>   In look, gesture or word.   [*They sit.*]
> *Martel.*   And such attention   100
>   As is due to the last and the best story
>   That ever was delivered will become you.
>   [*To* THIERRY] The grieved Ordella — for all other titles
>   But take away from that — having from me
>   (Prompted by your last parting groan) enquired   105
>   What drew it from you, and the cause soon learned —
>   For she, whom barbarism could deny nothing,
>   With such prevailing earnestness desired it
>   'Twas not in me, though it had been my death,

---

100. SD] Dyce (subst); not in Q1.   103. SD] this edn; not in Q1.

---

102. *delivered*] narrated.
103–42. *The ... sunk*] The doleful Ordella – the only appropriate adjective for her at that point – asked me what the cause of your groan as you departed was. I could not abstain from informing her, because she had such an eager desire to know the truth that I could have never hidden it from her even if my death should follow. After she (in whom all the good qualities of the women of antiquity resided, but not the bad ones) learned that the cause was that she had been determined by some higher power – though certainly an evil one – to meet death so that you could have an offspring, she looked up to heaven with no fear in her face, then she looked at herself, and finally she smiled, as though the joy she felt in doing something for you wanted to break out in spite of her grief of having to die and abandon you. After that, she took me by the hand (and for this reason I will always love my hand more intensely than I ever did before) and told me to come to you – a happiness that would be forever denied to her – and tell you that you loved her too much if you had decided to prevent the kingdom from having any children of yours as heirs to the throne, because all her worth depended on your love and her acceptance of it, and nothing else. Accordingly, as a way to repay that love and to show the world that she could not be the mother of your children not only for her fault but because it was not her destiny, and at the same time to demonstrate that she would never be envious of the happy woman who would give birth one day to your children, her quick death would make way for this new woman. Immediately after uttering these words, she used this knife on herself and fell to the ground, dead.
104. *take away*] detract something.
107. *barbarism*] barbarous cruelty, barbarity,
109. *'Twas*] that it was.

To hide it from her — she, I say, in whom 110
All was that Athens, Rome or warlike Sparta
Have registered for good in their best women,
But nothing of their ill, knowing herself
Marked out — I know not by what power, but, sure,
A cruel one — to die to give you children, 115
Having first with a settled countenance
Looked up to heaven and then upon herself
(It being the next best object) and then smiled,
As if her joy in death to do you service
Would break forth in despite of the much sorrow 120
She showed she had to leave you; and then, taking
Me by the hand — this hand which I must ever
Love better than I have done, since she touched it —
'Go', said she, 'to my lord (and to go to him
Is such a happiness I must not hope for), 125
And tell him that he too much prized a trifle,
Made only worthy in his love and her
Thankful acceptance, for her sake to rob
The orphan kingdom of such guardians as
Must of necessity descend from him; 130
And, therefore, in some part of recompense
Of his much love and to show to the world
That 'twas not her fault only, but her fate,
That did deny to let her be the mother
Of such most certain blessings — yet for proof 135
She did not envy her, that happy her
That is appointed to them, her quick end
Should make way for her', which no sooner spoke
But in a moment this too ready engine [*Shows a knife.*]

139. SD] *Dyce (subst); not in Q1.*

---

113. *ill*] evil.
116. *a ... countenance*] an expression on her face indicating a settled purpose.
129. *orphan*] i.e., which would become orphan if Thierry generated no offspring.
136. *her*] the woman supposed to become the mother of Thierry's children.
137. *them*] Thierry's future children.
139. *engine*] instrument, tool.

	Made such a battery in the choicest castle	140
	That ever nature made to defend life	
	That straight it shook and sunk.	
Thierry.	[*To the others*] Stay! Dares any	
	Presume to shed a tear before me? Or	
	Ascribe that worth unto themselves to merit	
	To do so for her? [*To* MARTEL] I have done. Now, on.	145
Martel.	Fall'n thus, once more she smiled, as if that death	
	For her had studied a new way to sever	
	The soul and body without sense of pain;	
	And then 'Tell him,' quoth she, 'what you have seen,	
	And with what willingness 'twas done, for which	150
	My last request unto him is that he	
	Would instantly make choice of one, most happy	
	In being so chosen, to supply my place,	
	By whom if heaven bless him with a daughter,	
	In my remembrance let it bear my name',	155
	Which said, she died.	
Thierry.	I hear this and yet live?	
	Heart, art thou thunder-proof? Will nothing break thee?	
	She's dead, and what her entertainment may be	
	In th'other world without me is uncertain,	
	And dare I stay here unresolved?	
	[*Rises and draws his sword.*]	
Martel.	O sir! [*Holds him.*]	160

---

142. SD] *this edn; not in Q1*.   145. SD] *this edn; not in Q1*.   146. Fall'n] *1711;* falne *Q1*.   160. SD1] Turner (subst); Draws his sword. Dyce; Draws. Weber; *not in Q1*.   SD2] Turner (subst); They hold him. Dyce; *not in Q1*.

---

140. *battery*] attack, assault.
choicest] most excellent.
144. *Ascribe*] attribute.
merit] be entitled.
147. *studied*] contrived.
158–9. *what ... uncertain*] Ordella committed suicide; hence, the fate of her soul after death might be damnation even though she killed herself for what she believed was a good cause. This is one of various moments at which the religious ambiguity of the play comes to the fore. Is the religious framework of the play pagan or Christian?
160. *unresolved*] undecided, uncertain.

SC 2]   THIERRY AND THEODORET   165

Brunehaut. Dear son!   [*They rise.*]
Protaldi.   Great King!
Thierry.   Unhand me! [MARTEL *does so.*] Am I fall'n
   So low that I have lost the power to be
   Disposer of my own life?
Martel.   Be but pleased
   To borrow so much time of sorrow as
   To call to mind her last request for whom   165
   (I must confess, a loss beyond expression)
   You turn your hand upon yourself: 'twas hers —
   And dying hers! — that you should live, and happy
   In seeing little models of yourself
   By matching with another. And will you   170
   Leave anything that she desired ungranted?
   And suffer such a life that was laid down
   For your sake only to be fruitless?
Thierry.   Oh,
   Thou dost throw charms upon me against which
   I cannot stop my ears. — Bear witness, heaven,   175
   That not desire of life nor love of pleasures,
   Nor any future comforts, but to give
   Peace to her blessèd spirit in satisfying
   Her last demand makes me defer our meeting,
   Which in my choice, and sudden choice, shall be   180
   To all apparent.
Brunehaut.   [*Aside*] How? Do I remove one mischief
   To draw upon my head a greater?
Thierry.   Go,
   Thou only good man, to whom for herself

---

161. SD1] *Turner; not in Q1.* SD2] *this edn; not in Q1.* fall'n] *1711;* falne
Q1. 173–4. For ... Oh, | Thou ... which] *Colman; Q1 lines* For ... fruitelesse?
| Oh ... which. 176. pleasures] *Q1;* pleasure *Q2.* 181. SD] *Weber (subst);
not in Q1.* 182–3. To ... Go, | Thou ... herself] *Colman; Q1 lines* To ...
greater? | Go, ... her selfe.

---

167. *hers*] i.e., Ordella's.
169. *little ... yourself*] See 3.1.48.
170. *matching*] pairing.
180. *sudden*] unexpected, unpremeditated.

    Goodness is dear, and prepare to inter it
    In her that was — O my heart! — my Ordella,   185
    A monument worthy to be the casket
    Of such a jewel.
Martel.   Your command that makes way
    Unto my absence is a welcome one,
    For but yourself there's nothing here Martel
    Can take delight to look on. Yet some comfort   190
    Goes back with me to her who, though she want it,
    Deserves all blessings.   *Exit.*
Brunehaut.   [*To* THIERRY] So soon to forget
    The loss of such a wife, believe it, will
    Be censured in the world.
Thierry.   Pray you, no more.
    There is no argument you can use to cross it   195
    But does increase in me such a suspicion
    I would not cherish. — Who's that?

       Enter MEMBERGE [*attended by* Guards].

Memberge.   One no guard
    Can put back from access, whose tongue no threats
    Nor prayers can silence, a bold suitor, and
    For that which, if you are yourself a king,   200
    You were made so to grant it: justice, justice!
Thierry. With what assurance dare you hope for that
    Which is denied to me? Or how can I
    Stand bound to be just unto such as are

---

192. SD2] *this edn; not in Q1.* 197. SD] *this edn; Enter Memberge. Q1.*
199. prayers] *Q1;* praises *Q2.*

---

 191. *want*] lacks.
 194. *censured*] judged.
 197. SD attended by *Guards*] Q1 indicates no entrances for any Guards, but there must be some by l. 223, when Brunehaut orders 'Drag hence the wretch', immediately bypassed by Thierry's 'Forbear'. The most likely point at which the Guards should enter is here, as borne out by Memberge's words ('One no guard / Can put back from access'), which would seem to suggest that the Guards have tried to stop her without harming her but that she has managed to enter the stage all the same, escorted by them (now awaiting orders on exactly how to handle the situation). Besides, it would be normal for guards to be on duty outside any room where the monarch was.
 199. *suitor*] suppliant.

      Beneath me, that find none from those that are   205
      Above me?
Memberge.   Theirs is justice: 'twere unfit
      That anything but vengeance should fall on him
      That by his giving way to more than murder,
      For my dear father's death was parricide,
      Makes it his own.
Brunehaut.   [*To* THIERRY] I charge you hear her not.   210
Memberge. Hell cannot stop just prayers from entering heaven.
      I must and will be heard. — Sir, but remember
      That he that by her plot fell was your brother;
      And the place where, your palace, against all
      Th'inviolable rites of hospitality;   215
      Your word, a king's word, given up for his safety;
      His innocence, his protection; and the gods
      Bound to revenge the impious breach of such
      So great and sacred bonds; and can you wonder,
      That in not punishing such a horrid murder   220
      You did it, that heaven's favour is gone from you,
      Which never will return until his blood
      Be washed away in hers?
Brunehaut.   [*To* Guards] Drag hence the wretch.
                  [*The* Guards *offer to seize her.*]

---

206. Theirs] *this edn;* There *Q2;* Their *Q1*.   210. SD] *this edn; not in Q1.*
212. heard. — Sir,] *Colman (subst);* heard Sir; *Q2;* heard, Sir; *Q1*.   223. SD] *this edn; not in Q1.*   223.1. SD] *Turner; not in Q1.*

---

    205. *that find*] the antecedent of 'that' is 'I' at line 203.
    206. *Theirs*] Q1 reads 'Their is', which Q2 changes to 'There is'. All previous editors have followed Q2. As terminal letters are frequently omitted in Q1 (see 1.1.106), emending to 'Theirs is' seems to be more appropriate than emending to 'There is'. The use of the possessive pronoun also provides a stronger connection between Thierry's and Memberge's speeches, in that 'Theirs' refers directly to 'those that are / Above', i.e., the gods. Memberge states that what has been happening to Thierry is the gods' just punishment for his failing to prevent or avenge Theodoret's death.
    209. *parricide*] killing of a near relative.
    210. *charge*] order.
    214. *where*] i.e., where he was murdered.
    216. *given up*] delivered, rendered.
    218–19. *such / So*] such.
    220. *That*] The antecedent is 'you' on the previous line.
    221. *did*] committed, perpetrated.

Thierry. [*To* Guards] Forbear. — With what variety
  Of torments do I meet? [*To* MEMBERGE] Oh, thou hast
    opened 225
  A book in which, writ down in bloody letters,
  My conscience finds that I am worthy of
  More than I undergo, but I'll begin
  For my Ordella's sake and for thine own
  To make less heaven's great anger. Thou hast lost 230
  A father, I to thee am so; the hope
  Of a good husband, in me have one, nor
  Be fearful I am still no man: already
  That weakness is gone from me.
Brunehaut.   (*Aside*) That it might
  Have ever grown inseparably upon thee. 235
  [*To* THIERRY] What will you do? Is such a thing as this
  Worthy the loved Ordella's place, the daughter
  Of a poor gardener?
Memberge.   Your son!
Thierry.   [*To* BRUNEHAUT] The power
  To take away that lowness is in me.
Brunehaut. Stay yet, for rather than that thou shalt add 240
  Incest unto thy other sins, I will

---

224. SD] *this edn; not in Q1*.   225. SD] *this edn; not in Q1*.   236. SD] *this edn; not in Q1*.   238. SD] *this edn; not in Q1*.

---

226. *writ*] written.
230. *make less*] diminish.
231–62. *the hope … wish*] This part is based on Grimeston, sig. D4ᵛ: 'Theodebert had but one only daughter, whom Thierry would take to wife … but Brunehaut, who desired greatly to see him master, but not to have a companion in this absolute authority, dissuades him from this marriage, inferring, to cover her hidden intent, that it was not lawful to marry his niece. Thierry, blinded with passion, who by a just judgement of God sought to die by poison of this viper by whose means he had done so much mischief, replies that the daughter of Theodebert was none of his niece, seeing that Theodebert was not his brother (being begotten by another father), reproaching Brunehaut that he knew no more than she had taught him, and upon this occasion she had encouraged him to kill him … Brunehaut, seeing herself taken by the nose and measured by the same measure she had measured others, resolves to prevent Thierry and to murder him. She therefore gives him a morsel mixed with a languishing potion, which caused him to consume of a bloody flux … Such was the tragic end of the troublesome life of Thierry.'

	With hazard of my own life utter all:	
	Theodoret was thy brother.	
Thierry.	You denied it	
	Upon your oath, nor will I now believe you.	
	Your protean turnings cannot change my purpose.	245
Memberge.	[*To* BRUNEHAUT] And, for me, be assured the means to be	
	Revenged on thee, vile hag, admits no thought	
	But what tends to it.	[*Exit.*]
Brunehaut.	[*Aside*] Is it come to that?	
	Then have at the last refuge. [*To* THIERRY] Art thou grown	
	Insensible in ill, that thou go'st on	250
	Without the least compunction? There, take that	
	[*Gives him the handkerchief.*]	
	To witness that thou hadst a mother which	
	Foresaw thy cause of grief and sad repentance	
	That so soon after blessed Ordella's death	
	Without a tear thou canst embrace another,	255
	Forgetful man.	[THIERRY *weeps.*]
Thierry.	Mine eyes, when she is named,	
	Cannot forget their tribute, and your gift	
	Is not unuseful now.	
	[*Wipes his eyes with the handkerchief.*]	
Lacure.	[*Aside*] He's past all cure:	
	That only touch is death.	
Thierry.	This night I'll keep it.	

246. SD] *this edn; not in Q1.* 247. Revenged] *F2;* Reuenge *Q1.* 248. SD1] *Dyce; not in Q1.* SD2] *Dyce; not in Q1.* 249. SD] *this edn; not in Q1.* 251.1. SD] *Weber (subst); not in Q1.* 256. SD] *this edn; not in Q1.* 258–61. Is ... cure: | That ... it. | Tomorrow ... full | Of ... mortal?] *Colman; Q1 lines* Is ... now. | He's ... death. | This ... it. | To morrow ... affliction. | Is ... mortall? 258. SD1] *Turner (subst); not in Q1.* SD2] *Turner; not in Q1.*

---

245. *protean*] changing, unpredictable.
249. *refuge*] resort.
250. *Insensible*] incapable of feeling or emotion.
252. *which*] who.
253–4. *thy ... That*] the cause of grief and sad repentance of you, who.
258. *unuseful*] useless.

Tomorrow I will send it you, and full	260
Of my affliction. *Exit.*	
Brunehaut. [*To* LACURE] Is the poison mortal?	
Lacure. Above the help of physic.	
Brunehaut. To my wish. —	
Now, for our own security, you, Protaldi,	
Shall this night post towards Austrasia	
With letters to Theodoret's bastard son,	265
In which we will make known what for his rising	
We have done to Thierry. — No denial	
Nor no excuse in such acts must be thought of,	
Which all dislike, and all again commend,	
When they are brought unto a happy end. *Exeunt.*	270

---

261. SD2] *this edn; not in Q1.*

---

261. *affliction*] i.e., tears.
262. *physic*] medical treatment or medical science.
264. *Austrasia*] pronounced as four syllables.
265. *Theodoret's ... son*] Cf. Grimeston, sig. D4ᵛ: 'of four bastard sons which Thierry had left, he chooseth him that pleaseth her best to install him king in his father's place'. The historical accounts mention *Thierry*'s bastard sons, not *Theodoret*'s. The change probably depends on the fact that alluding to Thierry's (historically attested) extramarital sexual relationships would have detracted from the highly virtuous depiction of his love for and devotion to Ordella.
266. *for ... rising*] to prepare the ground for his ascent to the throne.
267–70. *No ... end*] Brunehaut's closing words closely echo Machiavelli, *Prince*, 62: 'In the actions of all men, and especially of princes, where there is no tribunal to which to appeal, one must consider the final result. Therefore, let a prince conquer and maintain the state, and his methods will always be judged honourable and praised by all. For ordinary people are always taken in by appearances and by the outcome of an event.' On Massinger as 'a serious student of Machiavelli', see Gill. The passage is excerpted in Cotgrave, sig. S7ʳ, with the addition at the end of the half line 'Such powers has success', which is nowhere to be found in either Q1 or Q2. Its being part of another (lost) version of the play-text is suspect, given that it comes after the rhyming couplet that closes the speech and the scene, and it rather has the ring of a marginal comment by Cotgrave that was then rationalized as part of the quotation in the printing shop.

ACT 5

SCENE 1

Enter DE VITRY *and four* Soldiers.

de Vitry. No war, no money, no master; banished the court, not trusted in the city, whipped out of the country: in what a triangle runs our misery! Let me hear which of you has the best voice to beg in, for other hopes or fortunes I see you have not. Be not nice; nature provided 5 you with tongues for the purpose. The people's charity was your heritage, and I would see which of you deserves his birthright.
All Soldiers. We understand you not, captain.

SCENE 1] *Q1* (Act. 5. Scoe. 1). 6. tongues] *Turner;* tones *Q1.* 9. SP *All Soldiers*] *this edn; Omnes Q1.*

5.1.0.] I assign this scene to Field. Weber adds the setting: '*Night. A forest*'. As noted by McKeithan (148–9), the scene seems indebted to *1H4* 2.2. See Introduction, 16–17.

3. *triangle*] the one formed by 'court', 'city', and 'country', the three points of reference of the early modern economy and society.

our misery] The depiction of the plight of impoverished soldiers in peacetime is recurrent in the Fletcher canon, also appearing in *KNoK, Capt, Val, MadL, Loyal, SJVOB,* and *FalseO.*

6. *tongues*] Q1's 'tones' may seem acceptable in the sense of 'a particular quality, pitch, modulation, or inflection of the voice expressing or indicating affirmation, interrogation, hesitation, decision, or some feeling or emotion; vocal expression' (*OED* n. 5a), but *OED* cites only one instance as early as 1610 and nothing again until 1689; none of the cognate senses (5b–d) has anything earlier than 1680. Moreover 'tones' in the plural seems to be relatively rare: 5a cites no plural instances at all; 5b cites one from 1680. Hence, this would be a modern and distinctive usage, which has made me accept Turner's emendation.

7. *heritage*] 'that which comes from the circumstances of birth' (*OED* n. 4).

9. SP All Soldiers] Probably one soldier speaks, others indicate agreement (see Honigmann, 120–3).

de Vitry. You see this cardecu, the last and the only quintes- 10
sence of fifty crowns, distilled in the limbeck of your
guardage, of which happy piece thou shalt be treasurer.
[*Gives it to* 1 Soldier.] Now, he that can soonest persuade
him to part with't enjoys it, possesses it and, with it, me
and my future countenance. 15
1 Soldier. If they want art to persuade it, I'll keep it myself.
de Vitry. So you be not a partial judge in your own cause, you
shall.
All Soldiers. A match.
2 Soldier. [*To* 1 Soldier] I'll begin to you, brave sir. Be proud 20
to make him happy by your liberality, whose tongue
vouchsafes now to petition, was never heard before less
than to command. I am a soldier by profession, a gentleman by birth and an officer by place, whose poverty
blushes to be the cause that so high a virtue should 25
descend to the pity of your charity.
1 Soldier. In any case, keep your high style; it is not charity to
shame any man, much less a virtue of your eminence;
wherefore, preserve your worth, and I'll preserve my
money. 30
3 Soldier. [*To* 2 Soldier] You persuade? You are shallow;
give way to merit. [*To* 1 Soldier] Ah, by the bread of
God, man, thou hast a bonny countenance and a blithe,

---

13. SD] *Dyce; not in Q1.*   19. SP *All Soldiers*] *this edn; Omnes Q1.*   20.
SD] *this edn; not in Q1.*   you, brave sir. Be] *Q1 (subst);* you: Brave Sir, be
1711.   31. SD] *this edn; not in Q1.*   32. SD] *this edn; not in Q1.*   32-3. of
God, man] *Colman;* of a good man *F2;* of good man *Q1.*

---

10. *cardecu*] see 2.1.228.
11. *limbeck*] alembic, an early chemical apparatus used in distilling.
12. *guardage*] keeping, guardianship.
15. *countenance*] patronage, favour.
16. *want art*] lack skill.
17. *So*] as long as.
22. *vouchsafes*] condescends.
petition] ask humbly.
was] which was.
31. *shallow*] lacking argumentative depth.
33. *bonny*] jovial, smiling.
blithe] jocund, merry.

promising mickle good to a sicker womb that has trod a
long and a sore ground to meet with friends that will owe 35
much to thy reverence when they shall hear a thy courtesy
to their wandering countryman.

1 Soldier. You, that will use your friends so hardly to bring
them in debt, sir, will deserve worse of a stranger; wherefore, pad on. Pad on, I say! 40

4 Soldier. It is the Welsh must do't, I see. [*To* 1 Soldier]
Comrade, man of 'orship, Saint Tavy be her patron; the
gods of the mountains keep her cow and her cupboard;
may she never want the green of the leek nor the fat of
the onion if she part with her bounties to him that is a 45
great deal away from her cousins and has two big suits
in law to recover her heritage.

---

36. a] *Q1;* of *Q2.*   40. on¹] *Q2;* one *Q1.*   41. SD] *this edn; not in Q1.*

---

34. *mickle*] much.
sicker womb] stomach free from harm or danger.
38. *hardly*] hardily, harshly.
40. *pad on*] keep on walking, probably with a slight suggestion of practis-
ing highway robbery (cf. *OED,* v.1 5).
41. *It ... do't*] Brown (107) remarks that 'the English saw the Welsh as
disproportionately engaged in begging'.
42. *'orship*] worship. 4 Soldier speaks with a Welsh accent. Here, it is
conveyed through the omission of the initial consonant of the word (/w/).
This also occurs in *Pilgrim* 4.3.71: 'Pox o' thy 'orship!'
Saint Tavy] Saint Davy, David, the patron saint of Wales. 4 Soldier's Welsh
provenance is in this case signalled by having the voiced consonant /d/ lose
its voicing (i.e., become /t/).
her] 4 Soldier uses 'her' (ll. 42, 43, 67, and 47) and 'she' (ll. 43 and 45)
multiple times for the masculine singular pronoun. This is another linguistic
marker associated with Welshness. See Brown, 107.
44–5. *leek ... onion*] stereotypically associated with Welsh people at the
time. The leek is still a national emblem of Wales.
46. *cousins*] As E. Wyn James (pers. comm.) observes, the love of geneal-
ogy was another stereotypical trait associated with Welshness in the early
modern period. I am grateful to E. Wyn James for his help.
46–7. *has ... heritage*] 'The Welsh existed under a system of law which did
not recognize primogeniture, as did the English system. Indeed, only in the
sixteenth century did English law, following the incorporation of Wales,
declare partible inheritance in Wales illegal [through the Laws in Wales Acts,
also known as the Acts of Union]. The division of property among all the
sons (and sometimes daughters) seemed barbaric to the English. The Welsh
were in a transition between Welsh law and the newly imposed English law,
a transition that led to suits among heirs leading to increased litigation in
Wales' (Brown, 221–2).

1 Soldier. Pardon me, sir, I will have nothing to do with your
suits: it comes within the statute of maintenance. Home
to your cousins, and sow garlic and hempseed: the one   50
will stop your hunger, the other end your suits. *Gammawash,* comrade, *gammawash!*
4 Soldier. 'Foot, he'll hoard all for himself.
de Vitry. Yes, let him. Now comes my turn. I'll see if he can
answer me. [*To* 1 *Soldier*] Save you, sir! They say you   55
have that I want, money.
1 Soldier. And that you are like to want, for aught I perceive
yet.
de Vitry. Stand, deliver!
1 Soldier. 'Foot, what mean you? You will not rob the   60
exchequer?
de Vitry. Do you prate?   [*Threatens him.*]
1 Soldier. Hold, hold! Here, captain. [*Gives him the cardecu.*]
2 Soldier. Why, I could have done this before you.
3 Soldier. And I   65
4 Soldier. And I.

---

55. SD] *this edn; not in Q1.* 62. SD] *Turner; not in Q1.* 63. SD] *Dyce (subst); not in Q1.*

---

49. *it ... maintenance*] i.e., helping your suit would fall under the category of what the law forbids as 'maintenance', that is, 'the action of wrongfully aiding and abetting litigation; spec. support of a suit or suitor at law by a party who has no legally recognized interest in the proceedings' (*OED* n. 1a).

51. *end ... suits*] because hemp might be used to make both stout clothes (i.e., suits) and a rope with which the Welsh soldier might hang himself (and thus put an end to his lawsuits).

51-2. Gammawash] '[a] corruption, I suppose, of some Welsh word or words' (Dyce). David Willis (pers. comm.) suggests that this might merely be intended as gibberish Welsh, but it could also be a distortion of 'cymer watsh', literally translated as 'take watch' (i.e., on your guard, stand guard), 'watsh' being a fifteenth-century loan from English. I am grateful to David Willis for his help.

53. *'Foot*] See 3.2.103.
57. *like*] likely.
  aught] all.
59. *Stand, deliver*] 'a highwayman's order to his victim' (*OED* stand v. 4b).
62. *prate*] prattle.
SD] de Vitry probably threatens 1 Soldier with a weapon, which would explain why 1 Soldier concedes so quickly.

SC 1]   THIERRY AND THEODORET   175

de Vitry. You have done this? 'Brave man, be proud to make
    him happy'? 'By the bread of God, man, thou hast a
    bonny countenance'? 'Comrade, man of 'orship, Saint
    Tavy be her patron'? Out upon you! You uncurried colts,   70
    walking cans that have no souls in you but a little rosin
    to keep your ribs sweet and hold in liquor!
All Soldiers. Why, what would you have us to do, captain?
de Vitry. Beg, beg, and keep constables waking, wear out
    stocks and whipcord, maunder for buttermilk, die of the   75
    jaundice yet have the cure about you, lice, large lice, begot
    of your own dust and the heat of the brick kilns; may you
    starve, and fear of the gallows (which is a gentle con-
    sumption to't) only prefer it; or may you fall upon your
    fear and be hanged for selling those purses to keep you   80
    from famine whose monies my valour empties, and be
    cast without other evidence. Here is my fort, my castle of

---

68. of God, man] *Colman;* of a gode Man *Seward;* of God man *Q2;* of god man *Q1.* 73. SP *All Soldiers*] *this edn;* Omnes *Q1.*

---

70. *Out upon*] curses upon.
uncurried colts] ungroomed young horses, i.e., inexperienced people.
71–2. *walking ... liquor*] 'The metaphor is here taken from the old English blackjacks [i.e., black leather jerkins], made almost in the shape of a boot ... they were stiffened leather lined with rosin [i.e., a kind of resin], from whence a stiffened boot is called a jackboot' (Seward).
74–5. *constables ... whipcord*] Begging being illegal, beggars suffered repeatedly at the hands of the law in early modern England.
75. *whipcord*] a 'thin tough kind of hempen cord, of which whiplashes or the ends of them are made; in allusive use, the material of whiplashes' (*OED* n. 1a).
maunder] beg (cant).
75–6. *die ... lice*] Lice were considered a cure for jaundice. Cf. Thomson, Ὀρθομέθοδος, 124: 'Lice swallowed alive diminisheth (as is confirmed by some experimentally) the tincture of the jaundice'; Schröder, 154: '[Lice] are swallowed of country people against the jaundice.'
77. *brick kilns*] furnaces for baking bricks.
78–9. *consumption*] destruction.
79. *to't*] i.e., compared to it.
prefer] This verb 'is all right here, in the sense of "recommend" (*OED* [v. 9]). Starving will be recommended to the soldiers only by their fear of hanging, which', says [de Vitry], 'is really the easier death' (Turner).
81. *whose*] The antecedent is 'those purses' on the same line.
82. *cast*] condemned, convicted.

defence. Who comes by shall pay me toll; the first purse
is your *mittimus*, slaves.
2 Soldier. The purse? 'Foot, we'll share in the money, captain, 85
if any come within a furlong of our fingers.
4 Soldier. Did you doubt but we could steal as well as yourself?
Did not I speak Welsh?
3 Soldier. We are thieves from our cradles and will die so.
de Vitry. Then you will not beg again? 90
All Soldiers. Yes, as you did: 'stand and deliver!'
2 Soldier. Hark, here comes handsel. 'Tis a trade quickly set
up and as soon cast down.
de Vitry. Have goodness in your minds, varlets, and to't like
men. He that has more money than we cannot be our 95
friend, and I hope there is no law for spoiling the enemy.
3 Soldier. You need not instruct us farther: your example
pleads enough.
de Vitry. Disperse yourselves and, as their company is, fall on.
2 Soldier. Come there a band of 'em, I'll charge single. 100

Exeunt Soldiers.
[DE VITRY *withdraws.*]

Enter PROTALDI.

91. SP *All Soldiers*] *this edn; Omnes Q1.* 100. Come there a band of
'em] *conj Mason;* Come, there are a band of em *Q1.* 100.1. SD] *Seward;
Exe. Soldiers. 1711; Exit souldiers. Q1.* 100.2. SD] *Turner; not in Q1.*

---

84. *mittimus*] dismissal, notice to quit.
86. *furlong*] an eighth of a mile, 660 feet, 220 yards, or approximately 201 metres.
87–8. *Did ... Welsh?*] drawing upon the anti-Welsh racist trope circulating in sixteenth- and seventeenth-century England according to which being Welsh was tantamount to being a beggar come to the city to escape rural poverty, or even a thief.
91. *stand and deliver*] See 5.1.59.
92. *handsel*] 'first instalment of payment; earnest money; (also) the first money taken by a trader in the morning' (*OED* n. 4).
96. *no law*] i.e., 'no punishment by law' (Mason).
spoiling] robbing.
98. *pleads*] states the case.
99. *as ... is*] depending on their number.

Protaldi. 'Tis wonderful dark. I have lost my man and dare
    not call for him, lest I should have more followers than I
    would pay wages to. What throes am I in in this travel?
    These be honourable adventures. Had I that honest
    blood in my veins again, Queen, that your feats and these   105
    frights have drained from me, honour should pull hard
    ere it drew me into these brakes.
de Vitry. Who goes there?
Protaldi. Heigh-ho! Here's a pang of preferment.
de Vitry. 'Heart, who goes there?   110
Protaldi. [*Aside*] He that has no heart to your acquaintance.
    What shall I do with my jewels and my letters? My cod-
    piece? That's too loose. Good, my boots. [*Puts the jewels
    and the letters in his boots.*] — Who is't that spoke to me?
    Here's a friend.   115
de Vitry. We shall find that presently. Stand, as you love safety,
    stand!

---

103. travel] *F2;* trauaile *Q1.*   111. SD] *Dyce; not in Q1.*   112. letters] *Dyce;*
letter *Q1.*   113–14. SD] *Dyce (subst); not in Q1.*   116. love safety] *Q1;* love
your safety *Q2.*

---

101. *wonderful*] exceedingly.
    dark] The scene takes place at night, and the exceeding darkness is the
reason why Protaldi does not recognize de Vitry. True, de Vitry and the
Soldiers might also be disguised, but the text offers no evidence of this.
Perhaps de Vitry disguises his voice after recognizing Protaldi's at l. 120.
    man] servant.
    102–3. *more ... to*] i.e., thieves.
    104. *be*] are.
    104–5. *that ... blood*] another reference to Protaldi's erections for
Brunehaut.
    107. *these brakes*] this brushwood, this thicket.
    109. *Heigh-ho*] 'an exclamation usually expressing yawning, sighing,
languor, weariness, disappointment' (*OED* int.).
    preferment] advancement, promotion.
    110. *'Heart*] a corruption of 'by (or for) God's heart', a strong oath.
    111. *no heart*] no desire.
    112–13. *codpiece*] See 1.2.101.
    116–20. *Stand ... voice*] CF. *1H4* 2.2.47–9: 'Gadshill. Stand! / Falstaff. So
I do, against my will. / Poins. O, 'tis our setter; I know his voice.'
    116. *Stand*] See 5.1.59.

Protaldi. [*Aside*] That unlucky word of standing has brought me to all this. — Hold, or I shall never stand you.
de Vitry. [*Aside*] I should know that voice. [*To* Soldiers *within*] Deliver!

Enter Soldiers [*again*].

Protaldi. All that I have is at your service, gentlemen, and much good may it do you.
de Vitry. [*To* Soldiers] Zounds, down with him! Do you prate?
Protaldi. Keep your first word, as you are gentlemen, and let me stand. [*They approach him.*] Alas, what do you mean?
2 Soldier. To tie you to us, sir, bind you in the knot of friendship.
[*They bind him.*]
Protaldi. Alas, sir, all the physic in Europe cannot bind me.
de Vitry. You should have jewels about you, stones, precious stones.
1 Soldier. Captain, away! There's company within hearing. If you stay longer, we are surprised.
de Vitry. Let the devil come; I'll pillage this frigate a little better yet.
2 Soldier. 'Foot, we are lost: they are upon us.
de Vitry. Ha, upon us? [*To* PROTALDI] Make the least noise, 'tis thy parting gasp.

---

118. SD] *Dyce; not in Q1.*   120. SD1] *Turner; not in Q1.*   SD2] *this edn; not in Q1.*   121.1. SD] *Dyce (subst); Enter souldiers Q1.*   124. SD] *this edn; not in Q1.*   126. SD] *this edn; not in Q1.*   128.1. SD] *Dyce (subst); They tie him to a tree. Weber; not in Q1.*   137. SD] *this edn; not in Q1.*

---

118. *standing*] yet another reference to Protaldi's erections for Brunehaut.
119. *stand*] put up with, tolerate.
124. *Zounds*] a corruption of '(by) God's wounds', a very powerful and transgressive oath 'that had a similar force to bodily oaths in twenty-first-century English' (Munro, "Sblood!', 133).
Do you prate?] Do you prattle? This question might be addressed to Protaldi, but de Vitry is more probably inciting the Soldiers, who seem to be hesitating a little and do not get close to Protaldi until l. 126 ('Alas, what do you mean?')
129. *physic*] medicines.
130. *about you*] on you, in your pockets.
134. *frigate*] merchantman (*OED* n. 2a).

SC I]   THIERRY AND THEODORET   179

3 Soldier. Which way shall we make, sir?
de Vitry. Every man his own. [*Aside to* Soldiers] Do you hear? 140
    Only bind me before you go and, when the company's
    past, make to this place again. This carvel should have
    better lading in him. [*They bind him.*] You are slow, why
    do you not tie harder?
1 Soldier. [*Aside to him*] You are sure enough, I warrant you, 145
    sir.
de Vitry. [*Aside to them*] Darkness befriend you. Away!
                                                          Exeunt Soldiers.
Protaldi. What tyrants have I met with? They leave me alone
    in the dark, yet would not have me cry. I shall grow won-
    drous melancholy if I stay long here without company. I 150
    was wont to get a nap with saying my prayers; I'll see if
    they will work upon me now. But then, if I should talk in
    my sleep and they hear me, they would make a recorder
    of my windpipe, slit my throat. Heaven be praised: I hear
    some noise. It may be new purchase, and then I shall have 155
    fellows.
de Vitry. [*Aside*] They are gone past hearing. Now to task, de
    Vitry! — Help! Help! As you are men, help! Some chari-
    table hand relieve a poor distressed miserable wretch!
    Thieves, wicked thieves have robbed me, bound me!   160
Protaldi. 'Foot, would they had gagged you too: your noise
    will betray us and fetch 'em again.
de Vitry. What blessed tongue spake to me? Where? Where are
    you, sir?

139. we] *Q2;* she *Q1.*   140. SD] *Turner (subst); not in Q1.*   143. SD] *Dyce (subst); He is tied to a tree. Weber; not in Q1.*   145. SD] *this edn; not in Q1.* 147. SD] *this edn; not in Q1.*   147.1. SD] *1711 (subst); Exit souldiers. Q1.* 157. SD] *Dyce; not in Q1.*

142. *carvel*] the 'ordinary name from the 15th to the 17th cent., of a somewhat small, light, and fast ship, chiefly of Spain and Portugal, but also mentioned as French and English' (*OED* n. 1).
    143. *lading*] freight, cargo.
    145. *sure*] bound fast, unable to escape.
    148. *tyrants*] villains.
    149–50. *wondrous*] to a wonderful degree.
    151. *wont*] accustomed.
    155. *purchase*] booty.
    163. *spake*] spoke.

Protaldi. A plague of your bawling throat! We are well enough   165
   if you have the grace to be thankful for't. Do but snore
   to me, and 'tis as much as I desire to pass away time with
   till morning; then, talk as loud as you please, sir. I am
   bound not to stir, wherefore lie still and snore, I say.
de Vitry. Then you have met with thieves too, I see.   170
Protaldi. And desire to meet with no more of 'em.
de Vitry. Alas! What can we suffer more? They are far enough
   by this time. Have they not all, all that we have, sir?
Protaldi. No, by my faith have they not, sir. I gave 'em one
   trick to boot for their learning: my boots, sir, my boots!   175
   I have saved my stock and my jewels in them, and therefore desire to hear no more of them.
de Vitry. Now blessing on your wit, sir. What a dull slave was
   I dreamt not of your conveyance! Help to unbind me, sir,
   and I'll undo you: my life for yours. No worse thief than   180
   myself meets you again this night.
Protaldi. Reach me thy hands.
de Vitry. Here, sir, here. [PROTALDI *unbinds him.*] I could
   beat my brains out that could not think of boots. Boots,
   sir, wide-top boots! I shall love 'em the better whilst I   185
   live, but are you sure your jewels are here, sir? [*Searches*
   PROTALDI's *boots.*]
Protaldi. Sure, sayst thou? Ha ha ha!
de Vitry. So ho, hillo, ho!
Soldiers (*within*). Here, captain, here!   190

---

183. SD] *Dyce (subst); not in Q1.*   185. wide-top] *Q1;* wide topt *Q2.*   186–
7. SD] *this edn; not in Q1.*   190. SP] *1711 (subst);* Within souldiers *Q1.*

---

   165. *of*] on.
   bawling] 'making loud noise or outcry, vociferating' (*OED* adj. 2).
   175. *to boot*] in addition, with a pun on hiding the jewels in his boot.
   176. *stock*] money.
   178. *dull*] obtuse.
   179. *dreamt*] that dreamt, imagined.
   conveyance] contrivance.
   180. *undo*] unbind, but also ruin.
   189. *hillo*] 'a call used to hail a distant or occupied person' (*OED* int. a).
Cf. *Ham* 1.5.114–15: '*Marcellus.* Illo, ho, ho, my lord! *Hamlet.* Hillo, ho, ho,
boy, come and come!'

Protaldi. 'Foot, what do you mean, sir?

Enter Soldiers [*again*].

de Vitry. A trick to boot, say you? [*Takes the jewels out of* PRO-
TALDI's *boots.*] [*To* Soldiers] Here, you dull slaves: purchase, purchase, the soul of the rock, diamonds, sparkling
diamonds!

Protaldi. [*Aside*] I am betrayed, lost, past recovery lost. — As
you are men —

de Vitry. Nay, rook, since you will be prating, we'll share your
carrion with you. Have you any other conveyance now,
sir?

1 Soldier. [*Taking the letters out of* PROTALDI's *boots*] 'Foot,
here are letters, epistles, familiar epistles! We'll see what
treasure is in them; they are sealed sure.

[*Gives the letters to* DE VITRY.]

Protaldi. Gentlemen, as you are gentlemen, spare my letters
and take all willingly, all. I'll give you a release, a general
release, and meet you here tomorrow with as much more.

de Vitry. Nay, since you have your tricks and your conveyances, we will not leave a wrinkle of you unsearched.

Protaldi. Hark, there comes company! You will be betrayed.
As you love your safeties, beat out my brains; I shall
betray you else.

[DE VITRY *reads the letters.*]

de Vitry. Treason! Unheard-of treason! Monstrous, monstrous
villainies!

Protaldi. I confess myself a traitor. Show yourselves good subjects and hang me up for't.

191.1. SD] *Dyce (subst); Enter souldiers.* Q1. 192–3. SD] *Dyce (subst); not
in Q1.* 193. SD] *this edn; not in Q1.* 196. SD] *Dyce; not in Q1.* 197. men
—] *Colman;* men. Q1. 201. SD] *Dyce (subst); not in Q1.* 203.1. SD] *this
edn; not in Q1.* 211.1. SD] *Weber; not in Q1.*

193–4. *purchase*] spoil, plunder, booty (*OED* n. 8a).
198. *rook*] crow, a derogatory term for a greedy person.
prating] prattling.
199. *conveyance*] cunning device.
203. *sure*] fast, firmly.
205. *release*] 'written discharge or receipt' (*OED* n. 2b)
207–8. *conveyances*] contrivances.

1 *Soldier.* If it be treason, the discovery will get our pardon, captain.
de Vitry. Would we were all lost, hanged, quartered to save this one, one innocent prince. Thierry's poisoned, by his mother poisoned, the mistress to this stallion, who by that 220
poison ne'er shall sleep again.
2 *Soldier.* 'Foot, let us mince him by piecemeal till he eat himself up. [*Strikes* PROTALDI.]
3 *Soldier.* Let us dig out his heart with needles and half-broil him like a mussel. [*Strikes* PROTALDI.] 225
Protaldi. Such another, and I prevent you. My blood's settled already.
de Vitry. Here's that shall remove it. [*Strikes him.*] Toad, viper! [*To* Soldiers] Drag him unto Martel. — Unnatural parricide, cruel, bloody woman! 230
All Soldiers. [*To* PROTALDI] On, you dogfish, leech, caterpillar!
de Vitry. A longer sight of him will make my rage turn pity and, with his sudden end, prevent revenge and torture. Wicked, wicked Brunehaut! *Exeunt.* 235

---

223. SD] *this edn; not in Q1.* 225. SD] *this edn; not in Q1.* 228. SD] *this edn; not in Q1.* 229. SD] *this edn; not in Q1.* 231. SP *All Soldiers*] *this edn; Omnes Q1.* SD] *this edn; not in Q1.* 235. SD] *1711 (subst); Exit. Q1.*

---

220. *stallion*] Cf. Grimeston, sig. D4ʳ: 'and then had she got a young courtier called Protade for a stallion'.
who] The antecedent is 'Thierry' on the preceding line.
226. *Such another*] i.e., such another blow.
prevent you] thwart you by anticipating your actions (i.e., by dying on the spot).
settled] stagnant, coagulated.
228. *Here's ... it*] Here's the blow that shall stir your blood again.
229–30. *parricide*] killer of a near relative.
231. *dogfish*] a kind of small shark, applied opprobriously to a person.
233–4. *A ... torture*] If I see more of him, I'll kill him quickly out of pity, thus saving him from torture (an ironic foreshadowing of the death by torture he will actually suffer).
235. *wicked ... Brunehaut*] Cf. Grimeston, sig. D3ʳ: 'Brunehaut, a subtle and a wicked woman'.

[SCENE 2]

Enter BAWDBERT *and three* Courtiers.

1 Courtier. Not sleep at all, no means?
2 Courtier.   No art can do it?
Bawdbert. I will assure you he can sleep no more
   Than a hooded hawk. A sentinel to him
   Or one of the city constables are tops.
3 Courtier. How came he so?
Bawdbert.   They are too wise that dare know.   5
   Something's amiss. Heaven help all.
1 Courtier.   What cures has he?
Bawdbert. Armies of those we call physicians,
   Some with clysters, some with lettuce caps,

SCENE 2] *Weber; not in Q1.* 7–10. Armies ... physicians, | Some ... caps, | Some ... here | About ... him] *Colman; Q1 lines* Armies ... phisitians, | Some ... pills, | Twenty ... drench, | As ... him.

5.2.0.] Generally held to be a Fletcher scene. Weber adds the setting: 'Paris. A room in the palace'.
  1. *art*] skill.
  3. *hooded*] covered with a hood.
  4. *tops*] sound sleepers (*OED* n.2 1b).
  7. *physicians*] pronounced as four syllables.
  8. *clysters*] see 1.1.171.
lettuce caps] It seems indisputable that the reference here must be to 'a kind of cap supposed to have sleep-inducing properties'; it is not clear, though, 'whether the first element is to be apprehended as an instance of "lettice" or "lettuce". Lettuce was supposed to have a sedative effect ... and the "cap" referred to here may be a lettuce leaf placed on the head of a sleepless patient' (*OED* lettice cap n.). Yet it might also be a net cap, based on Nares (284), who quotes John Minshew's *Spanish Dictionary* to argue that 'a *lettice-cap* was originally a *lattice-cap*, that is, a net cap, which resembles *lattice* work, often spelt lettice'. Dyce is adamant that it must be a 'lettuce' cap: 'That the lettuce caps in our text mean certain applications of the plant lettuce, as a soporific, to the head of the patient, is, I think, evident.' He cites Parkinson: 'Galen showeth that the eating of boiled lettuce at night when he went to bed procured him rest and sleep ... the same is found effectual also with ... the juice thereof mixed or boiled with oil of roses and applied to the forehead and temples, both to procure rest and sleep and to ease the head-ache of any hot cause' (812). On balance, I think 'lettuce' is more likely than 'lettice'. Cf. also *Monsieur* 3.1.9–10: 'Bring in the lettuce cap: you must be shaved, sir, / And then how suddenly we'll make you sleep.'

    Some posset drinks, some pills, twenty consulting here
    About a drench, as many here to blood him.   10
    Then comes a Don of Spain, and he prescribes
    More cooling opium than would kill a Turk
    Or quench a whore i'th' dog days; after him,
    A wise Italian, and he cries: 'Tie unto him
    A woman of fourscore whose bones are marble,   15
    Whose blood snow water, not so much heat about her
    As may conceive a prayer'; after him,
    An English doctor, with a bunch of pot-herbs,
    And he cries out: 'Endive and succory,
    With a few mallow roots and buttermilk',   20

---

    9. *posset drinks*] drinks 'made from hot milk curdled with ale, wine, or other liquor, flavoured with sugar, herbs, spices, etc., and often drunk for medicinal purposes' (*OED* n. 1)

    10. *drench*] 'a medicinal, soporific, or poisonous draught' (*OED* n. 2)

    12. *opium ... Turk*] Early modern Europeans commonly believed Turks to be avid consumers of opium. Cf., e.g., Sala, 11: 'the Turks eat thereof [i.e., of opium] in great quantity almost every day ordinarily without any mischance or hurt to their bodies at all'; 12: 'But why the Turks devour opium on this fashion ought rather to be imputed unto an ordinary custom and common usage among them than to any other cause whatsoever'; 6–7: 'To eat opium in Turkey is no new thing, and the reason why it is used so amongst them is because they persuade themselves that it maketh them more adventurous and less fearful of dangers in war, so that when the Turk assembleth or mustereth any great army together, they make such havoc of their opium that they almost disfurnish the whole country.'

    13. *dog days*] the hottest days of summer, once deemed to be the least healthy period of the year.

    15. *fourscore*] eighty.

    19. *Endive and succory*] two herbs that were widely used for their therapeutic properties in the early modern period (succory being today better known as chicory). They were considered beneficial for a variety of ailments. They were believed, among other things, to 'comfort the weak and feeble stomach', to 'cool and refresh the hot stomach', to stop 'the lask or flux of the belly proceeding of a hot cause', to be 'good for the heat of the liver against the jaundice, and hot fevers, and tertians', to give relief to 'hot inflammations and impostumes, or gathering together of evil humours of the stomach, the trembling or shaking of the heart, the hot gout'; in particular, they were thought to mitigate 'the great inflammation of the eyes, being laid outwardly to the places of the griefs', while 'the juice of the[ir] leaves ... laid to the forehead with oil of roses and vinegar' would 'suage headache' (Dodoens, 3Avi^(r-v)), two uses that are compatible with Thierry's sufferings in the play.

And talks of oil made of a churchman's charity.
Yet still he wakes.
1 Courtier.   But your good honour has a prayer in store
If all should fail?
Bawdbert.   I could have prayed, and handsomely,
But age and an ill memory —
3 Courtier.   Has spoiled your primer.   25
Bawdbert. Yet if there be a man of faith i'the court,
And can pray for a pension —

Enter THIERRY, *on a bed, with* Doctors *and* Attendants.

2 Courtier.   Here's the King, sir,
And those that will pray without pay.
Bawdbert.   Then pray for me too.

23–4. But … store | If … handsomely] *Turner; Q1 lines* But … honor | Has … faile. | I … handsomely. 23. prayer] *Q2;* prayers *Q1.* 25. memory —] *1711;* memory. *Q1.* 26. i'the] *Q1;* i'th' *Q2.* 27. pension —] *Colman;* pension. *Q1.*

---

21. *oil … charity*] possibly a reference to an actual herbal decoction known as 'the oil of charity'. Cf. Woolley, C3ʳ⁻ᵛ: 'Take rosemary, sage, lavender, camomile, the lesser valerian, of each one handful; cut them small and put them into oil olive; let it be very thick with the herbs; let it infuse seven days in the sun; then take the glass wherein they are, and wind about the bottom a little hay, and set it into a kettle of seething water, and let it stand two hours; then strain it out and put in herbs, and do as before; so do three times; then put in valerian alone and do as before; then strain it and let the oil settle. Keep the clearest for Christians and the grounds and herbs for beasts.'

22. *wakes*] remains awake.

25. *ill*] bad.
primer] prayer book.

27. SD *on a bed*] In the early modern playhouses, beds would presumably have been brought on stage through the larger central stage door rather than the two flanking doors. It is striking that of the four King's Men plays that Walkley published in 1619–22, as many as three (i.e., all of them except for *Philaster*) feature crucial bed-scenes, the others being those in *Oth* 5.2 and *MT* 5.2. For an excellent study providing an informed and useful array of possible solutions regarding the potential staging of bed scenes, as well as the types of beds that might have been employed, in the early modern commercial theatre, see Thomson, 'Beds'. The canon of Fletcher and his collaborators offers at least two more scenes with sick men attended by physicians, namely *Monsieur* 3.1 and *Val* 5.2.

1 Doctor. How does your grace now feel yourself?
Thierry.   What's that?
1 Doctor. Nothing at all, sir, but your fancy.
Thierry.   Tell me,   30
   Can ever these eyes more, shut up in slumbers,
   Assure my soul there is sleep? Is there night
   And rest for human labours? Do not you
   And all the world, as I do, outstare time
   And live like funeral lamps, never extinguished?   35
   Is there a grave — and do not flatter me
   Nor fear to tell me truth — and in that grave
   Is there a hope I shall sleep? Can I die?
   Are not my miseries immortal? Oh,
   The happiness of him that drinks his water   40
   After his weary day and sleeps forever!
   Why do you crucify me thus with faces,
   And gaping strangely upon one another?
   When shall I rest?
2 Doctor.   O sir, be patient.
Thierry. Am I not patient? Have I not endured   45
   More than a mangy dog among your doses?
   Am I not now your patient? Ye can make
   Unwholesome fools sleep for a guarded foot-cloth,

---

29. *What's that?*] Prolonged lack of sleep is making Thierry hallucinate.
39. *immortal*] everlasting.
43. *upon*] at.
44. *patient*] pronounced as three syllables.
45–53.] Cf. *Val* 5.2.48–54: 'What can your doses now do, and your scrapings, / Your oils and mithridates? If I do die, / You only words of health, and names of sickness / Finding no true disease in man but money, / That talk yourselves into revenues – O! – / And ere ye kill your patients beggar 'em, / I'll have ye flayed and dried.'
47–50. *Ye ... ye*] I nourish you, I protect you, I take care of you benevolently and yet you cannot help me now, whereas you are usually able to cure 'Unwholesome fools' and 'Whores' – despite their wickedness, their immorality – because they pay you with valuable (possibly stolen) goods or with sex.
48. *Unwholesome*] morally corrupted.
   a ... foot-cloth] 'a large ... cloth, considered as a mark of dignity and state and laid over the back of a horse so as to hang down to the ground on each side' (*OED* 'footcloth' n. 2), which was richly 'ornamented, as with lace, braid, embroidery, etc' (*OED* 'guarded' adj. 3a).

> Whores for a hot sin offering, yet I must crave,
> That feed ye and protect ye and proclaim ye. 50
> Because my power is far above your searching,
> Are my diseases so? Can ye cure none
> But those of equal ignorance? Dare ye kill me?

1 Doctor. We do beseech your grace be more reclaimed:
   This talk doth but distemper you.
Thierry.   Well, I will die 55
   In spite of all your potions. One of you sleep,
   Lie down and sleep here, that I may behold
   What blessèd rest it is my eyes are robbed of.
                           [*An* Attendant *lies down.*]
   See, he can sleep, sleep anywhere, sleep now,
   When he that wakes for him can never slumber. 60
   Is't not a dainty ease?
2 Doctor.   Your grace shall feel it.
Thierry. Oh, never I, never! The eyes of heaven
   See but their certain motions, and then sleep;
   The rages of the ocean have their slumbers
   And quiet silver calms; each violence 65
   Crowns in his end a peace, but my fixed fires
   Shall never, never set. Who's that?

   Enter MARTEL, BRUNEHAUT, DE VITRY [*and*] Soldiers.

Martel.   [*To* BRUNEHAUT] No, woman,
   Mother of mischief, no. The day shall die first,
   And all good things live in a worse than thou art,

58.1. SD] *Dyce; not in Q1.*   67. SD2] *this edn; not in Q1.*

---

49. *crave*] beg.
50. *proclaim*] declare officially (to be doctors).
51. *searching*] inquisitive abilities.
54. *reclaimed*] The expression is taken from falconry: to reclaim a hawk means to call it or bring it back (*OED* v. 1a).
55. *distemper*] trouble, vex.
60. *he*] i.e., Thierry.
   wakes] remains awake.
61. *dainty ease*] delightful absence of pain.
66. *fixed fires*] eyes constantly open.
68. *Mother of mischief*] one of several alliterative insults to Brunehaut in the last scene. Cf. 5.2.89, 191.
69. *in a worse*] i.e., in a worse state.

   Ere thou shalt sleep. Dost thou see him?
Brunehaut.   Yes, and curse him, 70
 And all that love him, fool, and all live by him.
Martel. Why art thou such a monster?
Brunehaut.   Why art thou
 So tame a knave to ask me?
Martel.   Hope of hell,
 By this fair holy light and all his wrongs,
 Which are above thy years, almost thy vices, 75
 Thou shalt not rest, not feel more what is pity,
 Know nothing necessary, meet no society
 But what shall curse and crucify thee, feel in thyself
 Nothing but what thou art, bane and bad conscience,
 Till this man rest; but for whose reverence, 80
 Because thou art his mother (I would say
 'Whore'), this shall be — Do ye nod? I'll waken ye
 With my sword's point.   [*Jabs her.*]
Brunehaut.   I wish no more of heaven
 Nor hope no more but a sufficient anger
 To torture thee.
Martel.   See she that makes you see, sir, 85
 And to your misery still see, your mother,
 The mother of your woes, sir, of your waking,
 The mother of your people's cries and curses,
 Your murdering mother, your malicious mother.
Thierry. Physicians, half my state to sleep an hour now. — 90
 Is it so, mother?
Brunehaut.   Yes, it is so, son.

---

82. be —] *Turner;* be, *Q1.* 83. SD] *this edn; not in Q1.* 86. misery still see, your] *Q1;* misery, still see your *Colman.*

---

 70. *him*] i.e., Thierry.
 77. *society*] people.
 79. *bane*] that which causes death or ruin.
 82. *waken*] wake up.
 85. *she ... see*] she that gave birth to you (and so gave you all your senses, including sight).
 86. *still see*] be tormented with this state of non-sleep in which you cannot stop keeping your eyes open, to which Brunehaut has condemned you.
 87. *waking*] inability to sleep.
 89. *malicious*] full of hate, wicked.

  And, were it yet again to do, it should be.
Martel. [*To* Soldiers] She nods again; swinge her.
            [*They strike her.*]
Thierry.   But mother
  (For yet I love that reverence and to death
  Dare not forget you have been so), was this —   95
  This endless misery, this cureless malice,
  This snatching from me all my youth together,
  All that you made me for and happy mothers
  Crowned with eternal time are proud to finish —
  Done by your will?
Brunehaut.   It was, and by that will —   100
Thierry. O mother, do not lose your name, forget not
  The touch of nature in you, tenderness:
  'Tis all the soul of woman, all the sweetness.
  Forget not, I beseech you, what are children,
  Nor how you have groaned for 'em, to what love   105
  They are born inheritors, with what care kept,
  And, as they rise to ripeness, still remember
  How they imp out your age; and, when time calls you,
  That as an autumn flower you fall, forget not
  How round about your hearse they hang like pennons. 110
Brunehaut. Holy fool,
  Whose patience to prevent my wrongs has killed thee,
  Preach not to me of punishments or fears,
  Or what I ought to be, but what I am,
  A woman in her liberal will defeated,   115

---

93. SD1] *this edn; not in Q1.* swinge] *this edn;* swing *Q1.* SD2] *this edn; not in Q1.*   100. will —] *1711;* will. *Q1.*   105. have] *Bodleian;* are *Q1.*

---

 92. *were ... do*] should it be done again.
 93. *swinge*] thrash.
 102. *touch*] influence, trace.
 108. *How ... age*] '[a]nother metaphor from falconry. To imp a hawk is to insert feathers in his wings where he had been deprived of them in fighting with other birds' (Weber).
 110. *pennons*] 'long narrow triangular or swallow-tailed flag[s], usually attached to the head of a lance or a helmet, originally the ensign[s] of a knight under the rank of banneret, and later the military ensign[s] of lancer regiments' (*OED* n. 1a).
 112. *patience*] effort, perseverance.
 115. *liberal*] unrestrained by prudence or decorum.

    In all her greatness crossed, in pleasure blasted.
    My angers have been laughed at, my ends slighted,
    And all those glories that had crowned my fortunes
    Suffered by blasted virtue to be scattered.
    I am the fruitful mother of these angers,   120
    And what such have done read, and know thy ruin.
Thierry. Heaven forgive you.
Martel. She tells you true, for millions of her mischiefs
    Are now apparent. Protaldi we have taken
    An equal agent with her, to whose care,   125
    After the damned defeat on you, she trusted

                Enter Messenger.

    The bringing in of Leonor, the bastard
    Son to your murdered brother. Her physician
    By this time is attached too, that damned devil.
Messenger. 'Tis like he will be so, for ere we came,   130
    Fearing an equal justice for his mischiefs,
    He drenched himself.
Brunehaut.   He did like one of mine, then.
Thierry. Must I still see these miseries? No night
    To hide me from their horrors? — That Protaldi
    See justice fall upon.
Brunehaut.   Now I could sleep too.   135

---

    129. too, that] *Mason;* to that *Q1*.   132. then] *Q2;* thine *Q1*.

---

    126. *defeat on you*] ruin of you that she brought about.
    127. *bringing in*] accession.
    127–8. *Leonor ... brother*] See 4.2.265. The bastard sons of Thierry are unnamed in Grimeston. The name Leonor (a female name) is the playwrights' invention and might be intended obliquely to recall Concino Concini's wife, Leonora Dori Galigai. See Introduction, 15.
    128. *Her physician*] i.e., Lacure.
    129. *attached*] seized by legal authority (*OED* v. 1a). *OED* mistakenly quotes this example under heading 8a ('To join in sympathy, affection, or partiality *to* a person, place, etc.; to connect or attract intellectually or emotionally *to*. Usually in *passive*'). The mistake arises from the misunderstanding of the adverb 'too' as the preposition 'to'.
    130. *like*] likely.
    131. *equal*] impartial.
    132. *drenched*] drowned.

Martel. [*To* THIERRY] I'll give you yet more poppy.
                      [*To* Attendant] Bring the lady,
  And heaven in her embraces give him quiet.
                               [*Exit* Attendant.]

    Enter [*an* Attendant, *again, with*] ORDELLA [*veiled*].

  [*To* ORDELLA] Madam, unveil yourself.   [*She unveils.*]
Ordella.   [*To* BRUNEHAUT] I do forgive you.
  And, though you sought my blood, yet I'll pray for you.
Brunehaut. Art thou alive?
Martel.   Now could you sleep?
Brunehaut.   Forever.   140
Martel. [*To* Soldiers] Go, carry her without wink of sleep or
    quiet
  Where her strong knave Protaldi's broke o'th' wheel,
  And let his cries and roars be music to her,
  I mean, to waken her.
Thierry.   Do her no wrong.
Martel. No, right as you love justice.
Brunehaut.   I will think,   145
  And, if there be new curses in old nature,

---

136. SD1] *this edn; not in Q1.* SD2] *this edn; not in Q1.* 137.1. SD] *this edn; not in Q1.* 137.2. SD] *Dyce (subst); placed here Weber; Enter Ordella. following line 135 Q1.* 138. SD1] *this edn; not in Q1.* SD2] *Dyce (subst); not in Q1.* SD3] *this edn; not in Q1.* 141. SD] *this edn; not in Q1.* 145. No, right] *Weber;* Nor right *Q1.*

136–84. *Bring ... honour*] The sequence in which Martel presents Ordella to Thierry directly recuperates the theatregram of the veiled revenant woman from Euripides' *Alcestis*, together with aspects of the surprise reunion between Leontes and Hermione in *WT* 5.2 and the Lear–Cordelia reconciliation towards the end of *KL* 4.7. The structural trope of a grieving husband's acceptance of a veiled woman who turns out to be his allegedly dead wife reappears in *Malta* 5.2.88–147. See Introduction, 18–28, and Lovascio, 'Unveiling Wives'.
   136. *poppy*] known for its narcotic properties.
   141. *wink of sleep*] 'a (short) spell of sleep' (*OED* wink n.1 1a).
   142. *strong*] The adjective qualifies 'knave', not Protaldi. He is described as the resolute or steadfast (*OED* adj. 3) knave. Given that the play has shown Protaldi not to be particularly strong, this is also sarcastic.
   broke] broken.
   144. *waken her*] keep her awake.

  I have a soul dare send 'em.
Martel.   [*To* Soldiers] Keep her waking.
     Exit BRUNEHAUT [*guarded by* Soldiers].
Thierry. What's that appears so sweetly? There's that face —
Martel. [*To* ORDELLA] Be moderate, lady.
Thierry.   That angel's face —
Martel.   [*To her*] Go nearer.
Thierry. Martel, I cannot last long. See the soul   150
  (I see it perfectly) of my Ordella,
  The heavenly figure of her sweetness there. —
  Forgive me, gods! It comes! [*To her*] Divinest
    substance! —
  Kneel, kneel, kneel everyone! [*To her*] Saint of thy sex,
  If it be for my cruelty thou com'st —   155
  Do ye see her, ho?
Martel.   Yes, sir, and you shall know her.
Thierry. Down, down again. [*To* ORDELLA] To be revenged
    for blood,
  Sweet spirit, I am ready. — She smiles on me,
  O blessèd sign of peace.
Martel.   Go nearer, lady.
Ordella. [*To* THIERRY] I come to make you happy.
Thierry.   Hear you that, sirs?   160
  She comes to crown my soul. Away, get sacrifice
  Whilst I with holy honours —
Martel.   She's alive, sir.
Thierry. In everlasting life, I know it, friend.
  O happy, happy soul.
Ordella.   [*Weeping*] Alas, I live, sir,

---

147. SD] *this edn; not in Q1.* 147.1. SD] *Turner (subst); Exit* BRUNHALT *with* Gentleman *and* Guards. *Dyce; Exit* BRUNHALT *with a Guard. Weber; Exit* Brunhalt. *Q1.* 148. sweetly? There's that face —] *Colman;* sweetly there? That face — *conj Heath;* sweetely? there's that face *Q1.* 149. SD1] *this edn; not in Q1.* face —] *Colman;* face. *Q1.* SD2] *this edn; not in Q1.* 153. SD] *this edn; not in Q1.* 154. SD] *this edn; not in Q1.* 155. com'st —] *Seward;* comest, *Q1.* 157. SD] *this edn; not in Q1.* 160. SD] *this edn; not in Q1.* sirs] *Q1;* sir *Q2.* 161. soul. Away] *1711 (subst);* soul away *Q1.* 162. honours —] *1711;* honors. *Q1.* 164. SD] *this edn; not in Q1.*

---

  147. *waking*] awake.
  157. *Down, down again*] Everyone kneel, kneel again.

| A mortal woman still.
Thierry.   Can spirits weep too?   165
Martel. She is no spirit, sir; pray, kiss her. — Lady,
    Be very gentle to him.   [*She kisses* THIERRY.]
Thierry.   Stay, she is warm,
    And by my life the same lips — Tell me, brightness,
    Are you the same Ordella still?
Ordella.   The same, sir,
    Whom heavens and my good angel stayed from ruin.   170
Thierry. Kiss me again.
Ordella.   The same still, still your servant.
                               [*Kisses him again.*]
Thierry. 'Tis she! I know her now, Martel. — Sit down,
    sweet. [*She sits.*]
    O blessed and happiest woman, a dead slumber
    Begins to creep upon me. O my jewel!
                  Enter Messenger *and* MEMBERGE.

Ordella. Oh, sleep, my lord.
Thierry.   My joys are too much for me.   175
Messenger. Brunehaut, impatient of her constraint to see
    Protaldi tortured, has choked herself.
Martel.   No more,
    Her sins go with her.
Thierry.   [*To* ORDELLA] Love, I must die, I faint.

---

167. SD] *Turner; not in Q1.* 168. lips —] *Colman;* lips; *1711;* lips *Q1.* me] *Q1c;* not in *Q1u.* 169. SP Ordella] *Dyce; Mart. Q1.* 171.1. SD] *Turner (subst); not in Q1.* 172. SD] *this edn; not in Q1.* 177–81. Protaldi ... more, | Her ... faint. | Close ... deadly. | One ... dearest. | And ... woman] *Colman; Q1 lines* Protaldie ... selfe. | No ... her. | Loue ... glasses. | The ... deadly. | One ... kisse. | My ... now | Close ... too. | Thou ... woman. 178. SD] *this edn; not in Q1.*

---

165. *Can ... too*] Cf. *KL* 4.7.71: 'Be your tears wet? Yes, faith; I pray weep not.'
167. *she is warm*] Cf. *WT* 5.3.109: 'O, she's warm!'
170. *my ... angel*] i.e., Martel.
172. *Sit down*] Ordella probably sits on Thierry's bed, with no need for any further props.
176. *impatient of*] unable to endure.

  Close up my glasses.
1 Doctor.   The Queen faints too, and deadly.
Thierry. [*To her*] One dying kiss.
Ordella.   My last, sir, and my dearest. 180
            [*Kisses him.*]
  And now close my eyes too.
Thierry.   Thou perfect woman! —
  Martel, the kingdom's yours. Take Memberge to you,
  And keep my line alive. [*To* ORDELLA] Nay, weep not,
    lady. —
  Take me, I go.
Ordella.   Take me too. Farewell, honour. *Die both.*
2 Doctor. They are gone forever.   185
Martel. The peace of happy souls go after 'em. —
  Bear 'em unto their last beds, whilst I study
  A tomb to speak their loves whilst Old Time lasteth.
  I am your king in sorrows.
All.   We your subjects.
Martel. De Vitry, for your service be near us,   190
  Whip out these instruments of this mad mother
  From court and all good people. And, because
  She was born noble, let that title find her
  A private grave, but neither tongue nor honour. —
  And now lead on. They that shall read this story 195
  Shall find that virtue lives in good, not glory.
           Exeunt omnes.

      FINIS

---

180. SD] *this edn; not in Q1*. 180.1. SD] *Turner; not in Q1*. 183. SD] *this edn; not in Q1*. 184. SD *Die*] *F2*; Dies *Q1*. 189. SP *All*] *Weber*; Omnes *Q1*.

---

 179. *glasses*] eyes.
 183. *line*] lineage.
 187. *study*] think out, devise.
 188. *speak*] reveal, make known, manifest.
 whilst ... lasteth] forever.
 Old Time] also called (Old) Father Time, 'conventionally represented as an aged man carrying a scythe and frequently an hourglass; sometimes also as bald except for a single lock of hair' (*OED* 'time' n. 34b).
 189. SP *All*] See 5.1.9.
 194. *tongue*] eulogy (only instance recorded in *OED*).

APPENDIX 1
Press variants in Q1

Robert Kean Turner collated sixteen copies of Q1 plus the disjunct leaf C1 inserted in the copy in the Boston Public Library.[1] The copies collated by Turner are marked below with an asterisk (*). I have identified and collated a further six copies, which brings the number of all the extant copies of Q1 (to my knowledge) to twenty-two. These copies are as follows:

*BL[1] (British Library; 644.d.5)
*BL[2] (British Library; 841.b.1; trimmed at the foot in Sheet K, which affects the last one or two lines on each page)
*BL[3] (British Library; Ashley 83; a sophisticated copy associated with T. J. Wise: leaves B2, C1, D1, E2, and H3–4 have been exchanged with those in TxU[2])
*Bodl[1] (Bodleian Library, Oxford; 4° P 2(1) Art.BS; leaf [A2] from the quarto edition of Ben Jonson's *The Silent Woman* printed in 1620 by William Stansby has been inserted after the title page)
*Bodl[2] (Bodleian Library, Oxford; Mal. 243 (1); Edmond Malone's copy)
*CSmH (Henry E. Huntington Library; 60081)
*CtY[1] (Beinecke Library, Yale University; Eliz 13; trimmed, with some loss of catchwords and text in sheet K)
CtY[2] (Beinecke Library, Yale University; 1977 2598; several leaves torn and damaged in sheet B; a few headlines bled; sheet K slightly mutilated, with some loss of catchwords and text)
*DFo (Folger Shakespeare Library)
*Dyce (Victoria and Albert Museum, National Art Library; Dyce 25.A.33; Alexander Dyce's copy)
Hou (Houghton Library, Harvard University; GEN STC 11074; leaf [A2] and sheet D wanting)
Inner (Innerpeffray Library, F2; leaf E4 trimmed, with loss of headlines)
IU (Illinois University Library, 822 F63Tra; lacking leaf [A1] (blank); title page frayed and slightly torn (text unaffected); sheet K cropped, which slightly affects the text)
Leeds (Brotherton Library, University of Leeds; BC Lt BEA)

*MB (Boston Public Library; G.3966.21; uncorrected leaf C1 with manuscript corrections tipped-in, backwards, between C1 and C2; additional title leaf laid on to the rear pastedown; leaf [A1] (blank) wanting; James Halliwell-Phillipps's copy)
*C1 (disjunct leaf C1 inserted in MB)
*MWiW-C (Chapin Library, Williams College)
*NLS¹ (National Library of Scotland; 1.157(15); wanting leaf [A1] (blank); title page and leaf K4 mutilated, which makes it impossible to ascertain whether K (*i*) in that copy is in state 2 or 3)
*NLS² (National Library of Scotland; Bute.16)
PU (Kislak Center, University of Pennsylvania; PR2508.T3 1621)
*TCC (Trinity College Library, Cambridge; VI.9.80)
*TxU¹ (Harry Ransom Center Pforzheimer Library, University of Texas; Pforz 373)
*TxU² (Harry Ransom Center Wrenn Library Collection, University of Texas; Wh F635 621t WRE HRC Wrenn copy; a sophisticated copy associated with T. J. Wise: leaves B2, C1, D1, E2, and H3–4 have been exchanged with those in BL³)

All copies have been inspected during the preparation of this Revels Plays edition. My practice has been to check Turner's notes against the quartos he collated, and to supplement his observations with information from the six quartos that he did not collate. Mostly, my collation has confirmed Turner's findings, but it has also unearthed new facts. First, I have detected one press variant not recorded by Turner at 1.1.26, which is present in three copies (BL³, CtY², NLS²). Second, the copy in the Houghton Library at Harvard University (which Turner did not collate) includes an uncorrected leaf C1, which clearly reveals that the misspelled word at 1.2.121 is 'Muiſter', not 'Murſter' as hypothesized by Turner (the letter 'i' cannot be seen clearly enough beneath the handwritten correction in the disjunct leaf C1 inserted in MB). Third, Turner mistakenly listed the copy in the Harry Ransom Center Pforzheimer Library at the University of Texas as being in state 2 (corrected) at 4.1.96, while it is in fact in state 1 (uncorrected). Fourth, Turner took the word 'part' at 5.1.14 that is missing in one of the copies at the British Library as a press variant, but closer inspection reveals that the missing word is in fact the result of the paper being damaged. Finally, Turner considered 'barrenneſſe' (without a comma) at 4.1.162 to be the corrected state, with 'barrenneſſe,' (with a comma) being the uncorrected state. Unfortunately, this is the only press variant in H (*i*), so

APPENDIX I 197

that there are no collateral elements that might help one determine in which direction the adjustment occurred. However, the comma there is redundant (and it is difficult to believe that anyone inserted it belatedly), and the balance of comma vs no-comma surviving copies (five against seventeen) strongly weighs in favour of reversing Turner's judgement, which is what I have done.

These are the press variants that have been detected:

Sheet B (*outer forme*)
State 1: BL^3 (*containing leaf B2 from TxU^2, state 3*), CtY^2, NLS^2
State 2: BL^2, $Bodl^1$, PU
State 3: BL^1, $Bodl^2$, CSmH, CtY^1, DFo, Dyce, Hou, Inner, IU, Leeds, MB, MWiW-C, NLS^1, TCC, TxU^1, TxU^2 (*containing leaf B2 from BL^3, state 1*)

Sig. B1ʳ
head-title THE] *state 3;* THE *states 1 and 2*
1.1.1 tainturs] *state 3;* tainters *states 1 and 2*
1.1.14 'tis neceſſary] *states 2 and 3;* 'tis | neceſſary *state 1*
Sig. B2ᵛ
1.1.84 ſtaru'd] *state 3;* ſtarud *states 1 and 2*
1.1.107 deſpiſ'd] *state 3;* deſpiſd *states 1 and 2*
Sig. B3ʳ
1.1.121 Letchers, Leaches] *state 3;* Leachers, Letchecs *states 1 and 2*
Sig. B4ᵛ
1.2.37 here ſhe] *states 2 and 3;* here | ſhe *state 1*
1.2.52 Par'd] *state 3;* Pard *states 1 and 2*
1.2.61 an enimy] *states 2 and 3;* an nimy *state 1*
1.2.64 Himſelfe] *state 3;* himſelfe *states 1 and 2*

Sheet B (*inner forme*)
State 1: BL^3, CtY^2, NLS^2
State 2: $BL^{1,2}$, $Bodl^{1,2}$, CSmH, CtY^1, DFo, Dyce, Hou, Inner, IU, Leeds, MB, MWiW-C, NLS^1, PU, TCC, $TxU^{1,2}$

Sig. B1ᵛ
1.1.22 take] *state 2;* rake *state 1*
1.1.26 inflict] *state 2;* afflict *state 1*

Sheet C (*inner forme*)
State 1: C1, Hou
State 2: $BL^{1,2,3}$, $Bodl^{1,2}$, CSmH, $CtY^{1,2}$, DFo, Dyce, Inner, IU, Leeds, MB, MWiW-C, $NLS^{1,2}$, PU, TCC, $TxU^{1,2}$

Sig. C1ᵛ
1.2.105 vertuous traine] *state 2;* vertuoustraine traine *state 1*
1.2.119 a troope] *state 2;* a|troope *state 1*
1.2.121 Muſter] *state 2;* Muiſter *state 1*
1.2.130 *Martell,*] *state 2; Martell state 1*

Sheet E (*outer forme*)
State 1: Bodl[1,2], NLS[1], TCC
State 2: BL[1,2,3], CSmH, CtY[1,2], DFo, Dyce, Hou, Inner, IU,
Leeds, MB, MWiW-C, NLS[2], PU, TxU[1,2]

Sig. E2ᵛ
2.3.65 rare] *state 2;* care *state 1*
Sig. E4ᵛ
3.1.32 your] *state 2;* you *state 1*
3.1.35 iuice] *state 2;* iuce *state 1*

Sheet E (*inner forme*)
State 1: BL[2,3], Bodl[1,2], CtY[2], NLS[1,2], TCC
State 2: BL[1], CSmH, CtY[1], DFo, Dyce, Hou, Inner, IU, Leeds,
MB, MWiW-C, PU, TxU[1,2]

Sig. E4ʳ
Running title *Theodoret*] *state 2; Theoderet state 1*
2.3.172 *Exeunt:*] *state 2; not in state 1*

Sheet G (*outer forme*)
State 1: CSmH, Inner, TxU[1,2]
State 2: BL[1,2,3], Bodl[1,2], CtY[1,2], DFo, Dyce, Hou, IU, Leeds, MB,
MWiW-C, NLS[1,2], PU, TCC

Sig. G4ᵛ
4.1.96 with all] *state 2;* withall *state 1*

Sheet H (*inner forme*)
State 1: BL[1], CtY[1], Dyce, Inner, MWiW-C
State 2: BL[2,3], Bodl[1,2], CSmH, CtY[2], DFo, Hou, IU, Leeds, MB,
NLS[1,2], PU, TCC, TxU[1,2]

Sig. H1ᵛ
4.1.162 barrenneſſe] *state 2;* barrenneſſe, *state 1*

Sheet I (*inner forme*)
State 1: BL[2], CtY[1], DFo, Dyce, Inner, NLS[1], TCC, TxU[1,2]
State 2: BL[1,3], Bodl[1,2], CSmH, CtY[2], Hou, IU, Leeds, MB,
MWiW-C, NLS[2], PU

Sig. I3ᵛ
5.1.26 de-|fcend] *state 2;* def-|fend *state 1*

Sheet K (*inner forme*)
State 1: TxU²
State 2: Bodl¹,², Inner, MB, NLS¹ (?), TCC
State 3: BL¹,²,³, CSmH, CtY¹,², DFo, Dyce, Hou, IU, Leeds, MWiW-C, NLS², PU, TxU¹

Sig. K4ʳ
5.2.168 tell me brightneffe] *states 2 and 3;* tell brightneffe *state 1*
5.2.142 wheele] *state 3;* wheee *states 1 and 2*

Sig. K3ᵛ
5.2.115 defeated] *state 3;* defeeaed *states 1 and 2*

NOTE

1 Turner, 'Press-variants'.

APPENDIX 2
Overview of the historical events dramatized in the play, based on the *Chronique de Frédégaire* (seventh century)

Brunhilda (c. 543–613), also known as Brunechildis or Brunehault in the sources, was a Visigoth princess who became Queen of Austrasia by marrying King Sigebert I in 566. Sigebert was murdered in 575 by his brother Chilperic I, King of Neustria, at the instigation of his concubine Fredegund. After Sigebert's death, Brunhilda was captured and imprisoned in Rouen. Tensions and conflicts continued, Chilperic was killed (584), and in 592 the kingdoms of Austrasia and Burgundy were united under Childebert II through succession. When he died in 595, Burgundy passed to Theuderic II (587–613) and Austrasia to Theudebert II (586–612), with their grandmother Brunhilda acting as regent until they came of age.

Theuderic lived in Orléans, the capital of Burgundy, while Theudebert lived with Brunhilda in Metz, the capital of Austrasia, until he sent her away and she went to stay with Theuderic. From then on, the two brothers were frequently at war, with Brunhilda on Theuderic's side. Theuderic defeated Theudebert at Sens in 599, but they then made an alliance against their cousin Chlothar II, King of Neustria, and vanquished his troops at Dormelles, thus conquering a sizeable portion of Neustria (600–4). Shortly thereafter, set on by Brunhilda, the brothers resumed fighting against each other. Brunhilda was helped by her favourite and lover Protade. She decided to raise his status in the kingdom and conspired to have him appointed as Mayor of the Palace of Burgundy in 604. Protade was put in charge of Theuderic's army against Theudebert's, and Theuderic defeated Theudebert at Étampes. However, the soldiers did not want to continue shedding their countrymen's blood and killed Protade in his tent (606). They then forced the two kings to make peace. In 607/8 Theuderic married the daughter of the King of Spain, but Brunhilda rendered Theuderic unable to consummate the marriage. A year after the wedding, Theuderic deprived his wife of her dowry and sent her back to her father. In 610 Theudebert wrested Alsace from his brother, and Theuderic waged war on him again, defeated him, and deposed him in 612. Brunhilda had Theudebert confined in a monastery and executed. Theuderic thus became King of Austrasia too. He died of dysentery – perhaps poisoned by Brunhilda – while preparing for another battle against Chlothar and was therefore unable to complete his conquest of Neustria.

After Theuderic's death in 613, Burgundy and Austrasia passed to his son Sigebert II, who was only 12. Brunhilda then took on the regency of the kingdoms again. The nobles of Austrasia, however, dissatisfied with her politics, plotted against her. She was captured and handed over to Chlothar, who in the meantime had defeated Sigebert II and now accordingly ruled over the entire realm of the Franks. Chlothar accused Brunhilda of the death of ten kings of the Franks. She was tortured and then brutally executed.

APPENDIX 3
'The eldest son chargeth his mother with incestuous life': The Tale of the Lady of Cabrio in Fenton's *Tragical Discourses*

Geoffrey Fenton, 'The Impudent Love of the Lady of Cabrio with Her Procurer Tolonio, together with the Detestable Murders Committed between Them', in *Certain Tragical Discourses Written out of French and Latin* (London, 1567), 2Biii^r–2Bvi^r

... having one day the assistance of a fit time and place, in a gallery void of all company, he [i.e., the eldest son] preferred his opinion in this sort, not without an indifferent medley of shame and disdain appearing in all parts of his face: 'If it be a thing unseemly that a king should be disobeyed of his subjects, it is no less necessary, in mine opinion, that the prince avoid oppression of his people by power, for that a great fault in the one is none offence at all by reason of his authority, and the other sometime is exacted without just cause of blame. But, if it be a virtue in the majesty royal to be indifferent between the force of his power given him by God and the complaints of right in his vassals, why should it be an offence that the master or magistrate be put in remembrance or made to understand the points wherein he offendeth, seeing he hath no greater reason to yield justice to such as deserve punishment than bound in double sort to a wonderful care of integrity in living in himself, so as his authority and effects of upright conversation may serve as a line to lead the meaner sort serving under his awe to be in love with his virtues and commended for semblable sincerity and purity of life?

'But, for my part, good madam, were it not the remorse of an equal respect to your reputation and honour to all our house – and that my conscience hereafter would accuse me of want of courage and care to make good the virtuous renown of my dead father – I should hardly be forced to the terms of my present intent, nor my being in this place give you such cause of amaze and doubt of my meaning, for the duty which nature bindeth me to owe to the place you hold on my behalf and the law of obedience given by God to all children towards such as made them the members of this world makes me as often close my mouth against the discovery of the long grudge of my mind as I have great reason to impart the cause to your ladyship, who is touched more near than any other, that I would to God the thing whereof my mind hath given a judgement of assurance were as untrue as I wish it both far from mine opinion and void of a truth.

'Then surely should my heart rest, discharged of disquiet, and I dismissed from the office of an orator, which also I would refuse to perform if the importance of the cause did not force my will in that respect. Albeit, as the passions of the mind be free, and the spirit of man (howsoever the body be distressed with captivity) hath a privilege of liberty touching opinions or conceits, so I hope your wisdom, with the justice of my cause and clearness of intent, are sufficient pillars to support that which the virtue of natural zeal to yourself and dutiful regard to the honour of my ancestors moves me to communicate with you, chiefly for that the best badge of your own life and blood of your late lord and husband, my father, be distressed (as I am persuaded) by the secret haunt and unseemly glee of favour between the procurer Tolonio and you, whom God and nature have made a mother of such children that neither deserve such lewd abuse in you nor can brook his villainy in corrupting the noble blood wherewith they participate without vengeance due to the greatness of his poisoned malice.

'Wherein, good madam, as my dear affection to you wards hath made me so frank in warning you of the evil, so, if you give not order henceforth for the redress of that which I account already past every cause of doubt, you will come too short to cover that can be no longer concealed, when also small compassion will be used in the revenge of the injury. Neither can you in any sort complain rightly of me, in whose heart is already kindled a grudge of the wrong you have done to the nobility of us all, loathing withal the simple remembrance of so foul a fault, protesting unto you for end that, if hereafter you become as careless of the honour of your children as heretofore you have been void of regard to your own reputation, the world shall punish the abuse of your old years with open exclamation against your lascivious order of life, divesting you of all titles of high degree, and these hands only shall send Master Doctor to visit his process in the infernal senate, and preach in other pulpit than the highest theatre within the castle of Cabrio.' Which last threats argued a more mortality by his terrible regards of countenance, with broken words in his mouth, declaring sufficiently the vehemency of his passion.

All which as they persuaded the lady to dread a speedy execution of his anger (wherein her Tolonio should be chiefly distressed), so, being void of remedy in any fear she could prefer, she retired to the policy of feminine complaints, seeking to moderate the fury of his just choler by certain suborned tears and other dissembled arguments of dolour wherewith she seemed to fill each sinew and vein about her, continuing some space in that sorrowful contemplation, with her face upon the ground, casting dust and ashes upon her head (according to the desperate Persians, when they received any lamentable news), and, rising at last (as out of a qualm of heavy passions), replied to the exclamation of her son with these or such-like terms of counterfeit compassion:

'Were it not that innocence is a virtue sufficient of itself to answer all combats of unjust imputation, I should sure doubt of assistance in the defence of my cause and much less be able to clear the sentence of your sinister conceit against me. Neither had I reason to argue with you and less cause to enter into terms to justify myself, if in mine own integrity appeared not the absolute wrong you do to my present honour. And yet do I feel myself indifferently passioned between doubt and fear, for that your present choler, quarrelling with all offers of defence on my side, seemeth also curious to admit any credit at all in whatsoever I shall prefer to approve my guiltless life. For, if it be a virtue to be credulous in every report, you have reason to continue your grudge, or, if the view of your own eye had brought you to the sight of that wherein you presume a truth but by imagination, you were sufficiently absolved if you had already performed the end of your mortal enterprise. But, where your eyes argue against you (as partakers at no time of the likelihood of any such evil you have presently imagined), and yourself void of other witness than the information of your own partial conceit, let strangers be judges between the causes of your suspicion and the hard sentence you have passed of mine honour, and all the world that was privy to the course of my youth (when you were under the yoke and years of discretion) accuse the wrongs you do to the virtue of mine age, whose hoary hairs cry out of your present cruelty.

'Alas! Who is he that dare undertake the defence of this desolate widow if mine own children seek to set abroach my dishonour? What state or degree may be bold to repose credit with assurance in mine honesty when the fruit, congealed of the substance of myself, seemeth doubtful of my upright dealing? What expectation of faith, loyalty or good opinion is in any sort of strangers when the blood and blossoms of our own entrails enter into conspiracy against us? Our miserable condition and unhappy sex of ours, subject most (as it seemeth) to strange wretchedness when we account ourselves past the fear and malice of Fortune, who now – I see – beginneth her troublesome war, when we reappose most felicity and assurance in rest! It is now – alas! – that I find an experience of the common voice of the vulgar sort, confirmed also by consent of the ancient crew of the learned, that virtue is continually assailed with spite, envy and false imposition of crimes.

'Neither am I alone persecuted with the malice of all those mischiefs, although I only am oppressed with a present villainy whereof I never thought, and much less performed, any effect. How long – alas! – my son, have you joined in opinion with that fond sect, whose rashness in judgement hath made them oftentimes repent the sentence of their folly? Since when have you been so lightly persuaded of the reputation, constancy, and virtue of dames of honour? Do you measure their disposition by the vanity in yourself and villainy of such as credit only the instinct of their malicious brain? No! No! It is not the endeavour of ladies of my regard to practise in sensuality nor study in the vain delights of the flesh. And, for my part, methinks discretion should persuade you that the time and number of my years are not convenient to the follies whereof I felt no motion in the very flame and burning summer of my youth.

'You grieve with the familiarity between Tolonio and me, but chiefly because we use conference now and then in my chamber. Do not you know it is he by whose counsel are guided the whole affairs of the house? Or do you see his liberty enlarged since the death of your father, in whose time he practised in sort as he doth now and yet was he never jealous of his access hither at any hour? Had he not eyes to discern as far off as you, and his ears were as open to all reports as yours? Albeit he used discretion in judgement, neither could his heart – I am sure – digest half the villainy you have alleged if his surmise had been confirmed with a truth. But here – alas! – appear the points of my wretchedness, to fall into the danger of suspicion with him in whom I have reposed the quiet of my old years, and for the increase of whose wealth and patrimony I am in continual travail, both of mind and body. Wherein as the poor Tolonio (no less unfortunate than I, for that your grudge seemeth most heinous on his behalf) hath equal care to advance you by his advice and travail, so, besides your abuse to me (whom God and nature binds you to honour with all duty), you do double wrong to his faith and zealous intent towards you in returning his honest care with threats of no less mortality than shameful and cruel death, which, if it come in question by your rashness, what doubt bring you of his honesty, where now his name is of credit with the best of the country?

'And, for his part, if you give him the least inkling in the world of your displeasure, I warrant you his presence shall no more offend you in the house nor elsewhere, and then shall you know whether the favour he finds at my hands imports a meaning for your profit or to satisfy the pleasure of my vile and aged flesh; besides, the order of your affairs, both at home and in the senate, will try the difference between the commodity of his presence and hindrance that is sure to happen by his restraint of coming hither, when, my son, will also appear the care of your dear mother, whose diligence – alas! – deserveth better consideration than to be charged with the note of incontinence, which I protest afore God, with stretched hands and heart to the heavens, to have in no less contempt for the vileness of the sin than to see the wrongful conceit of such a villainy doth trouble you.'

Which she forgat not to accompany with all sorts of sighs and signs of dolour, intermeddled with such regards of dissembled pity in all parts of her face that, albeit he was past all doubt touching the truth of his own conceit, yet the tears of his deceitful mother moved him to admit her excuses, with such compassion of her sorrow that he seemed also to pass the pangs of her present passion; with protestation, under terms of great humility, that he grieved no less in that he had said than she had great reason to complain of the wrong he hath done to the renown of her virtue.

'Albeit', saith he (with a countenance of repentance), 'if you measure the force of my affection with the cause of my late plainness, your discretion – I hope – will construe my words according to the honest intent of my heart with excuse to my rashness, which you shall see hereafter so mortified in me that I will neither be so hasty to accuse, nor suspect without better advice.' For the which she seemed thankful unto him, with a present appeasement from anger, attending the offer of opportunity when she might prefer her son to a part in the tragedy which her wickedness had already begun upon his late father, for she was doubtful still of the young man and gave less faith to his words.

Index

a 1.1.48, 2.2.47, 2.2.105
abroad 2.3.159
abuse 1.1.22, 4.1.201
* Academe 1.2.90
accident 4.1.150
account 2.1.172
actor 2.1.14
Adelman, Janet p. 50
Adler, Doris pp. 31, 49
Aesculapius p. 93
affect 2.1.189, 2.3.163
afford 3.2.174
age 3.1.163
Aimoin of Fleury: *Historia Francorum* pp. 10, 13, 48
all-moving 3.1.127
allowance 1.1.31
amazement 2.1.121
angel 2.2.40
Appleton, William W. pp. 30, 49
apply 1.2.54
apprehend 2.3.146
apprehension 1.2.58, 3.2.51
art 5.2.1
ascribe 4.2.144
assume 4.1.173
astrolabe 3.3.4
astronomer 3.1.167, 3.3.12
atone 2.3.103
attach 5.2.129
aught 5.1.57

baffling 2.3.143
Baldwin, Thomas Whitfield pp. 24, 48
Bandello, Matteo pp. 17–18, 57
bane 5.2.79
bar 3.1.43, 4.1.176
barbarism 4.2.107
barren 2.1.260
bastinadoes 2.3.39
bastinadoing 2.3.149

battery 4.2.140
Bawdbert p. 32, Characters in the Play 10
bawdry 3.2.31
bawl 5.1.165
beadle 2.1.220
bear 3.3.12
bear up 2.1.320
Beaumont, Francis pp. 1, 3–7, 25, 28–9, 44–5, 47
  Pestle pp. 4, 50, 104
become 1.1.2, 1.1.108, 1.2.39
* bedder 1.1.86
beget 1.2.81, 3.1.43, 3.1.159, 3.3.34, 3.3.61
belike 3.2.45
Belloy, Pierre de: *Examen du discours publié contre la maison royale* p. 48
bell-ropes 2.2.47
bend 1.1.3
Bevington, David p. 68
Bible
  Eccles. p. 149
  Gen. p. 151
  Judg. p. 48
Blackfriars Theatre pp. 5, 134
Blamires, Adrian pp. 13, 31, 33–4, 48–50, 115, 118, 153
blanketing 2.3.54
Bliss, Lee pp. 28, 47, 49
blithe 5.1.33
Boccaccio, Giovanni
  Filocolo p. 27
  A Pleasant Disport p. 27
  Thirteen Questions p. 27
bond 3.3.2
bonny 5.1.33
Bowers, Fredson pp. 26, 48–9, 68
box 3.2.68
brakes 5.1.107

207

INDEX

'Branhowlte' p. 47
brat 3.2.167
brick kiln 5.1.77
bringing in 5.2.127
broker 1.1.86
Brown, Sarah Ann p. 173
browse 1.1.117
Brunehaut pp. 6–7, 10–18, 20–1, 29–34, 36–40, Characters in the Play 8
Buc, Sir George, Master of the Revels pp. 39, 47
Buchanan, George: *Jephthes* pp. 20–1
Burbage, Richard pp. 22, 24, 48

Caius, John: *Of English Dogs* p. 68
call on 2.1.7
callidus servus p. 108
Cameron, Kenneth Walter pp. 44, 51
* capon 1.1.163
cardecu 2.1.228
careful 3.2.159, 4.1.100
Carlson, Marvin pp. 24, 48
Carr, Robert, 1st Earl of Somerset pp. 38–9
Cartwright, Robert p. 49
carvel 5.1.142
cashier 2.1.61
cast 5.1.82
cater 2.1.61
cell 3.1.180
censure 4.2.194
Centaurs p. 110
challenge 1.2.74
chamber-wrestler 1.2.95
Chapman, George pp. 3, 50
charge 3.1.179, 4.2.210
Charles I p. 44
Charles's Wain 3.3.6
Chelli, Maurice pp. 3, 47
Children of the Chapel Royal p. 4
Children of the Queen's Revels p. 5
choice 2.3.113, 4.2.140
chop 3.2.77
Christopherson, John: *Iephthae* p. 21
Chronique de Frédégaire pp. 10–11, 13, 48

Clark, Sandra pp. 32–4, 36, 47, 49–50, 65
clerk 2.2.46
clip 3.1.78
cloister 1.1.145
Clubb, Louise George p. 47
club-fist 3.2.78
clyster 1.1.171
Coachman 3.3.5
Coatalen, Guillaume p. 49
codpiece 1.2.101
Colman, George p. 45
colt 1.1.176
* combat 2.3.133
Compagnoni, Michela pp. 37, 50
Concini, Concino pp. 8–9, 14–15
conduct 2.1.119
confine 2.1.236
confirm 4.1.224
conjure 2.1.320
Constable, Francis pp. 40–1
constellate 3.1.181
consume 4.1.6
consumption 5.1.78–9
conveyance 3.1.175, 5.1.179, 5.1.199, 5.1.207–8
convoy 4.2.38
* coral 2.2.45
cordial 1.2.75
Cotgrave, John: *English Treasury* p. 29
Cotgrave, Randle: *Dictionary of the French and English Tongues* p. 49
countenance 5.1.15
course 1.1.3
courser 1.1.150
covet 4.1.182
cozen 1.1.18, 4.1.215
crave 5.2.49
credit 1.1.35, 1.1.47
credulity 3.1.130
cullis 2.2.9
cunning 2.2.21
curtal 1.1.144

Darley, George p. 45
de Vitry pp. 6–9, 14–15, 17, 37, 43, 50, Characters in the Play 6
dear 3.2.61

declare 2.2.34
decoction 2.2.8
defame 2.1.145
defeature 1.2.125
Dekker, Thomas pp. 21, 50
delicate 2.3.113
deliver 4.2.102
Dessen, Alan pp. 95, 116
detection 1.1.43
Devereux, Robert, 3rd Earl of Essex p. 38
Diana 3.3.59
difference 2.3.103
direct 3.3.7
discharge 1.2.15
discourse 1.1.100
discover 1.1.100
dispose 3.2.106
distemper 5.2.55
Dodoens Rembert: *A New Herbal* p. 184
dog days 5.2.13
dogfish 5.1.231
Dori Galigai, Leonora p. 8
dose 1.1.171
dote on 4.1.58
* dowset 2.2.42
drench 5.2.10, 5.2.132
* drill 2.1.74, 3.2.7
Drummond of Hawthornden, William p. 29
ducat 3.2.41
* dull 2.3.17, 3.1.24, 4.1.62, 4.1.147, 4.1.198, 5.1.178
Dutton, Richard pp. 15, 39, 48, 50, 74, 129
duty 2.1.304, 4.2.50
Dyce, Alexander pp. 29, 45

easiness 1.1.36
Edwards, Robert R. p. 49
effect 2.1.83, 2.1.115
Elizabeth Stuart p. 41
else 2.2.32
* embryon 2.3.119
empoison 2.1.151
end 1.1.129, 1.1.45, 3.1.57, 4.1.150
endive 5.2.19
engine 2.3.167, 3.2.143, 4.2.139
enjoin 3.2.161

equal 5.2.131
ere 3.2.27
Eteocles pp. 20, 78
Euripides
　Alcestis pp. 9, 19–20, 22, 25–7, 49, 191
　Iphigenia in Aulis pp. 19, 21–2, 25
ever 2.1.124, 2.3.82
exemplified 3.1.53
exhalation 4.1.106

fair 2.1.149, 2.1.298, 4.1.46
fall 2.3.72, 3.1.176
fashion 1.1.100
Fauchet, Claude: *Recueil des Antiquités* pp. 10, 14, 16, 48
faulty 2.1.162
Fenton, Geoffrey: *Certain Tragical Discourses* pp. 17–18, 48, 57, 71, 202–6
Field, Nathan 3–5, 24, 27, 41, 47, 49–50
　Amends for Ladies pp. 3–4
　A Woman Is a Weathercock pp. 3–4
figure 3.3.7, 4.1.175
fillip 2.3.33
flame 3.2.180
Flavigny, Charles de: *Le Rois de France* pp. 16, 48
Fleay, F. G. pp. 3, 8, 14, 47
Fletcher, John pp. 1, 3–7, 9–10, 12–15, 19–22, 24–31, 34, 39, 43–5, 47–8, 50–1
　The Faithful Shepherdess p. 4
　Lieut p. 149
　Loyal pp. 6, 59, 171
　MadL pp. 21, 48, 59, 142, 149, 171
　Monsieur pp. 183, 185
　Pilgrim p. 173
　Princess p. 59
　Val pp. 30, 59, 171, 185–6
　A Wife for a Month p. 7
Fletcher, John, and Francis Beaumont
　Capt pp. 3, 171
　Cupid p. 6
　KNoK pp. 6, 25, 28, 41, 44, 103, 171
　MT pp. 6–7, 28, 30, 37, 40–1, 59, 185
　Phil pp. 6, 25, 28, 41, 50, 98, 185

INDEX

Fletcher, John, and John Ford
   The Noble Gentleman pp. 44, 51
Fletcher, John, and Nathan Field
   Four Plays, or Moral Representations, in One pp. 3, 5, 49
   Love's Pilgrimage pp. 3, 6
Fletcher, John, and Philip Massinger
   FalseO pp. 13, 59, 171
   LC p. 102
   Progress p. 60
   Proph p. 158
   SeaV p. 59
   SJVOB pp. 5, 149, 171
   SpCur p. 72
Fletcher, John, and William Shakespeare
   H8 p. 149
Fletcher, John, Philip Massinger, and Nathan Field
   Beggars' Bush pp. 3, 6
   Brother p. 60
   Corinth pp. 3, 102
   CustCount pp. 59, 158
   HMF pp. 3, 5, 92
   'The Jeweller of Amsterdam' p. 3
   Malta pp. 3–4, 6, 9, 27, 50, 191
   Rollo pp. 3, 6–7, 9, 13, 59, 63, 78, 142
foil 2.2.21
* foining work 2.2.121
fond 4.2.12
fondness 4.1.176, 4.1.198
'foot 3.2.103
foot-cloth 5.2.48
form 3.3.67
Forman, Simon p. 8
forswear 1.1.160
Frederick, Elector Palatine p. 41
Freebury-Jones, Darren pp. 3–4, 47, 51
freighted 1.1.36
fret 2.3.40
frigate 5.1.134
furlong 5.1.86

gage 2.3.96
Galant, Justyna pp. 32, 49, 150, 156
game 3.2.163
Gang of Four pp. 9, 47
gape 3.3.3
gelding 1.1.88
gelt 1.1.143, 4.1.44
Genest, John pp. 27, 49
Gentillet, Innocent: *Discourse upon the Means of Well Governing* pp. 13, 48
gilded 1.1.86, 2.2.13
give out 1.2.6, 1.2.113, 2.3.160, 4.1.229
give up 4.2.216
gladsome 3.1.69
glass 5.2.179
Globe Theatre p. 6
glorious 2.1.52
Glover, Arnold p. 45
goblin 1.1.168
Gossett, Suzanne pp. 41, 50
Goulart, Simon: *Mémoires de l'état de France* pp. 12, 48
Gowing, Laura pp. 36, 50
Grantham, Henry p. 27
Greatley-Hirsch, Brett p. 51
grievous 1.2.42
Grimeston, Edward: *A General Inventory of the History of France* pp. 10–14, 16, 21, 48, 57, 69, 79, 89, 111, 136, 168, 170, 182, 190
guardage 5.1.12
guarded 5.2.48
gust 1.1.114

ha ha ha 2.3.97
Hall, Kim F. p. 85
Hallissy, Margaret pp. 38, 50
handsel 5.1.92
hark 4.1.86
hatched in 2.2.65
'heart 5.1.110
heartstrings 4.1.147
heigh-ho 5.1.109
Heminges, William: *The Fatal Contract* p. 29
hemlock 3.1.35
Henslowe, Philip p. 5
Hensman, Bertha pp. 3, 47
Hercules p. 79

heritage 5.1.7
Herne, James p. 29
Higginbotham, Richard pp. 40–1
hillo 5.1.189
Hirsh, James E. p. 98
hollo 2.2.39
home 2.2.31
honest 1.1.165
Honigmann, E. A. J. p. 171
hooded 5.2.3
* hornbook 2.1.82
Horne, John p. 29
hospital 2.1.217
hot 1.1.1
Houghton, John p. 29
Howard, Frances pp. 38–9
Hoy, Cyrus pp. 1, 3–4, 46–7
humours, theory of pp. 62, 91, 96, 150

Ichikawa, Mariko p. 146
ill 2.1.165, 4.2.113, 5.2.25
immortal 5.2.39
imp out 5.2.108
impart 3.2.57
impatient 5.2.176
incense 2.1.153
indifferent 2.1.200
inhabited 3.1.98
insensible 4.2.250
instrument 1.1.10
Isle of Dogs 3.2.89–90
issue 3.3.27, 4.1.166

Jackson, MacDonald P. p. 46
Jackson, William A. p. 51
James I pp. 38–9
jaundice 5.1.76
jealous 1.2.3, 2.1.35
jennet 1.1.113
Jephthah pp. 19, 21, 48
Jocasta pp. 20, 78
Jonson, Ben
    The Alchemist p. 24
    Bartholomew Fair p. 5
    Catiline His Conspiracy p. 4
    EMO p. 74
    Epicene p. 4
    Poetaster p. 4
    Volpone pp. 4, 24

Josephus: *Famous and Memorable Works* p. 21
just 3.1.169

Karim-Cooper, Farah p. 85
keep 4.2.22
King's Men pp. 5, 9, 24, 41, 44
know 3.1.96
Koeppel, Emil pp. 21, 48

Lacure pp. 7–8, 13, 15, 32, 37–8, 43,
    Characters in the Play 11
lading 5.1.143
Lady Elizabeth's Men p. 5
laid up 4.1.2
Lamb, Charles pp. 29, 49, 149
lanceprisado 2.2.119
Lang, Andrew pp. 30, 49
Langbaine, Gerald pp. 45, 51
Le Long, Jacques p. 47
lecher 1.1.121
leech 1.1.121, 2.2.9
Leech, Clifford pp. 7, 12, 30, 34, 47–51
lettuce cap 5.2.8
level 1.1.72
lewd 3.2.16
liberal 5.2.115
like 1.2.29, 5.2.130
limbeck 5.1.11
line 5.2.183
Lodge, Thomas p. 21
loose 1.1.4, 1.1.6
Lord Admiral's Men pp. 21, 47
Lost Plays Database pp. 47–8
Louis XIII p. 8
Lovascio, Domenico pp. 47–8, 191
Lucan: *Pharsalia* p. 78
Luis-Martínez, Zenón pp. 31, 49
Lupić, Ivan p. 51
Luynes, Duc de p. 8

Machiavelli Niccolò: *The Prince* p. 170
made 3.2.76
malicious 5.2.89
man of war 1.2.100, 3.2.1
mandrake 3.1.2
mankind 1.1.119

INDEX

marble dew 3.1.2
Maréchal d'Ancre pp. 8, 14–15, 39, 47
Maréchal de Vitry pp. 8, 15
mark 4.1.35
Marlowe, Christopher p. 30
marry 2.2.39
Martel pp. 6–7, 16, 19–21, 26, 32–4, 37, 43, Characters in the Play 5
masque 3.1.117
Massai, Sonia pp. 44, 51
Massinger, Philip pp. 1, 3–5, 13, 43, 45, 47–8, 50
   Bondman p. 158
   Renegado p. 158
Massinger, Philip, and Nathan Field: *The Fatal Dowry* p. 3
Matthieu, Pierre: *La conjuration de Concino Concini* pp. 8–9, 14–15, 48
maunder 5.1.75
McDonald, Russ pp. 28, 49
McInnis, David p. 49
McKeithan, Daniel Morley pp. 12, 16–18, 48–9, 171
McManus, Clare p. 51
McMillin, Scott p. 51
Meads, Chris pp. 104–5
measure 4.1.130
Medici, Maria de' pp. 8, 15
Memberge pp. 10–11, 13, 26, 32, Characters in the Play 4
merit 4.1.142, 4.2.144
mew 2.2.28
mewed up 1.1.146, 3.1.86
mickle 5.1.34
miles gloriosus pp. 14, 82
mittimus 5.1.84
mix 3.1.41
modest 2.1.10
monstrous 1.2.98
Morley, Carol A. p. 12
morning star 3.3.3
Moseley, Humphrey p. 44
moth 1.2.102, 2.1.256
Mousnier, Roland p. 145
move 2.1.157
Munday, Anthony, and Thomas Dekker: 'Jephthah' p. 21
Munro, Lucy pp. 26, 48–9, 178

mushroom 2.2.117
* musket 2.1.75

natural heat 3.1.3
needful 4.1.195
Neill, Michael p. 26
Nero p. 85
Neville, Sir Henry p. 44
* night-dog 1.1.167
night-labour 2.1.47
nightmare 1.1.168
Nine Worthies p. 114
Niobe pp. 65, 111
north star 3.1.14

O'Connell, James J. Mainard p. 134
Oedipus pp. 20, 78
Okes, Nicholas pp. 40–1, 50
Old Time 5.2.188
Oliphant, E. H. C. pp. 29, 47, 49
opinion 2.2.80, 3.2.49
opium 5.2.12
optics 1.1.23
ordain 4.1.178
Ordella pp. 7, 13, 16, 18–20, 22–3, 26, 29–35, 43, Characters in the Play 3
outrage 3.2.73
Overbury, Sir Thomas p. 39
* overcome 2.3.134
owe 3.3.26

pad on 5.1.40
Panek, Jennifer p. 50
parapet 2.1.102
parcel 3.2.10
pare off 1.2.52
parish-top 2.3.45
parricide 2.1.132, 4.2.209, 5.1.229–30
parting 4.1.41
Paster, Gail Kern p. 133
patience 5.2.112
Patrick, Simon p. 13
Pavier Quartos p. 41
pay 2.1.190
Pearse, Nancy Cotton pp. 17, 19, 27, 34, 48–50
pennon 5.2.110
pennyworth 3.2.12
penthouse 1.1.20

Pérez Diez, José A. pp. 25, 48
perfect 4.1.170
period 3.1.101
persuade 3.2.114
petition 5.1.22
physic 4.2.262, 5.1.129
piece 2.2.70
pitch 2.3.75
Pitcher, John p. 48
plead 5.1.98
Pliny the Elder p. 116
poison 2.3.113
polecat 2.1.226
Pollard, Tanya p. 48
Polynices pp. 20, 78
poorly 2.2.100
poppy 5.2.136
posset drink 5.2.9
post 2.1.229
power 1.2.124
prate 5.1.198, 5.1.62
prefer 5.1.79
preferment 5.1.109
prefix 4.1.167
presage 3.2.123
prevent 5.1.226
prick up 1.1.139
primer 5.2.25
Private Libraries in Renaissance England p. 49
Privy Council pp. 39, 47
proceed 4.1.179
proclaim 5.2.50
proof 2.2.70
proper 2.1.51
Protade pp. 9, 12, 14–15
Protaldi pp. 5–7, 13–17, 20, 32–4, 37–8, 40, 43, Characters in the Play 9
protean 4.2.245
provide 1.2.99, 2.3.14
purchase 3.2.44, 4.1.7, 4.1.176, 5.1.155, 5.1.193–4
put on 3.3.21
put up 3.2.26

quench 3.1.3

race 1.1.120
rankness 1.1.90
rapier 3.2.76

rare 2.1.306, 2.3.65
Read Not Dead p. 6
reclaim 5.2.54
recompense 3.1.12, 4.1.109
redress 4.253
refuge 4.2.249
relation 2.1.9
release 5.1.205
relic 1.1.120
remiss 3.3.22
render 1.1.51
repair 3.1.169
repent 3.1.123
repine 2.1.53
reproof 1.2.18
reserved 4.1.195
resolution 3.3.28
resolve 2.1.230
resolved 2.1.150, 4.2.19
* retailed 3.2.63
rising 4.2.266
Rizvi, Pervez p. 3
Rochester, Joanne p. 48
Rocolet, Pierre p. 8
rook 5.1.198
Rose Theatre p. 47

Sala, Angelo: *Opiologia* p. 184
satisfaction 3.1.173
saucy 1.1.174, 3.2.64
scandal 2.1.155
scape 3.2.90
scarab 2.1.222
Schelling, Felix E. pp. 10, 30, 47, 49
searching 5.2.51
seared-up 2.1.141
see 1.1.119, 5.2.85, 5.2.86
self-blood 4.1.213
senseless 3.1.143
Serres, Jean de pp. 10, 12
set 2.2.84
set off 2.2.20
settled 5.1.226
Seward, Thomas p. 45
Shakespeare, William pp. 6, 25, 29–30
  1HIV pp. 15–16, 100, 171, 177
  A&C p. 67
  Coriolanus p. 37
  First Folio pp. 5, 41

Ham pp. 17–18, 37, 57, 62, 65, 108, 180
KL pp. 12, 16, 18–19, 22, 24, 26, 48, 100, 109, 191, 193
Macbeth pp. 16–17
MWW p. 68
Oth pp. 41, 108, 185
Shrew p. 108
WT pp. 16, 18–20, 22, 24, 26–8, 48–9, 191, 193
Shakespeare, William, and George Wilkins: *Pericles* p. 20
shallow 5.1.31
Sheldon, Ralph p. 29
Sherbo, Arthur p. 49
* shift 3.2.192
Shirley, James p. 44
shot 2.2.69
Shrank, Cathy pp. 42, 50
Shuger, Deborah p. 48
sicker 5.1.34
Sidney, Philip: *Arcadia* p. 92
sing 1.2.118
sirrah 2.3.140
sit 3.2.111
'slight 4.2.29
sniggle 2.2.6
society 5.2.77
son/sun, pun on 4.1.14
sow-gelder 1.1.175
speak 5.2.188
speeding 2.1.294
sphere 1.1.169
spite 3.2.82
spleen 3.2.94
spoil 5.1.96
sport 2.1.319
spot 4.1.51
Squier, Charles L. pp. 25, 30, 34, 48–50, 152
staid 2.2.16
* stallion bawd 2.2.110
stand 5.1.118, 5.1.119
state 3.1.177
Statius: *Thebais* p. 78
stay 2.2.100, 4.1.109, 4.2.44
steal 4.1.3
Steggle, Matthew p. 110
still 2.3.66, 3.1.61
stir 4.1.79, 4.2.87

stirring 4.1.1
stock 5.1.176
stockfish 3.2.65
stomach 3.2.20
Strachey, J. St Loe p. 45
strange 1.1.62, 2.3.55, 3.1.154
stranger 3.2.176
study 4.2.48, 4.2.147, 5.2.187
stump 2.2.44
style 2.3.65
succeeding 3.3.20
succory 5.2.19
suchlike 1.2.98
suffer 1.1.110, 2.2.80
sufferance 1.1.57
suit 1.2.76
suitor 4.2.199
superstition 1.1.51
sure 3.3.1, 5.1.145, 5.1.203
sway 2.1.187
* sweat 2.1.78
Swinburne, A. C. pp. 30, 49
swinge 5.2.93
syphilis p. 104

tainture 1.1.1
Tantalus p. 111
tax 1.1.1, 1.1.33
tear 3.1.2
tell 4.1.26
temper 2.3.86
Terence: *Andria* p. 108
text 2.1.201
Theodoret pp. 1, 3–10, 12–20, 22, 24–6, 28–33, 36–41, 44–5, 47, Characters in the Play 2
Thierry pp. 1, 3–26, 28–41, 44–5, 47. Characters in the Play 1
Thomson, Leslie pp. 146, 185
Thorndike, Ashley pp. 6–8, 12, 15, 47–8
tiger 1.1.129
tigress 1.2.41
Tillet, Jean du p. 48
toil 2.2.99
tongue 5.1.6, 5.2.194
top 5.2.4
touch 2.3.21, 5.2.102
Tourneur, Cyril pp. 3, 46
tragedian 4.2.60

INDEX

* trainer 2.2.39
transcend 2.1.87
transport 2.1.158
tun 2.2.120
Turner, Robert Kean pp. 40–1, 43, 45, 50–1, 195–9
turtle 3.1.42
tush 2.1.290
tyrant 5.1.148

Ulrich, Otto pp. 10, 12, 47–8
unaffected 2.2.23
uncurried 5.1.70
undo 5.1.180
undone 2.2.23
unhandsome 4.1.108
unhonest 2.2.23
unpatterned 3.1.52
unprovident 4.1.155
unresolved 2.1.130, 4.2.160
unsmooth 3.3.48
unspirited 2.2.22
unuseful 4.2.258
unutterable 2.3.37
unwholesome 5.2.48

varlet 1.1.140
vestal 1.1.153
Vicary Thomas: *English Man's Treasure* p. 104
Vignier, Nicholas pp. 12, 48
vouchsafe 2.3.79, 5.1.22

Waith, Eugene M. pp. 30, 49
wake 5.2.22, 5.2.60
waken 5.2.82, 5.2.144
waking 5.2.87, 5.2.147
Walkley, Thomas pp. 28, 40–1, 44
Waller, A. R. p. 45
Walton, Izaak: *The Complete Angler* p. 95

wandering 2.2.17
want 2.1.148, 3.1.121, 3.2.25, 3.2.43, 3.3.36, 4.1.122, 4.2.55, 4.2.191, 5.1.16
wanton 4.1.59
Ward, A. W. pp. 29, 49
wear 4.1.33
Weber, Henry pp. 6, 29, 45, 47, 49
Webster, John pp. 3, 30
Wells, William p. 3
Welsh people, stereotypes about pp. 173–4, 176
Werstine, Paul pp. 42, 50, 68
whipcord 5.1.75
Wiggins, Martin pp. 3, 6–9, 16, 46–9, 100
will 2.1.103, 2.3.33, 4.1.127
Williams, George Walton p. 68
Williams, Gordon: *Dictionary of Sexual Language* pp. 64–5, 67, 73, 80–1, 98–9, 103–4, 113
Williams, M. E. p. 47
Williams, Ralph: *Physical Rarities* p. 104
Willis, David p. 174
win 2.3.30
Wingfield, Richard p. 29
wink 3.2.118, 5.2.141
wonderful 5.1.101
wondrous 5.1.149–50
wont 3.1.77, 5.1.151
Woolley, Hannah: *Supplement* p. 185
worm-eaten 2.1.86
worthy 4.1.185
wrought upon 2.1.288
Wymer, Roland pp. 31, 49
Wyn James, E. p. 173

Zounds 5.1.124

EU authorised representative for GPSR:
Easy Access System Europe, Mustamäe tee 50,
10621 Tallinn, Estonia
gpsr.requests@easproject.com